Celibate
Fabulous & Fearless

Monica R. Carter, M.B.A.

This book is a work of non-fiction in accordance with the author's memory; however, some names were changed to protect the identity of certain individuals.

CLF Publishing, LLC.
9161 Sierra Ave, Ste. 203C
Fontana, CA 92335
www.clfpublishing.org
(909) 315-3161

Copyright © 2014 by Monica R. Carter. All rights reserved. No portion of this book may be reproduced, stored in a retrieval system, or transmitted by any form or any means electronically, photocopied, recorded, or any other except for brief quotations in printed reviews, without the prior permission of the publisher.

Cover Design by Senir Design. Contact information info@senirdesign.com.

Photographs of Monica R. Carter by Charrita Rainey, CRP Photo & Design. Contact information - charritar@gmail.com.

ISBN # 978-0-9960815-0-4

Printed in the United States of America.

Dedications

This book is dedicated first to my **Heavenly Father** who knew me before I was born and never took His hand off my life. I also dedicate this book to my family. First, in *loving memory* of my maternal grandparents and uncle, who would be so proud of me.

Mr. Eugene & Mrs. Lucille Gordon
Mr. Derek (Dusty) Gordon♥ *(RIP - 5/12/14)*

Grandmother Jean, the matriarch of the family, you have always loved me and been there for me. Thank you for keeping me fabulously dressed, teaching me etiquette, and to be well spoken and mannered. My creativity came from you, which has made me unique.

Dad Michael, despite your illness, I have always felt your love, and if you could, you would have moved mountains for me. Thank you for loving me, bringing me into this world, and being the smartest, most handsome, ambitious and most fearless person who never gave up on life. Through your life, I have learned no matter the cards you are dealt, God will always see you through.

Second dad Chris, you have never been overbearing or treated me like a stepchild. Thank you for always providing for the family, giving us a foundation of a Christian lifestyle and keeping us consistent in the word of God. I really appreciate the love and support you have given me during the most difficult times in my life.

Mom Vicki, thank you for giving me life, providing for and loving me unconditionally. There is nothing like a mother's love when it is time for battle. Thank you for your words of wisdom, support and encouragement. I cannot thank you enough for keeping me active as a child, with being a girl scout, in ballet, tap dancing classes and much more. Being exposed to many diverse environments has made me the woman I am today. Thank you for being an awesome mom!

Brother Lil' Chris, although we are like night and day, you are stuck with me. You have always been a loving brother and friend. Thank you for all your love and support.

Aunt Lynn, I know you would move the sun, moon and stars for me if you could. As I grew up, and still today, whatever I needed you made a way to provide it. You always trusted my word that I would pay the car notes on my first two BMW's you co-signed for in my early twenties. Thank you for all your love, words of wisdom and encouragement throughout my life and keeping me Runway Fabulous! It is also such a blessing to know all of your friends know I am Lynn's pride and joy.

♥Uncle Dusty, thank you for always being a phone call away and being my candy supplier for my grade school business that you knew nothing about. You always picked me up from pre-school and at least three times a week we would eat "Shrimp Fried Rice." Now I know why I love rice so much. Every birthday, I could always count on seeing the latest movie and eating all the sweets I desired. Thank you for trusting me and co-signing for my first car. I miss you so much already and the great conversations we always had together. You always loved me unconditionally and had my back. I know you are smiling in heaven and are no longer in pain. I am certain you are one of God's precious angels. Love you forever and always. RIP!

Aunt Darcel, thank you for ensuring my summers were always fun in St. Louis, by going to all the water and amusement parks. When I was a young child, you picked me up from pre-school whenever needed. Thank you for taking care of me, buying me clothes for school and loving me.

Aunt Cheryl, thank you for exposing me to the latest oldie jams back in the day. You know, when you used to be in the basement with your boyfriends, I would sit on the stairs and listen to the latest groves. We used to have so much fun at the skating rink, and I enjoyed mixing my popcorn and barbeque potato chips. Thank you for picking me up from school, buying me the latest gear for the school year, and for loving me.

Uncle Gramp, you never really said much, but when you did, you always gave me sound advice and I appreciate it. Thank you for watching out for my dad and being there for him.

Uncle Joe and Aunt Maxine, thank you for inspiring me to get my real estate license and to build wealth, which you have done so well. I aspire to live comfortably like you both when I am in my 70's.

Uncle Charles (Chuckie), no matter what direction I turn, you have always supported me. You have no idea how your words of encouragement have helped me get through many challenging days.

To a whole host of cousins, thank you for your love and support. Lastly, I dedicate this book in loving memory of my great uncles Wilbert and Jimmy and great aunts Mary and Bernice, aunt Jerri, godmother Mary Ann, uncle Lonnie and great grandparents.

I love you all!

Acknowledgements

I acknowledge that God alone, who creates great works into masterpieces, gets the glory for this divinely-inspired book that will draw men and women closer to Him. I thank God for transforming me to fulfill the eternal purpose He has for my life. I could not have made it this far without His unconditional love, strength, grace and mercy in my life. God, you are worthy to be praised each and every day of my life, and I am humbled that I am the chosen one to deliver this message to many people in the world who are in bondage from sexual immorality.

Further, I would like to acknowledge my senior pastor Dr. Kenneth Ulmer (a.k.a Bishop) and First Lady Togetta Ulmer at Faithful Central Bible Church (FCBC) for welcoming me to the ministry. Words cannot explain how much your sermons each week have blessed me. I express my gratitude for you allowing me to quote some of your remarks from the services that have been such a blessing to me, as I know those sermons will be a blessing to others. God knew what I would need and when I would need it, when He blessed me with you two. I look forward to where God is taking me, and from your teaching, I am no longer afraid to move from season to season when God says it is time! Thank you and God bless you both.

Pastor William A. Garrett and First Lady Garrett at The Way, The Church. Thank you for being there for me when I was growing up and as a young adult. God knew I needed the duo in you two: one who is compassionate and the other giving me tough love. Without the foundation God laid for me through you both to live a righteous life, I could not have made the transition to FCBC and maintain a righteous lifestyle. Words cannot explain how much I appreciate all of your words of encouragement, guidance, and support during the rough times in my life. I must say, you two would call the crew, if someone were to mess with Monica. I appreciate your everlasting support. God spoke through Pastor in order to save my life during my tragic situation. I would not be alive today, if God would not have given you a word for me. Thank you and God bless you both! You both will always have a special place in my heart!

Dr. Cassundra White-Elliott, my publisher, thank you for taking this project on and using your God-given talents to bring my story to light. Your time, encouraging words, advice and guidance have been such a blessing, and I'm ready to take on the world!

Thank you, Senir Dacillo, my graphic designer, for creating a fabulous cover, and Tim Quick, Bestbuck Sites for branding MRC Enterprises, LLC and creating my phenomenal website design!

Red14Films, Adam Cushmanovich, Rocco Rivetti and Gilles O'Kane. Thank you for creating my Cinematic Book Extravaganza for the world to visualize my life story. You guys are the best, and I can't thank you enough.

My friend and fitness trainer Reggie "The Machine," thank you for pushing and motivating me when I did not have the strength to workout. Your skills, nutrition plan, and tough love are unimaginable and much appreciated. I owe my results all to your care for your clients and dedication to make me look and feel fabulous!

God has truly blessed me with wonderful friends who have seen it all in my life and know me well. Thank you for being there for me through the good and bad. I cannot name one friend without naming another, so you know who you are that has a special place in my heart, and when I was down you lifted me up, and when I was up, you encouraged me to go higher. This type of love from a friend is priceless, and I thank you all!

Contents

Introduction		9
Chapter 1	*Show Me State*	11
Chapter 2	*Going to Cali*	17
Chapter 3	*Saved and Fearless*	25
Chapter 4	*Entrepreneur Spirit*	35
Chapter 5	*It's Time for Ministry*	47
Chapter 6	*All that Glitters is not Gold*	59
Chapter 7	*The Transition*	83
Chapter 8	*Watching the Clock*	91
Chapter 9	*The Dating Scene*	113
Chapter 10	*Finally Mr. Right*	121
Chapter 11	*Answer the Call*	219
Chapter 12	*Ten Reasons to Avoid Premarital Sex*	223
Chapter 13	*My Life on Display*	225
Conclusion		231
About the Author		233

Introduction

> *"For this is the will of God, your sanctification: that you abstain from sexual immorality; that each one of you know how to control his own body in holiness and honor, not in the passion of lust like the Gentiles who do not know God."*
>
> -1 Thessalonians 4:3-5 ESV

Have you ever wondered, *God, why am I not being blessed, not financially stable, emotionally and spiritually drained, lusting after someone I can't stand to be around, always a booty call and feeling used?* If these questions and others like it have ever gone through your mind, you are not alone. Many Christian men and women feel this way, while many others have felt this way at least one time or another. If you are scratching your head and wondering if the question refers to both men and women, yes, men can be a "booty call" as well. According to 1 Thessalonians 5:23 ESV, man consists of three parts: spirit, soul and body. Therefore, anyone who possesses a body can feel used and be used for his/her body.

Feelings of being used for one's body are caused when men and women of God participate in sexual immorality, such as fornication and adultery. Sexual sin is the only sin you can commit against your own body, and when you do so, you create unholy soul ties with those whom you are not married. God knows the challenges of sexual immorality amongst believers, as He states in 1 Corinthians 7:2 ESV: *"But because of the temptation to sexual immorality, each man should have his own wife and each woman her own husband."* This does not mean a person should get married just to have sex. As you will learn, I personally know where that leads to from my own experience and from the years of speaking with many men and women.

Because God made sex for marriage, single Christians are supposed to live a "celibate" lifestyle. However, many of them have not made the decision to be celibate, due to its unpopularity. While speaking to many Christians, I have learned they have been told many disturbing statements by others, such as being celibate is definitely not popular (which it is not), it is not cool, no one will marry you without testing the goods, you are considered square, or something must be wrong with you. Because of these negative statements, my "goal" in writing this novel is to let all my single brothers and sisters in Christ know you can be *"Celibate Fabulous & Fearless!"*

Of course, the devil will place people in your path to make you feel just like the earlier comments; however, you have to always consider the source of who is saying these foolish things. Anytime you are uncertain about exactly what God wants you to do, ask yourself, "What does God say about fornication and adultery?" God's words are your only source for direction, clarity, and instruction. God makes no mistakes, and He certainly does not create anything less than fabulous and fearless in His sons and daughters.

God has placed me in the depths of unchartered waters with sharing my life story. My story is not a buttoned-up Christian story; rather, my life has been full of ups and downs. But, I want people to know, even though there have been ups and downs, God has never forsaken me. He has placed me in many uncomfortable seasons, and it was all for this day: to inspire, encourage, and share with other Christians the love of God despite adversity, tragedy, heartache, humiliation and many disappointments. I am thankful because in each season of my life, God has always given me grace and mercy and has developed me to grow to the next level in Christ and in my personal life.

IT'S TIME FOR A PROMOTION, SINGLES! Many of us who have already experienced fornication would say, "If I could do it all over again, I would remain a virgin until marriage." Well, if you have ever made that statement, it is never too late. God is clear about sexual sin. One way that has helped me abstain from sex is to consistently renew my mind day and night in the word of God, which renews your strength. I learned later in life, it is very important to surround yourself with "like-minded people." I do not care how strong you are; in most cases, you will become a product of whom you socialize with.

It is my prayer that if you are a single Christian who is not living a celibate lifestyle, your mind and spirit will be charged to adhere to the instructions given to us in God's word. When you do so, the blessings of God will flow in your life as you walk in obedience. Remember, obedience is better than sacrifice. *"But Samuel replied: 'Does the LORD delight in burnt offerings and sacrifices as much as in obeying the LORD? To obey is better than sacrifice, and to heed is better than the fat of rams'"* (1 Samuel 15:22 NIV).

Chapter One
The Show Me State

> *"You saw me before I was born. Every day of my life was recorded in your book. Every moment was laid out before a single day had passed."*
>
> -Psalm 139:16 KJV

"The Show Me State," St. Louis, MO, is where I was born. As the scripture above says, God knew me before I was even born and the events that were going to take place in my life. He knew my beginning from my ending and everything that would transpire in between. I often wonder if God gave us all a chance to read the script of our lives to provide us with insight to what our experiences would be in the future, if we would try to detour from His plan or would we simply trust Him to lead, direct and guide us. Hummm??? Detouring from God's word in my life has been my motto. I had opted to live my life my own way and to cut corners most of the time. When I cut corners and at every failed attempt, He reminded me, "Until you do it my way, you will not enjoy the ultimate blessings I have in store for you." God is gracious and merciful. He does not want to see us fail, but at the same time, He has given us free will. He said in Deuteronomy 30:15 KJV, *"See, I have set before thee this day life and good, and death and evil."* It is up to us to choose life and good.

Growing up in St. Louis from one to four years of age, I experienced nothing but happy times. My dad Michael and my mom Vicki were married, and I came into the world when they were twenty years old. My dad had several interests keeping his attention. He was an entrepreneur, a student studying to be an attorney, and a model, among so many other things. My mom, on the other hand, was a dentist technician and a college student. Even in the midst of their careers that kept them occupied, both of my parents were elated that I arrived to add another dimension to their lives. Although they were young and unsure of what parenting would bring, they were excited to have a bouncing baby girl to shower their love upon. At the time I was born, we lived with my paternal grandmother Jean, for a short period of time. Later, my parents and I moved into our own apartment.

I was told that as a child, I was extremely spoiled by my dad, who would allow me do whatever I wanted. Let me paint a picture for you to show you exactly how spoiled I was. My dad purchased a pair of black clunky shoes for me, and I was particularly fond of them. They were my favorite shoes. I wore them with every dress (whether they matched or not), and they can be seen in most of my baby pictures. Whenever my grandmother Jean would see me wearing those shoes, she would ask my dad, "Michael, why would you let her wear those shoes when you know they are despicable?" He would smile and respond, "Because Monica wanted too!" It did not matter to him; he just wanted to make me happy. To add to my spoiled character, I was very particular about what I wore. I only wanted to wear dresses, and when I had on a dress, no one could hold me, except my dad.

I was the youngest of all the grandchildren and the third grandchild on my mom's side of the family. Being the new baby in the family means I received all the love and attention from everyone. Can you say, "SPOILED"?

My mom and dad have several sisters and brothers, who were all very good to me. I also had a whole host of cousins, great aunts and uncles who all lived in St. Louis. With all the love that was showered upon me, you probably can imagine there was a little drama when I came into the world. Who was going to spend the most time with 'little' Monica? Of all the people who loved spending time with me, one of a few people I loved spending time with was my maternal grandpapa Eugene, who passed away after I graduated from high school. Monica could do no wrong in Papa's eyes. If I wanted to go to space, he would try to figure out a way to take me.

On the other hand, his wife, my grandma Lucille, was more of the disciplinarian. But, I could do whatever I wanted when she was watching her soap operas all day. When her soaps were on, her eyes were glued to the television and less attention was paid to what I was doing. While my grandma Lucille loved her soaps, she despised Papa smoking cigarettes. So, when I found out he would sneak into the basement and smoke, we made a deal that every time I caught him smoking, he would pay me a quarter, or I would tell Grandma Lucille. So basically, I received at least one dollar each week.

As a child, when I hung out with Papa, one of my favorite experiences was when he would take me to White Castle. I loved to eat there. To this day, whenever I visit a city that has a White Castle, it is the first place I dine.

My grandpapa and my dad were not the only ones to spoil me and treat me like their little princess. My uncle Dusty, aunts Darcel and Cheryl, on my mom's side, were always taking me places. They loved to take me to the skating rinks, water parks and amusement parks. When they were hanging out with me, they loved to dress me like a baby doll. They were in junior high, high school, and I was their real life baby doll. We had loads of fun with all the adventures we would enjoy. My grandmother Jean, who was the shopper, did more than her fair share of spoiling me too. She always kept me in the finest of everything, and so did all of her boyfriends. Anything that a young girl could think of, she purchased for me. For my third Christmas, she bought me a full-length white fur coat, with matching gloves and hat. Shall we say 'fabulous' at three years old? My grandmother Jean had all the ladies talking about us when we would shop at Neiman Marcus or Sax Fifth Avenue. Not only did she shop for me, she spent a lot of quality time with me. Time is something that is irreplaceable, and I cherish those memories.

While I was very young, she taught me how to play every card game you could imagine, such as Spades, Gin Rummy, Tonk, etc. I even knew how to play backgammon. When I would lose, I would always tell her she was cheating. That was my spoiled attitude rearing its head. Sometimes, I would even beat her friends and make a little money for my piggy bank.

My aunt Lynn is another person who loved spending time with me and me with her. When we were together, she would always take me shopping. I did not get to see her too often, but when we did see one another, we would have a lot of fun when she came to town or when I would visit her in Houston, TX for the summer while growing up. We would take road trips from Houston to St. Louis, and I would talk the entire way. I do not know how Lynn tolerated me talking the entire time, but she was a principal and loved children, so spending time with me was a joy for her. Lynn was in college when I was born, and shortly thereafter, she married a NFL player. And of course, her husband, my new uncle, spoiled me too. I remember my uncle giving me a white life-size rabbit and I loved it. Spoiling me just seemed to be automatic with everyone who came in contact with me.

Most of my family was very much present in my life and enjoyed spending time with me. However, my uncle Gramp (my father's brother) was a ladies' man and very busy, so I do not remember spending too much time with him. As I got older, I spent a lot of time with my cousins, both older and younger. I really enjoyed spending time with all of my grandparents, uncles, aunts and cousins. My childhood in St. Louis was pleasant and full of love. My family loves me dearly, and I, in turn, love them as well.

A Little Girl's Worst Nightmare

Every daughter wants to be "daddy's little girl," and that I was. As I stated earlier, my dad loved me so much that he would do anything for me. But one day, that would all soon come to an end. My nightmare happened one day when my dad was hanging out with friends. My dad and his friends hung out from time to time and enjoyed one another's company, either on the weekend or after a long day's work. That time, however, was different. Someone decided he/she wanted to do him harm, so a chemical was placed into his drink or marijuana. (Don't act like no one else was smoking marijuana in the 70's☺. It was a popular pastime.)

When my dad arrived home later that day, he told my mom he felt weird. The next thing she knew, my dad was going ballistic, and he ended up giving her a black eye. That was all she wrote for my mom. She packed up our things, and she took me to Papa's house. That type of behavior was not like my dad. He had never put his hands on my mom before that day. Once my grandmother Jean learned of what had transpired, she checked my dad into a psychiatric treatment center to get evaluated. Sadly, he was later diagnosed with Schizophrenia at twenty-four years old.

My mom and everyone in my family were devastated. It truly broke their hearts to see my dad become ill. It changed all of our lives. I was too young to really understand the impact my dad's absence would have on me. I would ask where my dad was and would cry at times because I could not see him. Can you imagine how devastating that was for me to be with my dad all the time and then all of a sudden not to have him as a part of my life the way he had been before? What made it worse for me was I did not really understand the magnitude of how that would change my life then and in the future. Talking about how your life can change in a blink of an eye. I remember my aunt Lynn always telling me my dad loves me as I grew up and saying if he could he would do anything for me.

My dad is very smart and was very ambitious, and I often wonder what my dad would have become if he had not fallen ill. My mom immediately became a single parent at twenty-four years old. I still had my dad, but he could not do the things he used to with me, and it was very confusing. No one ever really explained to me my dad was ill or what his condition was.

Eventually, all I heard was that my dad was crazy. I tried to erase those words from my mind. What was even more depressing and confusing was no one ever sat down with me to explain what was going on. In the 1970's, Schizophrenia was not talked about, and most people did not understand the illness. It was considered taboo, and people acted as if though it did not exist. The reality is this illness effects many people, mostly very intelligent people, and it could happen to the most successful person without any warning.

In 2014, society still frowns upon this illness, but what people do not realize is we are all God's children no matter if one of us has a disability or not. He created each and every one of us. Although we may choose not to fellowship with Him or worship Him, He still has His hand on our lives. He orchestrates everything behind the scenes. My mother was not raised in the church, so we did not attend a church. However, my grandmother Jean would take me to a Catholic church, and all I remember was always having to stand up and sit down multiple times during the service. I can only imagine how my mom was feeling suddenly not being in my dad's life any longer and making a life-changing decision that would hurt and disappoint our family members. Even though my mom and I were not active in a church at a young age, God was always by our sides. Remember, He knew all of this was going to happen before the day ever came. The scripture below says God will help you in times like these.

> *"Fear not, for I am with you; be not dismayed, for I am your God; I will strengthen you, I will help you, I will uphold you with my righteous right hand."*
>
> -Isaiah 41:10 NIV

My mom is very brave, and I really want to thank her for not leaving me behind with family members, like many parents do after a life-changing event in their lives. As you read the next chapter, as it unfolds, you will understand what I mean.

Tips from Lessons Learned

1. Do not sweep life-changing matters under the rug with children. Bring the issues to the forefront, face them, and discuss them, especially with the people involved.
2. Parents, be honest with children about serious matters, particularly when it effects them.
3. Take the time to explain any life-changing events to people around you, so others can know how to deal with them.
4. Allow the child to see an ill parent. This will alleviate the child feeling uncomfortable when being around the parent.
5. Help the child navigate through life by knowing how to answer questions about the absence of a parent.

Chapter Two
Going to Cali

> *"Have I not commanded you? Be strong and courageous. Do not be frightened, and do not be dismayed, for the Lord your God is with you wherever you go."*
>
> -Joshua 1:9 ESV

After all the drama and sadness of having to leave my dad, due to the effects of his illness, my mom decided to relocate us to Los Angeles, CA. Mom's car at the time was a two-door 1975 Green Mustang, and my papa helped us pack all of our things and put a trailer on the back. He drove my grandma Lucille, Mom and me to Los Angeles, to live with our cousin, whom we call Boo. Boo lived in a four or five-bedroom house with her husband Nate (Rollo), from the television show *Sanford and Son,* and their four daughters and soon-to-be newborn son, Lil' Nate.

Again, I was too young to really understand everything that was going on, but I could feel when things were uncomfortable for us. Upon our arrival, Papa and Grandma Lucille made sure we had everything we needed. Then, they flew back to St. Louis. It was the saddest day, and they did not want me to leave St. Louis. To make matters worse, for a long time, my dad did not even know where my mom and I lived. At the time, he was really young and was not taking his medicine. That caused him to act out a lot. If he had taken his medicine, he would have been able to operate in a somewhat 'normal' state.

As always, I made myself at home, in my new environment. I had never been a shy child, and I was always talking to anyone I could. Once my mom started to get out and look for a job, the party was on. My youngest cousin April was jealous because now there I was on the scene. I was younger and cuter than she was, and I was getting all the attention in the house. April was furious. I had stolen the show!

One day, I was sitting in my high chair booster seat minding my own business. I was too big to be sitting in the booster seat, as I had outgrown it. Out of nowhere, April came by and knocked me backwards. In what seemed like slow motion, I fell out of the chair and a glass from the counter fell on my face and broke.

The pieces of glass went everywhere. Unfortunately, one of the pieces cut me right above my right eyebrow. Rollo was hot as fish grease, and April received the beating of her life. I was rushed to the hospital and received stitches. Later, when I was in junior high school, we learned a piece of glass had not been removed, and it formed a small cist that my doctor had to remove.

The incident in the booster seat was the final straw for my mom. At that point, she decided it was time to look for an apartment. After searching for some time, she found one that was suitable, and we finally moved. After a short period of time, every kid on the block knew me. I have always been an extrovert, leader, never a follower, and always made my existence known.

While living in our new apartment, my mom eventually found Pastor Fred K. Price's church, which was located at the time on Crenshaw Blvd. Pastor Fred K. Price has now been elevated to Apostle Price and now owns the old Pepperdine University campus in Los Angeles, and he converted it into a church. I attended church with my mother, but I felt the church was not in me. I was not aware why I needed the word of God. At the time, I did not have a complete understanding of how to apply the word of God to my life. Not only was I immature (young) in the natural, but I was immature in the things of the spirit.

My spiritual immaturity was no reflection on Apostle Price, because he was (and is) an "in-your-face and tell-it-like-it-is pastor." The teachings were always great. To this day, he still is an awesome pastor. In addition to attending church services, I attended Faith Christian School (FCS), which included grade levels pre-K to sixth grade. I attended FCS until fifth grade and had many friends while I was in attendance. I had four close friends; we always hung out together. We were even in the Brownies and Girl Scouts together. While at FCS, I also met my friend Delania, and we are still very close friends today. One of the four friends would become a well-known actress and is doing well today.

Every summer, I would fly alone on TWA. I began this tradition at five years of age. I would fly to visit my family in St. Louis and my aunt Lynn, who eventually moved to Houston. I was never a clingy child, so I looked forward to seeing the stewardesses at TWA to talk their ears off and to seeing my dad. At times though, I was a little fearful, because I really did not know how he would react while I was with him. The bits and pieces of conversations I had heard from family members had me scared.

Once my dad learned where we were living, he used to call my mom and say he was coming to Los Angeles. She knew he was not taking his prescribed medications, so she figured his coming to visit us was not a good idea. My dad is very intelligent. All he needed was our home or my school address, and he would know how to find me.

Later, I transitioned to LaTijera Magnet Elementary School. That was really a great move for me, not to mention my friend Delania was a student there. During that time is when I met my then best friend Vivian. Also during that time, I had so many other friends from school, my neighborhood and social activity groups.

Smart and Talks Too Much

At my new school, parent-teacher night finally rolled around. During my mother's conferences with my teachers that night, the only issue my teachers stated they had with me was that I "talk too much." Every teacher complained to my mom saying, "Monica always finishes her work early, but then she starts to disrupt everyone else." With my outgoing personality, I would always sit in front of the class; I never liked to sit in the back of any classroom.

Despite all of my talking, Ms. Kelly was the only teacher who recognized the ambitious leadership skills I possessed at a young age. So, when I was in her class again, she pretty much made me her "teacher's pet." Basically, I was her 'little' assistant. Ms. Kelly would give me duties, such as passing out assignments, pencils, writing questions on the board, and walking around to assist other students after I was done with my work. It was always fun for me to assist her. Helping Ms. Kelly and the students gave me a sense of purpose. Each day, I could not wait to go to Ms. Kelly's class to help others. I guess it has always been in my DNA to motivate and inspire others to succeed. This has always been my greatest gratification. I was always an "A" student, but it was always something burning inside of me to do more than just attend school.

During my break from school, around the holidays, my mom and I would bake homemade cookies. Afterward, I would take the cookies and sell them in the neighborhood. This also brought joy to me and others, plus the profits filled my bank account. My mom always kept me busy, whether it was with ballet, tap dancing class or girl scouts, not to mention I had slumber and birthday parties or attended other friend's parties. I was never bored as an only child, and I was very mature for my age.

One day to my surprise, I was walking out of school, and I thought I saw my dad in front of the school. When I got home, I quickly shared the information with my mother. I said, "Mama, I think I saw my dad." She said, "Girl, your dad is in St Louis." She basically dismissed what I had said. Not long after having that brief conversation, my dad climbed our balcony wanting to see me. At the time, it was scary for me and my mom to see my dad behave that way. Others found his behavior unsafe for us to be around. Today though, I understand my dad was ill, but he desperately wanted to see his daughter, so he had hitchhiked from St. Louis, MO to Inglewood, CA to find his daughter. My dad wanted so much to hold me in his arms that he hitchhiked a few times. My mom would always contact my grandmother Jean, and she would fly him back home.

At school when people would talk about their dads, I would not say anything. I was embarrassed, hurt, and ashamed. I always wondered, *Why did this have to happen to my dad?* From my disappointments and hurts, I began to block out not having my biological dad in my life. My attitude caused it to appear to some that I did not need a dad or I did not care. But the reality is, it has always bothered me. Every little girl needs her father, because that is who will teach her how a man is supposed to treat her. And, a father will be there for her to support, protect, and encourage every decision in her life, including the decision of her future husband. Of course, God has given women a discerning spirit, but a biological father definitely has his place in the family and in his children's lives.

In the absence of my father, I thank God even more for my mom being in my life. It was just she and I for a long time, and she did an awesome job as a single parent. Because she was receiving money each month (due to my dad's illness) and working, we always had a roof over our head, food and enough money for my extra-curricular activities.

Although my mother was a single parent, she was not without a support system. We always had someone in our family who was willing to help. For example, my uncle Dusty moved from St. Louis to Los Angeles, to live with us. He and I used to hang out a lot. He used to take me to the candy store and to the movies on every birthday. We had so much fun. I used to tell Dusty that I needed to take candy to school every week, so he would buy me big bags of candy for school. I would then take the candy, put a few pieces in zip lock bags, and sell them at school. I was the "candy girl." One day, my little business closed abruptly.

In passing, Dusty mentioned to my mom he had purchased candy for me. In her surprise, she asked, "For what?" Dusty answered, "Monica needs candy at school." Boy was I in trouble, but she could not really be mad at me for making some pocket change. I had always been a little entrepreneur and always had ideas about how to make money at a young age.

You Are Not My Daddy

During that same time frame, I remember my mom having a boyfriend named Sam. One day, I wanted to go skating with my cousins, but to my surprise, he told me I could not go. That was the first time I was able to say, "You're not my daddy!" My outburst did not help matters at all. The next thing I knew, he was trying to whip me, and I said, "You're not whipping me." Eventually, my mom stopped dating him, and I was glad, because I did not like him at all.

The next thing I knew, Christmas was every day in our house when my mom met a man named Eddie. He would take us to the movies in limousines, and I could eat any type of candy I desired. He purchased my mom a new Cadillac with an eight-track cassette tape player, and Tina Marie's "Squarebiz" was always in rotation. I thought for sure Eddie was Santa Claus, and we were moving up like the Jeffersons. He used to sit me on his knee and sing songs, give me stacks of one dollar bills, and whatever I wanted, he would buy it. But one day, Santa disappeared, and my mom told me he went back to the North Pole. Now, she did not really think I believed that story.

My mom eventually met a man named Chris, when I was about nine years old. Chris worked at McDonald Douglas and was doing very well. Chris and my mom were really just friends in the beginning. Because of their friendship, Chris would babysit me while my mom would go on dates with other men. Every time I went by Chris' house, he would be playing oldies music and cleaning. Chris would also pick me up from school. When Chris would arrive to LaTijera, he would pull right in front, get out of his long old school classic car, which was a bucket, and yell, "MONICA!" Being Miss Popular, I always tried to play it cool with my friends, so they would not see me getting into the bucket. I would let everyone walk off before I walked over to the car.

One day I had finally grown tired of the embarrassment, so I said, "Chris, please don't yell my name when you come to pick me up. I see you, and I know to come to the car." Chris was always so mellow, and he did not really pay much attention to my antics. He just kept right on being good to me.

> *"Whoever restrains his words has knowledge, and he who has a cool spirit is a man of understanding."*
>
> -Proverbs 17:27 ESV

Every day Chris picked me up, he knew I wanted to eat at McDonald's, and he told me later in life he would sometimes have to save to ensure he had the money for McDonald's. (Awe, thank you Chris for making my day.) Chris did not have any children, so I was like his child at the time. Chris is the youngest of two brothers and one sister. I will always remember him being nice to me, even though I was a brat at times. I had really become spoiled because it had always been just my mom and I, and then a new person had joined our family. As time progressed, I noticed my mom and Chris starting to get closer. Then, he started staying over a little later and later. I used to lie in my mom's bed and chat with her. This was our normal everyday activity. But then, I noticed she started kicking me out of her room earlier. Now, I know why!!!

Tips from Lessons Learned

1. Do not avoid the sick parent. Make arrangements for him/her to spend time with the children.
2. Conduct on-going conversations with your children and find out what they are feeling. This will help to avoid shipwrecks later and will provide an outlet for the children to express their feelings.
3. Continue to let children know how much they are still loved, even in the midst of life challenges.
4. If a child has a void of a parent in his/her life, continuously inform him/her even though his/her mom or dad is not around, it does not mean he/she does not love the child.
5. Ensure the child understands there is nothing to be ashamed or embarrassed about, due to one of his/her parents having a mental illness.

Monica R. Carter

Chapter Three
Saved and Fearless

> *"Then I will give you shepherds after my own heart, who will lead you with knowledge and understanding."*
>
> -Jeremiah 3:15 NIV

One beautiful and bright Sunday morning, Chris walked to the corner from where we lived and came back home to get my mother and me, so we could attend The Way, The Church. I was about twelve years old, and The Way, The Church was a new experience for both my mom and me, because it was much smaller than Crenshaw Christian Center Church. When we casually walked inside the church, there were five people in the sanctuary, not including us. Pastor Garrett and First Lady Garrett were conducting the service. I could tell it did not matter to them if there were five people or five hundred people. They were serious about praising the Lord and giving Him all the glory. We joined that day. Chris was raised in church, so that was his foundation. To him, it was not an option for us to not attend church and not have the Word in our family.

Soon after we began attending the church, Pastor Garrett was not in favor of Chris and my mom cohabitating, so he married them. He wanted them to be in right standing with God. Later in the year, they had an official wedding. Of course I was not that happy, and in the wedding pictures, anyone could see my sadness. Growing up, I did not know how I was supposed to act or feel in a blended family and how I should treat a stepfather. When you are a young child and you have been accustomed to only having one primary parent and then someone comes in new to the family, you feel as though your life is being invaded or you do not feel important as you once did. Another way to look at it is- the child does not get all the attention he/she once received. This is how I felt when Chris came into our family. It was not that Chris and I did not get along or despised one another. He was getting some of my mom's attention when before it was all mine.

Little did I know the way I treated Chris would come back to haunt me by God showing me how it feels to be a stepparent. In hindsight, looking back on my behavior, I must say it is embarrassing. As an adult, I understand it is very important for the man to have a family meeting when blending a family, whether it is the man's child or not. The man is the head of the household and should lead the conversation. The man should sit down with the entire family and explain what is going on and how each parent's love will not change for the child, just because the adults are getting married. This will remove any ambiguity or uneasiness the child may be feeling, and everyone involved will have a sense of comfort.

As you will read in later chapters, I was a stepmother and was about to be a stepmother again. From my experiences with a stepparent and as a stepparent, there will always be a challenge when real talk is not engaged in when two families are blended together.

The good thing for me was, Chris was never a disciplinarian, and he always supported me if my mom was to get mad at me for something I did, such as throwing away the forks and knives in the trash, because I did not want to wash them. I hated washing dishes, especially when food was left on the plate and placed in the sink. I would ask, "Can't someone just empty the food off the plate and then put it in the sink?" When they did not, I would just bypass the entire process.

While my family was making the adjustments of being a blended family, we still attended church. I was very much unaware the Word was being placed in my spirit each week. By that time, our church had moved to an actual church facility, because we wanted to grow as a ministry. Pastor Garrett and First Lady Garrett are the type of ministers that will leave no one behind. They are determined for you to hear and understand the Word. If you did not understand, they were always available to help you. Let me just say, God knew what I needed growing up, and He put Chris in our lives to direct us to the right shepherds. Growing up as a child, I thought I knew it all, and no one could tell me anything. Who knows anything about life as a teenager? Teenagers have a tendency to believe they have arrived when it comes to having knowledge about how the world works. The sad reality is they do not know half of what they think they know. As a teenager, I was never bad, just obstreperous at times. My grades were never an issue, and I believe because I was an only child for a while, I was always around adults a lot of times, which made me the center of attention and turned me into "Queen" Monica!!!

At The Way, The Church was the first time we were really consistent with attending church. And more and more, as time went on, I started hearing about fornication at a young age, but still I did not understand the impact fornication really had on one's salvation, spirit, body and soul. I was still a virgin, so those sermons seemed to be unimportant to me at the time. Little did I realize, that information would greatly impact my future. The Word was always great and entertaining, and I loved to attend church growing up.

Then as a church family, we moved across the street to an office building where during the week traffic school was held. We held church in one of the office spaces. That was when the church membership increased. Every summer, we would have a church barbeque, and it would be so fun. Later in life, I would return back to this office building, which would be a life-changing experience for me by "watching my clock." You will find out in later chapters how and why when watching your clock can lead you into making bad choices in life.

When I was growing up in the church, there were not a lot of children who I could fellowship with, so I mostly hung out with friends on the outside, who did not attend church. My friends who attended Catholic school were in the fast lane, and I used to tell my mom just because a person attends a Catholic school does not mean he/she will be square. You must be a leader and not a follower wherever you go, and I was definitely a leader.

Even though most of my friends did not attend church, at a young age, I would always invite them to hear the awesome Word from my pastor. Some would come, and some would not. The main reason most of my friends would come was to hear Chris sing, as he was a lead singer and had a great voice. I believe Chris thought he was one of the Temptations, because he would jump off the stage, sing in the aisles and the church would be rocking. Our church eventually grew, and we ended up in a building that held about 200-400 people, and that was where we remained throughout my tenure at the church.

Saved By the Bell

I continued to be a student at LaTijera where all of my teachers loved me. My friends and I had a lot of fun with theatrical plays, cheerleading and being great students. Delania, Raquel, I and others would hang out. My friend Vivian did not attend LaTijera, but we would see each other on some weekends. Delania's mom would let us do anything we wanted when we were at her house.

When we were about fourteen, Delania had a boyfriend, who was already out of high school. Raquel and I would spend the night over Delania's house. When we spent time there, we would hang out with much older people, rather than people our own age. One of our favorite pastimes was going to Uncle Jam's Army, which was a large dance/DJ experience with young adults.

One night, Raquel and I were supposed to be staying at Delania's, but we learned Delania was going to spend the night at her boyfriend Shawn's house. She asked us if we wanted to come. Raquel and I excitedly responded, "Yeah, that should be fun." We had no idea there would be two of Shawn's older friends over there as well. I called my play sister Ann, as I was so excited that we were hanging out.

I told Ann, "Guess what? Raquel and I are at Delania's boyfriend Shawn's house, and we just ordered pizza. He has a few of his friends here, and we're going to spend the night." I was very excited. She said, "How old are these guys?" I said, "About 18 or 19, I think." She asked, "And they live alone?" I said, "Yeah. They are grown." I did not understand why she was asking so many questions. I was young and did not have a clue that was not a good situation for us.

Ann responded very casually, "Oh, yeah? Where does he live?" I gave her the address, and she said, "Okay, call me if you need me." About fifteen minutes later, Shawn's buzzer rang, as if someone was at the front gate of his apartment. To my surprise, it was you know who: my MOM! Yikes!

Mom said, "Tell Monica and Raquel, if they do not get their butts outside in five minutes, I'm going to call the police." Shawn was upset, to say the least.

He said, "You two have to leave. I don't want any trouble." We were so scared, and I knew for sure I was in hot water. We went outside and got in the car. My mom was steaming. I could almost see the steam coming from her ears. She yelled, "Raquel, I'm going to call your mother and tell her what you were doing, and Monica you're getting a huge whipping." We sat there quiet as mice, and we knew talking back and complaining was not in our best interest.

When we got home, my mom called Raquel's mom and told her what we had been up to. Raquel's mom told my mom to whip Raquel right along with me. Chris witnessed it all. He pleaded with my mother, saying, "Come on, Vicki. Don't whip them!" But nothing anyone could say could make my mother stop. She was upset and disappointed. That was the first and last whipping I ever received.

Raquel stayed over that night, and we laughed about the situation later. But we still had no idea what we could have gotten ourselves into. I am certain those guys did not want to play hopscotch with us. Those guys could have tried to take advantage of us, but thank the Lord, for He assigned Ann to watch over me.

> *"For he will order his angels to protect you wherever you go."*
>
> -Psalm 91:11 NIV

A New Addition to the Family

I finally made it to high school, and boy was I the show stopper. I was a great student; therefore, the principal Dr. Freeman would always give me free lunch, nutritional snacks and basically whatever I wanted. Besides being intelligent and having a beautiful feather hairstyle, I was always fashionable and loved cheerleading, not to mention, my boyfriend Dejon was the finest and tallest guy on the basketball team.

Every summer when I went to Houston and St Louis, my family would take me shopping. After those shopping sprees, I would have many clothes for the school year. I was never without anything I needed or wanted. Also, I would always have a summer job at a Harry A. Meyer Center for disabled children, among other places. I really enjoyed working there every summer. The children really enjoyed me and my friend working there, because I would create fun activities for everyone. Some of the children's disabilities consisted of Down Syndrome and Hydrocephalus (known as water head babies).

While I was at the center one day, my friend Chelsey kept disturbing Jimmy who has Down Syndrome. He finally grew tired of her antics, so he flipped her over and ripped her Guess overalls. That was the funniest thing I had ever seen and boy was she mad. His parents reimbursed Chelsey for the overalls, and that was the last time she disturbed him. I guess you could say Chelsey learned her lesson.

One summer, I convinced the director of the center to let us go to Magic Mountain. She said, "Okay Monica, but do not put them on any roller coasters." I said, "Okay." But I was thinking to myself, *How can we go to Magic Mountain and not get on any roller coasters?* So, we went and we got on the Gold Rush, one of the smaller roller coasters.

Boy, were they screaming in fear! But they had so much fun. At the end of the summer, it was time for my job to end. It was always so hard for me to leave them, and I would miss them for quite a while afterwards.

For all the summer jobs I had, I would just type a letter for my mother to sign and would then find my own jobs through the school district. I was always a go-getter while growing up. I was simply unstoppable and felt there was not anything I could not accomplish.

Before long, my mom was telling me she was pregnant and having a baby boy. This came as somewhat of a shock, for I had been the only child for nearly fourteen years. I had always wanted a sister, so when she initially told me the baby was a boy, I was not too excited. Shortly after my shock and disappointment wore off, I began to get excited and thought it would be cool to have a younger brother. The downfall was we were going to be at least fourteen years apart, give or take a few months. As a teenager, who has time to play with a little baby or even want to stay home and babysit?

Sure enough, as I had suspected, my role was to babysit at times. But that was only when my mom could catch me at home. It was not as though I was at home babysitting every weekend, but when I was at home I would. My brother, whom we call Lil' Chris, was a blessing in my life. Even though, we are like oil and water, he is a great younger brother. He is more of an introvert, mellow and laid back, while I am an extrovert and have never been shy in any way.

When Lil' Chris was about five years old, my parents and I noticed he would always tune his little radio to the Jazz station. Lil' Chris loved music. It was at that age when he started to take piano, flute and lessons for many other instruments. Throughout middle school and high school, Chris was always in the school bands. When he was in high school, he used to play several instruments in the University of Southern California (U.S.C.) major band. He even traveled with a few of the band members to do private gigs. After high school, he continued at U.S.C and was a member of their band for several years. Music continues to be Lil' Chris' passion.

My First Time

At age seventeen, I had sex for the very first time with Dejon. He was a virgin, and I could tell he was getting peer pressure from his friends to have sex. He was saved and raised in the church, but he was not associating with Christ-minded people. As teenagers, we were so in love, but we were oblivious of the consequences for violating God's word. I went to his house after school, and I do not even know how it happened. One thing led to the other. I must say, it definitely was not worth losing my virginity, and unfortunately, it was not at all what I expected. It was not special like some girls dream it will be, but that is because God says sex is pleasing to Him after the wedding ceremony, not before.

Being celibate is more of a challenge once you have already experienced sexual intercourse and then you want to become celibate afterwards. It is much easier to remain a virgin and not be exposed to sex. I encourage all virgins and non-virgins, if you are going to commit your life to Christ, abstain from sex until you get married. We were created in the image of God, and this is how God says it should be - period. This alleviates any sexual urges you may experience and it is honorable unto God, and when you abstain from engaging in sexual intercourse, you are not creating unholy soul ties to each person you are having sex with. You will learn the dangers of "unholy soul ties" in later chapters.

When men and women fornicate and break up, they have a lustful desire for that person, because their souls are connected. God made sex for marriage to keep couples connected. Therefore, my brothers and sisters in Christ, it is a dangerous game to have pre-marital sex.

Additionally, with the rise of sexually transmitted diseases, being celibate is the way to go. There are so many women whose minds are messed up, because they have given their prized possession away and now the man does not want them anymore. Unfortunately, all some men want to do is sample the treasure, and then they are ready to move on. Rewards will be plentiful when you follow the word of the God.

> *"For this is the will of God, even your sanctification, that ye should abstain from fornication."*
>
> -I Thessalonians 4:3 ESV

As my senior year in high school continued, most of my classes were electives, and the one class I enjoyed the most was my cooking class. The teacher for this class was a weird woman named Ms. Graham who always looked like she just rolled out of the bed, never combing her hair. As a practice, my appearance was always chic, and I think Ms. Graham may have been a little jealous of me. I noticed she always wanted me to wash the dishes after class. After a while, I started to feel like she was not being fair with the distribution of duties.

One day, I wore a pair of leather pants, and when she asked me to wash the dishes, I said, "I can't wash dishes today." Ms. Graham became belligerent and called me a heifer and said, "You are going to wash the dishes!" I then excused myself from the class, and I quickly told Mr. Freeman, and I could not wait to tell my mom. My mom went up to the school the next day to meet with the teacher and told her to never call me anything but my name. Mr. Freeman was not pleased with Ms. Graham's lack of professionalism, so she was reprimanded.

Despite a few challenges here and there, high school was always fun, and I would not change anything. After graduating though, I would have gone to a university, such as Harvard or Stanford, instead of hanging around people who were not so ambitious and who thought college was never a good idea. My aunt Lynn was a great supporter. She always encouraged me and wanted me to experience a university outside of Los Angeles. She even offered to pay for my college education. I wish I would have attended a university out of state, because I know it would have been a great experience for me to collaborate with a large diverse group of students from all over the world. However, I always say God had me right where I was supposed to be, in order to get me to where He needs me to be!

Tips from Lessons Learned

1. Remain a virgin until marriage – the rewards are great.
2. If you are not a virgin, maintaining a celibate lifestyle will set you free and protect you from many consequences from sexual sin.
3. Do not get caught up by peer pressure to have sex or find yourself just having sex for activity.
4. Socialize with like-minded Christian men and women.
5. Teenagers need accountability partners with which to discuss their personal matters.
6. Renew your mind day and night to strengthen your walk with Christ, no matter your age.
7. Have conversations with your children about sex when appropriate, and the importance of remaining a virgin until they fully understand the benefits and consequences if they do not adhere to God's word.
8. Encourage youth to experience an out-of-state college.
9. Identify who your children's spheres of influences are.
10. Discuss the Word with your children periodically to ensure they understand what they hear in church.

Monica R. Carter

Chapter Four
Entrepreneur Spirit

> *"But these things I plan will not happen right away. Slowly, steadily, surely, the time approaches when the vision will be fulfilled. If it seems slow, do not despair, for these things will surely come to pass. Just be patient! They will not be overdue a single day."*
>
> -Habakkuk 2:3 TLB

After high school, as I mentioned, I could have attended any university I wanted. However, there are at least two reasons why I did not go away to college right away. First, I did not desire to leave my mom, and second, I always yearned to be an entrepreneur. So, instead of returning to the classroom after graduation, I created a company called "Monica's Creations." I fashioned accessories and placed Swarovski Crystals on glasses, pendants, hair clips, etc. I dispensed the items in two stores one of my friends owned.

A couple of my friends were my models, and I would create the items and bequeath them unto my friends to wear. I presented them with my business cards to distribute when they were adorned with my products. The intended goal was marketing for my business. My friends would give the potential buyers my business card to inform them of where they could purchase items of their own. Distributing business cards is for one purpose and one purpose only- to enhance one's client base by gaining additional clients.

However, one of my friends at the time, whom I met in high school, said she was at a party, and everyone was asking her where she purchased the accessories. She graciously told them, "My friend makes them." I inquired, "Well, did you give them my card?" To my bewilderment, she told me, "They did not ask for it." I said, "WHAT?" To say the least, I was shocked and somewhat perturbed. As you can imagine, that was my last time giving her anything free to wear. I realized she did not have my best interest at heart. She had no intention of helping me increase the revenue for my business.

I have always had the creativity to make accessories and other products, but I did not have the financial support to continue with my business or the resources to take it to the next level. Before the designer Tarina Tarantino launched her line, I was designing numerous accessories before the 'bling' even became popular.

To this day, I bedazzle my clients' Christian Louboutins and other accessories with Swarovski Crystals, and, of course, my own as well. I spend countless hours creating and putting the 'wow' factor on the simplest items. My passion causes me to not grow tired of making beautiful luxurious accessories. Ten hours will pass by without me taking notice. Having my own fashion line has always been my dream, but again I did not have the resources to do so, and the people I knew who could have connected me never did. This is the norm in our culture, which is extremely disappointing. Despite what man does or does not do, I now know I should always look up to God, for He will put the right people in my path.

While working to build my company to the level it did reach, I worked a few jobs right after high school. Then at twenty years old, I met my godmother, Mary Ann Mitchell, who was an entrepreneur and CEO of a multi-million dollar company, which she and her husband started in their garage over twenty years ago. I worked for her for a short while and learned a lot about business acumen and corporate and financial structures.

Mary Ann wanted me to focus on business and I did; however, I was young and wanted to enjoy life as well. So, instead of putting the necessary hours into working and establishing a secure foundation, I spent a lot of time partying with many of my friends. We had our routines. For example, every Sunday, my play cousin Inga, Vivian, Delania, Tammy, whom I met right out of high school, several other friends and I frequented a night club called the Red Onion. Back then, the Red Onion was the place to be on Wilshire Blvd in Los Angeles. I was not twenty-one years old to get into a night club, but a friend of mine gave me an ID to use, and I did not even resemble the person on the ID, but security would overlook that very important detail. I could not wait to be an adult, and my mom and other family members would always tell me, "Do not rush to be grown. Enjoy your young life while you can, because when you get grown, real life starts." Unbeknownst to me, later in life I would remember those words so vividly and wish I would have listened to all the wise women and men in my life. If only I could rewind time!

Panicked Mom

During that same timeframe, I met Justin at the Red Onion. He was extremely handsome and a ladies' man. Justin was about six feet four, with chocolate-colored skin, and coal black curly hair. His skin was smooth as a baby's, and he always dressed and smelled so good. I was cognizant he was not good for me, but he was a smooth talker, and I was reeled in, as were many other women. I considered myself an adult and mature, but some men, especially if they are older than you, know how to flatter young girls. I was twenty years old, living life and having fun. I had no cares or concerns in the world. Some of the girls who would hang out with me and my close friends did not have any dreams or aspirations. The only dreams they had were to be employed at a job and get entangled with a man who could fulfill their needs. Ever since I was a teenager, I always aspired to be successful, to live well and help others in the process.

Justin and I had so much fun hanging out. Every time we went out, he tried his best to have sex with me. I never fell for it at first, because I knew he was a ladies' man. But one night at his house, the chase was over, and he conquered me. This is clearly an example of having casual sex. Being young and not accountable to anyone in the church can lead one to make bad choices. We continued to date and hang out, but the time we spent together started to become less frequent.

As time passed on, I went to my gynecologist one day for a checkup, and he said, "Did you know you are a few months pregnant?" I exclaimed, "WHAT??? Pregnant, are you sure, Doctor?" He said, "Yes, you are." Words escaped me. Finally, after regaining my composure, I asked my doctor, "What were my options?" He said, "You can have the baby, or you can have an abortion." I was livid, and I could not think clearly. I told him I needed to inform my mom, and I was completely at a loss of understanding because I had been taking my birth control pills. He said, "Well, you must have missed one."

I called Inga first and told her I was pregnant. She was so emotionless. Her immediate response was, "Let's just go have an abortion." I responded, "No, I need tell my mom, because I'm so scared and wouldn't know what to do with a baby." Besides, I most certainly did not want to tell Pastor and First Lady. I was unaware what scripture says about abortion, and I could not imagine giving birth to a baby at twenty years old.

Moreover, all I could think about was everyone in my family who would be disappointed in me. I kept asking myself, *What am I going to tell my mom?* It was ironic that I was focusing on my mother and family, when the most important persons I should have been concerned about pleasing was God and the Lord Jesus Christ. Who cares what others think? It is always most important to know what God says in His word.

At that time, my mom worked at the Neiman Marcus corporate office. I called my mom while I was at the doctor's office and said, "Mom, I'm a few months pregnant." My mom was hysterical and could not believe what she was hearing. She was not upset per se. She was more worried about me, and she did not know what to do. She insisted I meet her at our residence, and she left work. When she got home, she called her close friend Misty to come over.

Misty is as close to me as an aunt and is a great confidant to my mom. Misty is from Compton, CA and is very street savvy. When she arrived, she inquired about our choices in dealing with the situation at hand. I told them I did not want to have a baby, because I knew I was not adequately prepared to raise a child. My mom was still very confused; she really was just ambiguous about what to do.

At that point, although we continued to attend church every Sunday, church was not in me. For me, it was more of a routine, but I was not really focusing on the Word and making it a part of my lifestyle. All I knew was I would not know the first thing about raising a baby. Misty then picked up the phone and made an appointment for us to go to an outpatient hospital where they would perform the abortion. My appointment was scheduled for the next week. On the day of the procedure, my mom and Misty waited for me in the recovery area. Once the operation was completed, we left and ate pizza, as if though nothing had occurred.

My mom and I never shared the incident with anyone. Unless she told Chris, I do not know if anyone ever knew. I told Justin I had an abortion after the fact, because he would have wanted me to keep the child, and that was out of the question. Justin was livid and said he did not believe in abortions. I felt horrible after the procedure, and he made me feel even worse after our conversation. I soon would learn what God says about unborn children, no matter if they are conceived out of wedlock.

"Children are a gift from God."

-Psalm 127:3 ESV

As I developed in the Word through my continued church attendance, I inevitably became spiritually wiser. As a result of greater spiritual maturity, I repented of my sins and asked for God's forgiveness for the abortion. After I repented, there were times our adversary would still remind me that I killed a child, and I would feel horrible. During those moments, I would lean on what I learned in the Word: God has already forgiven me. Now, I can share this information with you. If you had an abortion and are still feeling terrible about it, the devil is tormenting your mind. If you have not repented of your transgression, I suggest if you are a born-again believer to repent-today. Once you repent of your sins, God will forgive you and He will blot out your sins. If you have already repented, God has already forgiven you. Now, it is up to you to let the guilt go and move progressively forward with your life. Now that you have been informed of the truth, you can do better in strengthening your relationship with Christ. It is similar to the saying, "Once you know better, you do better."

"Repent therefore, and turn again, that your sins may be blotted out."

-Acts 3:19 ESV

A Breath of Fresh Air

I ended the relationship with Justin, but I continued working with Mary Ann at her company, and selling my accessories. I was feeling better about myself and wanted to engage in a little excitement. Ethan, a friend of mine, whom I had known for a few years, called me on a Friday and asked if I wanted to go to an exquisite party a physician in Beverly Hills was hosting. Desiring to do something exciting, I consented. I immediately called Delania, Tammy and Vivian to accompany me to the party. I thought it would be exhilarating for us to hang out together, as it had been a while. As I was getting dressed, I slowly gave myself a thorough assessment. I was pleased with what I saw because as always, I looked amazing. I have always been the type of person that likes to stand out in a crowd. I have never adorned myself with anything that someone else would wear at any gathering that I have attended. My style is truly unique.

When we arrived to the party, we were all looking beautiful and walked in like we owned it. The doctor, who was hosting the party, had a fabulous house, and there were food and drinks ever present. No one would leave hungry or thirsty. I had a Margarita that evening, which was rare, as I never was a person who drank or even liked to drink. I took two sips, and that was it. As Vivian, Delania, Tammy and I traversed through the crowd of people and enjoyed ourselves, I started to notice a few of the men whispering and admiring us, while pointing their fingers in our direction.

Shortly thereafter, the waitress came over to offer my friends and me a free drink. I told her I would like a "Shirley Temple." I did not want another Margarita, and "Shirley Temples" are my signature drink. I always ask the bartender put it in a martini glass as if I am really having a drink. As the waitress was taking my drink order, she leaned over and said, "An attorney named Cramer wants to dance with you. Here's his card. He wanted me to give it to you." I was quite taken aback. I said, "Oh boy. I guess since he sent his little card over I'm just going to jump into his arms?" I paused for emphasis and continued, "Tell him to come and introduce himself to me and ask me to dance." The waitress laughed and agreed, "I heard that." I was bougie and pretentious in those days. My attitude was- how dare he want me to come over to him. Cramer took about thirty minutes to walk over and ask me to dance. He said he wanted to see how long it would take me to come over to him. I guess he found out I was not coming at all.

We danced the entire night, and he kept the drinks advancing to my friends. My other friend Lindsey, who was dating Ethan, had arrived by then. We were all having a wonderful time and did not want the night to end. My girls were dancing, drinking and teasing all the men in the room. Cramer asked for my number and said he would like to take me to dinner. I consented, and we went to Spagos, on Sunset Blvd. on our first date, which is a very exquisite venue. I was twenty-two, and Cramer was thirty-two years old. Cramer was really the calm in my storm. He really helped me stay focused and was an advocate for education. Coming from Nigeria and working so hard to start his own practice in Beverly Hills, he did not have time to expend aimlessly. He was all business and very focused, yet he still knew how to relax and unwind.

I loved how Cramer was really ambitious, and despite how busy he was, he would always make time for me. Quite frequently, Cramer would take me to the most exquisite restaurants, shopping on Rodeo

Drive in Beverly Hills and wherever else I desired to go. He gave me his credit card to use, but before I charged anything, he required me to get his permission. That was fine with me. After all, it was his money. He definitely had a right to say how it was spent. It was not anything for Cramer to purchase me a $1000 dress or $500 pair of shoes. Seeing how I liked fashion, not just for the name or for show, it was always my desire to have a line of quality clothing. Quality, versus quantity, is most important to me. Besides, since I was born, I have always worn quality apparel, so the way Cramer would splurge on me was nothing new in my life. Believe it or not, although I love fashion, I hate to walk around in stores. To alleviate my discomfort, Cramer made sure we had shoppers that would call us to tell us what was hot in the stores. In my opinion, walking around in malls and stores is such a waste of time.

Cramer was very generous, and he always wanted to ensure I looked beautiful for him. Cramer is a Salvatore Ferragamo man, which is my type of guy. I like a clean cut man, not one who is flashy and wears designer logo printed shoes. That is not classy to me at all. In his generosity, Cramer helped purchase more product for me to create my accessories, so I could sell them to all his doctor, attorney and business colleagues. Trust me, he was frugal like me. And even though we both love the finer things in life, we rarely paid full price for anything. So, for him to invest in my business was huge. Even though he invested money in my dream and wanted me to succeed, his ultimate goal was for me to go back to college.

With Cramer's encouragement and that of others, I enrolled in college. At one point, I wanted to be a nurse. Then, I decided on becoming a doctor, until I actually dissected a cadaver who donated her body to science. Although I was not fearful of the task, that was not my passion. Cramer wanted me to be an attorney, and looking back, I wish I had attended law school to become a fearless attorney. That was not God's plan for me, and God had me exactly where I was destined to be.

> *"I will instruct you and teach you in the way you should go; I will counsel you with my eye upon you."*
>
> -Psalm 32:8 ESV

Just as Cramer made a difference in my life, I would always reciprocate any way I could. Some of the things I did to make his life easier were to type up his cases, organize his office, analyze data and answer calls, if we were in his office on Saturdays. God has given me several abilities, and I have always known that I can do all things through Christ that strengthens me. This is what God put in me at an early age, even without me fully knowing at that time what the word of God says about your talents and abilities. Even though the age difference was ten years between Cramer and me, I was mature for my age in some ways, and Cramer would soon find out how mature I was in the kitchen.

One Saturday morning, I desired to cook something special for Cramer. While he was lying down asleep, I went into the kitchen. As I began to prepare the food, I noticed I did not have enough cooking oil. So, I poured what I had in the skillet and turned the fire on low, so it could begin to heat up, while I rushed to the store. I figured with the fire being low, it would be safe. Because Cramer was asleep, he had no idea I had gone to the store. The store was only around the corner, but when I returned within approximately twenty minutes, several firemen had arrived. There was smoke billowing from the house. When Cramer saw me, he screamed at the top of his lungs, "WHAT WERE YOU THINKING? You almost burned the house down, and I could have died from the smoke!" I apologized profusely. He eventually calmed down. I was so embarrassed. What I had done was definitely immature, and I clearly did not have a sense of responsibility in the kitchen. It was apparent to me I had some growing up to do. After that fiasco, it took Cramer a while to trust me in the kitchen, especially when he was not there.

Cramer and I took our relationship slowly and were not intimate for at least six months, but I knew the day would come that he would make a move. On a warm Saturday evening, we attended his friend Dr. Alan Adwadul's wedding in Newport Beach, CA and Alan insisted we stay the night at his plush beach house. The ambiance in that home definitely set the right tempo. When we arrived, there were red roses in the hallway leading into the bedroom, and sexy black LaPerla lingerie was laid out on the bed for me. I was so nervous and wondered to myself, *How can I get out of this one?* Cramer's facial expression said, *Don't even think about it!* He began to pour himself a glass of his signature drink Louis XIII that Alan gave us as a welcome gift, which cost about $1000 a bottle at that time.

Cramer began to give me a nice back massage, and it was all over. All I can say is that night was amazing. The next morning, I still did not feel convicted. Yes, of course, I went to church. I was connected to the ministry, but the Word was not in me or the desire to live a righteous lifestyle. And because it was not, I could not see anything wrong with fornicating. The next day at church, First Lady could not keep her eyes off me, as if she knew I had fornicated the night before.

> *"And I will give you shepherds after my own heart, who will feed you with knowledge and understanding."*
>
> -Jeremiah 3:15 ESV

Cramer and I continued to have some fun times, and when Crustaceans in Beverly Hills first opened in 1995, we dined there every Friday. We would meet his colleagues there for dinner, and sometimes, it would be just the two of us. Crustaceans has been my favorite restaurant since it opened. I must say, Cramer spoiled me and set the bar high for my future relationships. He even took my grandmother Jean and me to Yamashiro's in Hollywood Hills, CA one evening for dinner when she was visiting me. Cramer had just purchased a new Hummer and Porsche, and he wanted to show it off to anyone and everyone. My grandmother really enjoyed herself and liked Cramer a lot.

Later in the year, I went on to work for a Fortune 500 company as a human resources professional. Cramer was so excited when I acquired the job. He said, "Monica, you really need to finish college, because it's going to be blessing to you one day." My boss David, at the time, also encouraged me to go back college, along with a few people in my family. I finally adhered to everyone's concerns and enrolled in college again.

By working over sixty hours a week and attending college at night for my undergraduate degree, our relationship suffered, but Cramer was more concerned about me graduating. Periodically, I would see my friends, but for two years when I started graduate school at night, my party days were over, because work and school were really time consuming and demanding. Cramer and I still kept in touch, and he would reach out and check on me from time to time. He was one person I could call anytime, and he would do anything for me.

Whatever I needed, he was always there to provide it. He would not invest fully into my business unless we were married. I was not ready for marriage, nor did I want to marry him. With Cramer being a Nigerian, he was very controlling and jealous, and I knew if I married him, I may as well wear a sheet over my head, because he always made suggestions about what I should wear and where I should go. He was never abusive. It was just the nature of his culture. The women never had an opinion, and that is how it was. I could not see myself living that way, but I did miss Cramer when we started to drift apart. He loved me much more than I loved him. I did love him, but not with the same intensity as he loved me. I guess you can say I was not in love. Of course, we all have thought we were in love with someone, but the truth of the matter is you do not realize it until you finally experience real love. Cramer was an integral part of my life. He taught me a lot about business, life and always had my back. He was definitely what I needed in that season.

> *"There is a time for everything, and a season for every activity under <u>heaven</u>:*
> *-a time to be born and a time to die,*
> *-a time to plant and a time to uproot*
> *-a time to kill and a time to heal,*
> *-a time to tear down and a time to build*
> *-a time to weep and a time to laugh*
> *-a time to mourn and a time to dance*
> *-a time to scatter stones and a time to gather them*
> *-a time to embrace and a time to refrain,*
> *-a time to search and a time to give up,*
> *-a time to keep and a time to throw away,*
> *-a time to tear and a time to mend,*
> *-a time to be silent and a time to speak,*
> *-a time to love and a time to hate,*
> *-a time for war and a time for peace."*
>
> -Ecclesiastes 3:1-8 ESV

Tips from Lessons Learned

1. When you repent of your sins, remember God forgives you, but the devil will always try and torment you. Stay focused on God's word.
2. Being celibate will alleviate unholy soul ties and many other unnecessary issues mentioned in this chapter.
3. Do not be flattered by things a man can buy you, which could inevitably compromise your salvation, values and walk with God.
4. God will provide all your needs if you submit your life to Him.
5. Avoid temptation by not sleeping in the same bed with someone who is not your spouse – this is something I would compromise over and over again all my life.
6. Surround yourself with people that are where you want to be and can mentor you to get there.
7. First, ask God for His vision for your life and set a plan. Then, execute that plan, and God will make a way for you. Do not wait for people to help you. God will bless you on your way and put the right people in your path.
8. Be diligent, determined and disciplined in the word of God.
9. Do not lean unto your own understanding about the Word. Continue to seek knowledge and understanding in areas where you are ambiguous and struggling.
10. Your ultimate judge is God! Do not be concerned about what others think about mistakes you have made. The Christian community will not be able to vouch for you on judgment day, only the Lord Jesus Christ.
11. Seek out someone at church who you have a relationship with that will hold you accountable for your actions. Not a 'yes' person, but someone who will tell you the truth and have your best interest, never telling you only what you want to hear.

Monica R. Carter

Chapter Five
It is Time for Ministry

> *"Obey your leaders and submit to them, for they are keeping watch over your souls, as those who will have to give an account. Let them do this with joy and not with groaning, for that would be of no advantage to you."*
>
> -Hebrews 13:17 NIV

After dating Cramer, it was time for me to be liberated and to experience life to the fullest capacity, which to me included going out to party. Prior to each party, getting my hair styled was an absolute requirement. I had a reoccurring weekly appointment to get my hair styled. That was beyond excessive and was an unqualified time robber. Who has time to sit in the beauty shop until one a.m.? For each appointment, I would be in the salon for extensive periods of time. When I was with Cramer, he did not prefer for me to spend my time in such a manner. He saw it as a complete waste of time. In retrospect, there is so much more I could have done with the hours I spent under the dryer, having breakfast, lunch and dinner there and catching up with many friends. I must admit my priorities were not in order.

My hairstylist and friend Colette has been styling my hair for twenty-five plus years, since I was seventeen years old. Colette's shop was very popular in Beverly Hills. Colette is still the most talented hairstylist in Los Angeles. Tammy, Delania, Vivian, Colette, Gena, Rochelle, Tanya and many of my other friends used to frequent any club scene we wanted and just revel in life. Reggae music was very popular at the time, so we would frequent Reggae, R&B, Jazz concerts and comedy shows. Even after breaking up with Cramer, we remained in contact, and he sponsored anything I may have needed. He would even purchase my plane tickets at times when I wanted to travel. In my early twenties, it was party time, and the same is true for most young adults. But if I could do it all over again, I would have chosen to surround myself with people who would have kept me focused on my entrepreneurial aspirations, college and all my future endeavors. But, I have lived and learned to never have regrets, only lessons learned and always thanking God for the time I have left to make wiser decisions.

When I was in my twenties, I had so many friends, or shall I say people I thought were my friends. Everything I have experienced has revealed who my real friends are. As I began to become more mature, people whom I thought were friends began to be in less frequent contact with me and me with them. There are seasons in time when some friends may not be suited for your lifestyle, and I have definitely seen friends removed from my life as my seasons have changed. That is not necessarily a negative thing. God has each person in our lives at the time he/she needs to be there.

During that time in my life, I was starting to spend more time becoming involved in the ministry. As mentioned, Pastor and First Lady were no nonsense. They taught the Word, lived by the Word, and expected each member to do the same or to at least make an honest effort. Yes, they understood we are all human and prone to err, but they expected to see improvements in our lives and walking in accordance to what we had been taught to the best of our ability.

My mom was in the ministry, and Chris was in the choir, as mentioned. I would attend church with my girlfriends or most times by myself. I would never permit any of my male friends to accompany me to church, because I made that mistake once and vowed to never repeat it again. Pastor and First Lady would always position themselves by the front door after service and greet the guests after service. On one particular Sunday, I brought a male friend and because I was like a daughter to my pastors, they felt comfortable to confront anyone I knew. They asked my friend, "So, who are you?" He answered, "I am a friend." First Lady asked, "What kind of friend are you?" Pastor did not give him a chance to respond before he said, "Do not start nothing, won't be nothing." He said that to say- if you mess with my daughter, we are going to have problems.

I laughed it off and walked very quickly out the door. Then the next Sunday, Pastor's sermon was about women having male friends. I was completely embarrassed because I knew he was talking to me and anyone else who had 'friends.' But I did understand he was doing it for our own good. What type of pastor would he be if he did not lead and guide us according to the word of God? He said, "I know what kind of friends they are. Ladies, do not waste your time just being someone's friend. You should date to be married."

I heard Pastor's speech, but I was too young to give serious thought to marriage. However, his sermons each week started to convict me about my sexual sin. I began to think about the life I was living before God and what type of example I was setting before my friends outside of church, because I did not have any church friends.

The friends I hung out with were all fornicating (I am not judging them), but for them it was no big deal. None of them were hearing the Word like I was on a consistent basis. My consistent hearing of the Word gave me a burning desire to want to change, but it was quite the opposite for my friends. I was having a foundation of God's truth instilled in me, while my friends were accustomed to living life according to the world's standards. With all that I heard each week in church, I had an opportunity to be an example for them. Instead, I had one foot in the church and in the world.

The truth of the matter is, I really started to enjoy the Word and going to church. Pastor taught us the Word in abundance and gave us assignments to memorize scriptures. Each year, the congregation read through the entire Bible during our own meditation time. Although I did not realize it, with many of these assignments, my mind was being renewed day and night, and my life was being transformed.

> *"And be not conformed to this world: but be ye transformed by the renewing of your mind, that ye may prove what [is] that good, and acceptable, and perfect, will of God."*
>
> -Romans 12:2 ESV

I could have easily continued to conform to the ways of the world by the company I was keeping, but the word of God is powerful- more powerful than a two-edged sword (Hebrews 4:12 ESV), and it cut away all that God wanted to separate from my life. The Word was beginning to cut away old patterns and habits.

At my church, Pastor was very careful about welcoming just anyone to work in the ministry. He wanted to ensure ministry workers would enhance the lives of others and not contaminate. If anyone wanted to work in the ministry, he/she was required to endure a laborious process to join. The first step was for one to complete an application. The application included several questions, such as:

Do you use drugs? Have you committed adultery, if married? If so, does your spouse know about it? Have you fornicated in the past twelve months? Are you addicted to porn? Do you hold any grudges against anyone?

Of course, I tried to avoid completing that application for a while. One could not work in the ministry if he/she was involved in any type of sexual sin. I knew I was fornicating, so I did not participate in ministry right away, because at the time I was not fully ready to make the commitment to give up sex and live a Christian lifestyle. I was enjoying my activities immensely, but all the while Jesus had been speaking to me about committing to the word of God and being faithful. I was also very aware of the scripture about falling and getting back up.

> *"For a just [man] falleth seven times, and riseth up again: but the wicked shall fall into mischief."*
>
> -Psalm 24:16 KJV

Yes, Jesus does say you are forgiven when you repent; however, even when I learned of these scriptures, I was still rebellious and did not want to obey the Word. I still wanted to live life by my terms, and often times, I would take these scriptures for granted, not thinking I could be in a tragic situation, where I might not be able to repent of my sins.

> *"If we deliberately keep on sinning after we have received the knowledge of the truth, no sacrifice for sins is left."*
>
> -Hebrews 10:26 NIV

> *"Flee from sexual immorality. All other sins a person commits are outside the body, but whoever sins sexually, sins against their own body."*
>
> -1 Corinthians 6:18 NIV

> *"The acts of the flesh are obvious: sexual immorality, impurity and debauchery; idolatry and witchcraft; hatred, discord, jealousy, fits of rage, selfish ambition, dissentsions, factions and envy; drunkenness, orgies, and the like. I warn you, as I did before, that those who live like this will not inherit the kingdom of God."*
>
> -Galatians 5:19-21 NIV

Pastor, for what seemed like an entire year, was always preaching on fornication and adultery. During women's meetings, on every second Saturday of each month, First Lady would speak about sexual sin. I was exhausted from hearing about fornication. You are only tired of hearing about what you are guilty of doing. It seemed every time someone preached, he/she was preaching on sexual sin. I knew deep down, the Holy Spirit was convicting me about my actions and the conviction was becoming overwhelming.

At first, I tended to ignore these sermons and was jubilant when church ceased for the day. However, that really did not make the reality of what I was doing depart. I guess, one could say, the truth injures. I wanted what was done in the dark to stay there. In addition to hearing about my sins, I also felt the impact of them in different areas of my life. I remember reminiscing about how I always tithed, but my tithing was similar to investing and never securing a return on my investment (ROI). If you are tithing and committing sexual sins, you will not receive a return on the seed you planted, and you should not work in the ministry, because you do not want to interrupt the blessings of the ministry. As a result of my sins, I was not being blessed financially, spiritually or emotionally.

As time progressed, my desire to participate in the ministry grew stronger, but I knew my lifestyle of fornication was still present. To my surprise, I found out, if you are a volunteer for the ministry, you did not have to complete the very detailed ministry application. Whew! While intermittently volunteering in various ministries, I noticed some of the ladies would stare me up and down if my shirt was a little low cut in the front or my skirt was a little above my knees. I thought my attire was appropriate at church and quite frankly more stylish than others who attended. Obviously, there were those who did not agree with my perception. As you can imagine, someone occasionally had something to say. I would never show cleavage, wore mini-skirts or intended to be disrespectful. At times, I would be so irritated with some of the ladies, which on several occasions caused me to rescind on my commitment to volunteer. My perception of working in the ministry never included drama. Remember, my family and I had been at that church before any of those women, so in my mind, they were powerless. I am sure you will agree my thinking was demented.

When some people work in the ministry, they do it to cover up their sins. I think they believe their work is some type of atonement. No matter if you think you are fooling Jesus by trying to compensate for sinful acts, He sees everything. He knew what I was going to do before I did it, and He witnessed every act I have ever committed. First Lady was the one I used to hide from. She would see me walking down the hallway and bellow my name, "MONICA!" My heart would begin beating rapidly, and I would say, "Yes, Ma'am." She would say, "Your top is a little low. Have you been fornicating?" I would respond, "No, I have not," knowing I had been indulging in immoral sexual activities to satisfy my sexual cravings. However, I was hesitant to admit it to First Lady.

First Lady would mostly focus her attention on me, and I would always wonder, *Why is she was always picking on me?* I did not know the answer to that question at the time, but I later learned God assigned her to me. He knew I needed someone in my face that was fearless and would keep her eyes on me.

Not only would I become nervous when she would yell my name, but everyone who was around would be nosy and try to hang around to hear what she was going to say to me. When I would tell my friends about my Sundays, they would say, "I would not put up with that, and that is why I would not want to get involved in a church." Those responses were just excuses, but I can see how most people would not want to be confronted in that tone by their first lady, but again that is who Jesus assigned to me, and He knew it was what I needed. I am grateful for every question she asked and for the love and concern she showed me.

Virtuous Woman

Pastor is a great teacher, and when First Lady preached, I really enjoyed it. She was straight to the point and never wavered on what she believed. The message was always given at the right time and ranged in topics from the Proverbs 31 woman, to men and women relationships, to sexual sins, etc. Ladies, the image of the virtuous woman is what Jesus longs for us to be. All of the verses from Proverbs 31 are awesome. However, there are a few that so many women are oblivious to in this day and time. Several of these overlooked verses include:

> "^{10}Who can find a virtuous woman? For her price is far above rubies. ^{18}She perceiveth that her merchandise is good: her candle goeth not out by night. ^{23}Her husband is known in the gates, when he sitteth among the elders of the land."
>
> -Proverbs 31:10, 18, 23 KJV

Verse 10 says, "Her price is far above rubies." Jesus is basically saying to women everywhere, "When you fornicate, by answering an invitation to sleep with a man you are not married to, you are lowering your standards." Remember, sexual intercourse is only for the marriage bed. It hurts my heart when I see women taken advantage of by men or when she herself does not see her own self-worth. This is clearly demonstrated when she freely gives up her precious goods for a moment of pleasure or to be someone's mistress. When unmarried people have intercourse, they combine their souls with someone who is not their husband or wife. This creates unholy soul ties from one person to the next. The only person our soul should be tied with is that of our spouse.

In making these statements, it is not my intent to judge any woman who has done any of these things. As you have already read, my life has been laid out, and it has been clearly stated that I have fornicated. Therefore, my statements do not come to condemn but to let all women know the truth or to at least remind them of the truth. Through the writing of this book, it is my goal to ensure women know their self-worth and to stop settling for a piece of a man.

All women were made in the image of God, and He wants us to experience all that He has for us. Although this particular verse speaks specifically about women, men also have value and should treat their bodies as the temple of God and refrain from immoral sexual activities.

Verse 18 says, "Her merchandise is good." Hallelujah! When I heard Pastor Ron's wife on *Preachers of L.A.* tell Loretta "her merchandise is good," I stood to my feet and shouted out, "Absolutely!" Ladies, we have what men want, but when women give away their best merchandise making it plentiful for men to get, this lowers the standard and value of our goods. Men figure if they do not get what they want from one woman, they can and will call another one, whether it be Mandy, Lisa, Jackie, Tracy or whomever, because these women do not know how precious they are. Ladies, let us raise the bar of our self-worth and standards and start to receive the ultimate blessings God has for us.

Verse 23, "Her husband is known in the gates." Sounds like Boaz to me! Ladies, many of us have settled for less than what God has for us in the area of relationships. We have allowed ourselves to be involved with men who are not equally yoked with us, and we have suffered the consequences of our actions. But, the good news is it is not too late to set things in their proper order. It is important to understand, Jesus has prepared someone just for us, and when we settle for someone we know is not for us, we will miss out on who God has prepared just for us. Even if we meet someone and it does not work out, what God has already ordained for you, no one can destroy. Ladies, men are hunters, not women. Please know you are the prize, and believe me if a man wants you, he will do everything in his power to conquer you. So, be patient and wait on God.

> *"So they are no longer two, but one flesh. Therefore what God has joined together, let no one separate."*
>
> -Matthew 19:6 KJV

Mocked by Friends

Finally, I completed the application to join the ministry. I was excited and ready to serve God. I started as a greeter, to greet the members and the guests as they entered into the church. This position was just right for me. It fit my personality well. I am an extrovert, so I like to socialize and serve. Week by week, I purposed to learn every member's and visitor's name. People feel special when the church ministry acknowledges them on a first name basis. The hospitality industry has been using these standards for years, and it works well in developing a healthy rapport with their clientele. Great customer service is important to me, and I always want people to feel at home. I was on fire for the Lord and was never late for my post. I respected my church, the position I held, and God's people. To me, it was a win-win situation. I was fulfilling a need in the ministry and using my talent of motivating and inspiring others as they walked through the door.

My spiritual development was starting to mature, and I would tell all my friends what I had learned each week in church. Just as every new babe in Christ, I was starting to crave the Word and learn more about becoming an image of God, even though I was not a new Christian. I was truly bubbling over with my newfound love for the Lord, and I was happy to share with anyone who would listen.

My friends could tell there was a change in me. Unfortunately, some of them did not quite understand how God was transforming me by the power of His Word. They often tried to ridicule me in front of others, but that was never a good idea. Although I was saved and on fire for the Lord, God was still working on me, and often times, my response would be fierce. Some of my friends would say, "Hey, Mother Theresa" and make Christian jokes. Or, when there were men around, someone would announce, "She's celibate," and then everyone would get on the subject and make a joke of it. At first, I used to get irritated and defensive, but after a while, I just ignored them. If anything, I was disappointed because they did not see the value in living a chaste life.

When people start to transition from secular to godly living, others will always watch their every move and come against them. When people ridicule others for living according to the word of God that is the devil trying to discourage them and get them off focus. If I wore a pair of shorts, some of my friends would laugh and say, "Oh, Mother Theresa can wear shorts?" I would respond with laughter and say, "Yes, because Mother Theresa is fabulous and blessed!"

Even though the Lord had a hold on me, I still had to show my friends a thing or two. One Saturday night, my friend Kisha had a pole dancing party. Many people do not know Pole Dancing is great exercise, and you have to be in great shape to do it. All of the women had sexy fictional names, and mine was "Candy." There were about fifteen of us, and we were competing to see who had the best pole dancing moves. There were five men, who were family members of Kisha's, who had the responsibility to judge the dancing. Some of the girls were huffing and puffing out of breath after completing their routine. I was patiently waiting for my turn, because I was about to take things to the next level.

When it was my turn, they began to go into an uproar yelling, "Where is Mother Theresa? It is your turn." At first, I was Mother Theresa, but after I showed my moves, they started to call me by my dancing name for the evening "Candy." I went from the top of the pole to the bottom and swung around with some floor dances. It was evident their skills had nothing on mine. I told them, "Ladies, you are lucky the Lord has a hold on me. All phenomenal things come from Him!" I won the prize and left them with their mouths open.

My friend Tandy has a pole dancing studio, and often times, a few of my friends and I would go there for some great core exercises and to engage in girl talk and have a good time.

As I would talk about fornication with my friends, they thought abstaining from pre-marital sex was foolish and that celibacy does not work in these days. I met with Pastor to inform him of the challenges I was having with friends and the topic of fornication. He gave me a list of scriptures to share with friends in case the matter arose again. He also told me I should not negotiate the word of God with them. He instructed me to just share the Word and move on. He said, "You can't get into debates with friends about what the Bible says. You can only give them knowledge and understanding, but they will have to make the decision to believe or not. There is no need for you to get upset about their behavior." After I spoke with him, I understood I was doing my job by enlightening them on the Word similar to Jesus putting Pastor in my life to give me knowledge and understanding.

> "Then I will give you shepherds after my own heart, who will lead you with knowledge and understanding."
>
> -Jeremiah 3:15 NIV

One thing I did notice, as my friends would start to have financial or relationship issues, they would always call me for advice. At first, I would respond sarcastically and say, "Wow, you are calling Mother Theresa for help? The other day you were just clowning me." However, Jesus convicted and reminded me when my brethren reach out to me in need, I am to help them.

> *"The heartfelt counsel of a friend is as sweet as perfume and incense."*
>
> -Proverbs 27:9 NIV

Tips from Lessons Learned

1. Always put God first in every aspect of your life; the ultimate reward is inheriting the kingdom.
2. It is important to always surround yourself with great people at church who you can trust.
3. Do not be discouraged when you decide to live a righteous lifestyle. Your friends may mock you, but they are learning from you. Be patient with them, as they have struggles like we all do.
4. God sees all things, even when we are being sneaky and cutting corners. We are only delaying our blessings from God.
5. You cannot serve the world and God. The best gratitude you can ever have is serving God.
6. Building a relationship with your pastor and/or first lady can make all the difference in the decisions you make in your life. They are here to feed you with knowledge and understanding and help you stay on the right path.
7. Renewing your mind in the Word day and night is critical to maintaining a righteous lifestyle.
8. Participating in the ministry is all a part of you serving God and making more disciples.
9. Women and men, please do not devalue yourselves by allowing the opposite sex to use your body. Your body is God's temple, not a visitors' center or a flight layover.
10. God says, "Your merchandise is good" and "priceless." Do not devalue your self-worth, ladies.

Monica R. Carter

Chapter Six
All that Glitters is not Gold

> *"Let no man deceive you with vain words: for because of these things cometh the wrath of God upon the children of disobedience."*
>
> -Ephesians 5:6 KJV

At that juncture in my life, everything was fabulous. I was really enjoying being in the ministry and serving the people of God. Furthermore, I was still working at the Fortune 500 Company, working over sixty hours a week, going to school at night and driving my James Bond two-seater BMW Roadster convertible. In between working, attending evening classes, and studying, there was no time for any fun, because I was determined to complete my undergraduate and graduate degree within four to five years. After some time, my diligence paid off. I completed both programs of study as planned. While some of the classes were challenging with the enormous amount of homework assignments, English and math have always been my best subjects, so those classes were not difficult to complete.

After completing my degrees, I found my daily routine becoming repetitious, and I needed some excitement. My friend Meagan called me from time to time, and we would go to dinner or private functions. She always knew the hottest spots to relax and have a good time. Meagan is approximately eight years older than I, and she is a prominent real estate professional. Most of my friends were older than I was. I eventually began socializing with people who were more successful, because I aspired to be an entrepreneur, millionaire, and to resign from corporate America one day. Meagan was divorced by the time we met. She always kept a few boyfriends who would take good care of her, but, of course, she made her own money and was not dependent on anyone.

Meagan called me one day and asked, "Are you still under Cramer's spell?" I said, "Ha-ha. We chat from time to time, and he will always be there for me, but we are not a couple." At that time, Cramer was building a hotel in Nigeria and traveled back and forth a lot. Some of my other male friends would take me out when I had time, but because of my schedule, life was hectic. I did not have much time for socializing, even though I desired to.

She continued by saying, "Well, my man Phil has a friend named Jon I want you to meet." With curiosity, I asked, "How old is he, and what's his profession?" I really wanted to see where she was going with her suggestion. I requested more details. Meagan dated old men, and I was not interested in dating my father! She laughed and said, "Girl, he's about thirty-five, and that's only ten years older than you. Phil said Jon owns several businesses and is a really nice guy." I inquired, "How does Phil know he's a nice guy?" We both began to laugh. Meagan replied, "Apparently, Jon saw you at my birthday party and asked Phil who you were. He thought you were beautiful, sexy and classy. You know how you usually light up the room with your bubbly personality." All I could say was, "Yes indeed!" After we had a good laugh, I finally said, "Well, let me get back to you, because I will not be available for a few weeks." Three weeks later, we all went out to dinner.

The Introduction

One Friday evening, we all assembled at Meagan's house to decide where we would go to dine. Meagan, knowing my preference, realized if he asked me I was going to say Crustaceans. Phil was already there when I arrived, and both Phil and Meagan were looking dapper as always.

The doorbell rang, and we thought it was Jon, but it was a delivery guy with five dozens white roses with one red rose in the middle. Meagan said, "Awe baby, I love those roses. That was so nice of you." She was grinning from ear to ear. Phil shook his head and said, "Babe, I did not have those delivered." You should have seen Meagan's face. The smile that once covered it suddenly disappeared as quickly as it had come. She is very fair complexioned, and she turned beet red. The deliveryman said, "These are for Monica." I was flabbergasted. As I stood there in utter surprise, he asked me to read the note. The note said: "I look forward to meeting you. Thank you for taking time to have dinner, Beautiful." And, it was signed Jon!

I was shocked and at a loss for words. However, my pastor has always taught me men are hunters, and they will go after whatever they want and go out of their way to please a woman. Jon was exemplifying exactly what Pastor had said. Prior to our first date, he had already moved into action. Although I am not someone who particularly cares for roses, I thought he was a gentleman, and I appreciated the gesture.

Shortly thereafter, Jon walked in the door. Phil felt outdone and made his position clear. He said, "Jon, man you always trying to do the most." With impeccable charm, Jon responded, "I would do anything for this beautiful woman." I said, "Isn't that sweet? Thank you so much for the lovely roses." He politely responded back with, "It is my pleasure. I wanted to ensure you knew you are very special." Meagan and Phil were about to lose consciousness with all the flattery that was going on.

> *"A man who flatters his neighbor spreads a net for his feet."*
>
> -Proverbs 29:5 ESV

Jon was not someone I would say, "Oh, he is so fine." He was handsome in his own way. Jon stood five feet ten, was a toned 185 pounds, had Chinese slanted eyes and chocolate-colored skin, with a nice grade of hair. He was clean cut, sharply dressed, smelled good, had white teeth, was very charismatic and well spoken.

Meagan all of a sudden was in a hurry. With an attitude, she said, "Let's go. I am hungry, and since Monica received the roses, where would the princess like to go?" Meagan was nice at times, but would prefer all the attention be on her, and at times she would love to throw shade. Jon said, "You are right. Where would my princess like to go?" Before I could answer, Meagan and Phil said simultaneously, "CRUSTACEANS!" I agreed, "Absolutely."

We all rode together with Jon in his new black on black Phantom Bentley. Jon opened my door and placed my legs in the car. I was pleased he did, because it would have been a disappointment if he expected me to open the door myself. While we were driving, I was thinking, *He must do very well for himself to drive this car*. There are many cars, such as Mercedes and BMW, men drive, so they can fake it until they make it, but if a man drives a Bentley, he can afford it.

Phil and Meagan were in the back seat making drinks, and Jon had Jay Z (Jigga) tuned into the sound system. At one time, I had been fond of Jigga, but at that point, I mostly listened to my gospel CD's, because I was on fire for the Lord and trying to stay focused. As we rode along, I felt a little uncomfortable and desired to know more about Jon to ensure I was not wasting my time.

Jon began to ask me questions, such as where I was employed and resided, if I had any children, and whether or not I had a boyfriend. I informed him of my situation with Cramer and how we were great friends. Jon said, "That's cool that you two are still friends. Most breakups do not end well, and people are not amicable with one another."

I returned the favor and asked him questions as well in an effort to learn more about him. I asked if he had any children, a girlfriend and about his profession. He had two children, had never been married, had just broken up with his girlfriend, and is an investor who buys/sells real estate. I sarcastically remarked, "You must sell a lot of real estate!" He ignored my sarcasm and said, "Yes I do, but not only residential homes. I own commercial buildings, strip malls and many other type of commercial properties." We all made small talk and laughed while enjoying the ride to dinner.

After arriving and being seated at dinner, we all had a stupendous time. Jon was acting as though I was his woman already. Besides that, I noticed he was very popular. He knew every other person in the restaurant, no matter the ethnicity. The staff knew me very well, only because I had been patronizing their business since Crustaceans opened. Jon introduced us to his Cuban friends, and they told Phil and Jon they were going to steal Meagan and me from them. We all laughed, but I could tell Jon did not find it hilarious. Then, his friends left.

When Jon went to the men's restroom, Phil said, "My man likes you, Monica." I asked, "How do you know Jon likes me?" Phil answered, "I have known Jon for a long time, and he does not allow any woman he just met to ride in his Bentley." I said, "He is just trying to show off." Phil said, "Oh, no. He has no reason to show off. Jon has it going on and can get any woman he wants." I said, "Well, I guess that makes two of us, because I can get any man I want." Jon arrived back to the table just as I was finishing my comment and replied, "Well, those other men will not have a chance." After making his comment, he laughed it off, but I knew he meant every word of what he said.

Flattered with Gifts

When Jon sat down at the table, he had a quaint box in his hand. He said, "This is for you, Beautiful." Meagan was taken aback, "Oh, my goodness. This is killing me, Jon. If you are spoiling Monica this much on the first date, you will not have any more surprises for her as you continue to date." Then, Phil said, "You are going to give up some goods tonight, Monica." I could not believe what my ears were hearing. I looked at him with a stern look on my face and said in a matter-of-fact tone, "That will not be happening." Meagan then opened her big mouth and said, "That's for sure, because Monica is celibate." Phil disagreed, "Oh, please. Jon is going to hit that." His tone said he knew for sure something sexual would be taking place between Jon and me later that night. Jon said, "Man, hold up. Why are we talking about this woman's personal business at the table? That's not cool." I have never seen Phil shut his mouth so fast. I was steaming hot. It was not that I was ashamed of being celibate, but that was my business to share with him, not Meagan's.

I turned my attention back to the gift and away from my sex life and said, "Jon, you did not have to give me a gift. The roses are more than enough." He said, "You deserve much more than this." He just overlooked the 'celibate' statement and acted as if though it had never been said, and he showed no interest in talking about it. When I opened the box, I was surprised at what I saw inside: a diamond pinky eternity ring inside. I said, "I can't take this." He said, "It is no big deal. I want you to have it." I was thinking, *I really hope he does not think he's going to sleep with me, because he will be sadly mistaken.* I took the ring home but did not wear it for a long time.

As the night passed along, dinner was great, and we all continued to laugh and have a satisfying time. Not to mention, we ate well, and Jon paid the bill. Drinking alcohol was not my forte, except for a special occasion to toast a celebration. When I did have a drink, it was only a few sips of Moet. While everyone else had drinks that night, I had my favorite "Shirley Temple" in a martini glass. I must admit it was a fantastic time out with friends. I was on cloud nine and having so much fun.

> *"But I am afraid that as the serpent deceived Eve by his cunning, your thoughts will be led astray from a sincere and pure devotion to Christ."*
>
> -2 Corinthians 11:3 NIV

After dinner, they wanted to relax at a lounge, but I needed to get home to rest for church in the morning, as it was already twelve midnight. Jon did not force the issue, and as we were driving back to Meagan's house, he asked me when he could see me again. I told him I would let him know because with school and work, my schedule was full and did not allow a lot of free time. He said, "I am busy as well, but I will make time for you." He opened my door, kissed me on my cheek and escorted me to my car.

Before I arrived to my home, Meagan was calling me to share what Jon had spoken to her and Phil. Meagan said, "Girl, he loves you. He told us he would do anything for you, and he's glad you are a church girl." I said, "Girl, he just met me, and I am sure he has many women." She replied, "I do not think so. Phil only knows his ex-girlfriend, and supposedly, she is crazy in love with Jon." I remained optimistic and said, "Well, he seems nice, but I need to see what he is all about. He mentioned he went to church, but I never heard of the church he attends. He talked a lot about God, but I think he knows I attend church and now because of your big mouth, he knows I am celibate." I continued, "Meagan, in the future, please let me tell my good news. Okay?" She said, "Okay, girl. I am sorry." I asked her if she was aware he was an investor and owns large commercial properties. She answered, "Phil mentioned he owns property and a real estate office." I said, "Okay, girl. Let's chat tomorrow at church." Meagan had begun attending my church a few years prior, and she really enjoyed the sermons.

After our dinner out, I did not call Jon. Nevertheless, he paged me every day. Yet, I did not respond for a week. My older girlfriends have always told me not to call back right away. When I called Jon back after a week, he was not ecstatic. He said, "So, it is like that?" I asked, "What do you mean?" He responded, "I called you a week ago, and you are just now calling me back." I said, "Oh, my apologies. I have been so busy, and by the time I get home, I am exhausted." He asked, "What if I did you that way?" I said, "I would think you were busy."

With my final response, he changed the subject and asked me when we could go out again. I said, "Jon, let me just be honest. I am really busy with work, school and church. Right now, I barely have time for myself." He was not letting up too easily. He continued, "Well, you have to make some time and enjoy your life. So, how about we get together in two weeks?" He was persistent, to say the least. I said, "Okay, I will add you to my schedule, and let's see how it works out." He then asked, "Can I at least come and take you to lunch one day?" I said, "Sure, that's fine."

Jon took me to lunch from time to time, and we had many opportunities to get to know each other and talk about our family, friends and growing up. If we were ever discussing church, I was always the one to bring up the subject and ask questions. He would never mention anything about church, which I thought was bizarre. Silly me, I was about to be twenty-six years old, and I was clouded by all the excitement. School and work were my life, so he was refreshing. Jon was slowly pulling me closer to him. It was clear we were unequally yoked, and I should have followed the Holy Spirit and ended what would be the beginning of a nightmare to come.

> *"So flee youthful passions and pursue righteousness, faith, love, and peace, along with those who call on the Lord from a pure heart."*
>
> -2 Timothy 2:22 ESV

It's My Birthday

Jon had no idea our second date was my twenty-sixth birthday. I did not want to inform him, because I knew he would desire to do something grand, and I did not want him expecting sex from me. Jon was very romantic and loved to make me feel like a princess, which I loved. As we were driving along Pacific Coast Highway listening to his favorite Jay Z, Frankie Beverly & Maze and other music, Jon said he needed to make a quick stop at his friend's house in Malibu, CA.

As we made our way there, I asked him if he listened to gospel music, and he said, "No, not really, but I am not opposed to it. What artists do you like? I will purchase the CDs." I provided him with a few artists' names, and he said, "Okay, next time we go out, I will have some gospel music for you." Eventually, we pulled up to a breathtaking house, which had valet parking in the front. I said, "I can stay in the car until you come back." He said, "No way. Please come in with me, so I can introduce you to my friends." When we entered, people were eating and listening to music. He introduced me to everyone, and they were cordial.

Jon went downstairs with his friend, came back within fifteen minutes, and then we left. I noticed he had a backpack and soon as the car came up, he threw it in the trunk. I did not give it deep thought, but I was curious as to what was in the backpack.

We headed to a nice romantic dinner on the beach in Malibu. The dinner table had white roses and candles all around the table. In the middle of the table was a card with 'Happy Birthday' on it. I was completely caught unaware. Barely able to find words, I asked, "How did you know it was my birthday?" He answered, "Meagan told me." I should have known Meagan could not hold water. He then inquired, "Monica, why didn't you tell me it was your birthday? I just found out today, and I could have done something far better than this." I said, "I did not want to make a big deal out of it. My friends are giving me a party tomorrow, so this is fine." He said, "Okay, well do not feel like you cannot tell me things, because I would have done something extraordinary for you." I said, "No worries. This is great."

Jon said, "So, open the card and let's order dinner." I opened the card, and he wrote he was glad to have met me and hoped we can be more than friends soon. The bottom of the card had a little pocket, and in it was $1500. He said, "Go buy yourself something nice." I said, "Jon, look. I have only known you for a few weeks, and these lavish gifts are very much appreciated; however, I live a completely different life than you. I am saved and living a lifestyle of Christianity. I do not want to continue to take these gifts and leave you to have expectations of me."

He responded, "No way, Monica. I do not have any expectations of you. I really like you and appreciate your values. I have the ability to do whatever I want for you, so just enjoy the moment for once in your life. Besides, most women are always asking for money, and I love the fact you never ask, which makes me want to do more for you, Beautiful." I said, "Well, I was raised with the understanding a man should know what a woman needs; therefore, a woman should not have to ask." He said, "Exactly my point!" I was thinking to myself, *Oh boy, what am I getting myself into? At some point, he's going to want more from me than just my cute smile.*

We went on to enjoy the evening, and it was great. Then, he said, "Your eyes are so beautiful and hypnotizing. Those sexy eyes are pulling me closer to you." Next thing I know, he kissed me on my neck. I was thinking, *Lord Jesus, help me now.* I said, "Let's stop kissing, because this is too much for me."

The weather had begun to cool down, so we prepared to leave. While we were driving, Jon asked when he would see me again, and I said I would let him know very soon.

Afterward, I was really trying not to think about him, but I thought about him all day every day. That kiss was always at the forefront of my mind. Being celibate was new for me and even though my mind said, "You are going down the wrong path," my flesh was crying for more. Then, I thought about what the Lord said about repenting of my sins.

> *"If we confess our sins, he is faithful and just to forgive us our sins and to cleanse us from all unrighteousness."*
>
> -1 John 1:9 ESV

The Good Time Charlie

Finally, I called Jon the next week to say hello, and we talked for nearly an hour. He said he would be traveling and would be back in about seven days, and he would like to see me when he returned. We continued to spend time together, and I began to tell my friends about him.

About two months into our friendship, he asked me if I wanted to be his woman. I asked him how he was going to handle my lifestyle, because he was not celibate, and I had not heard him ever say he went or was going to church. He said not to worry about that and he loves me. I asked, "You love me?" He said, "Yes. I have deep feelings for you." We kissed passionately, and I said, "Okay." Then I emitted a sigh, as if to say, *Lord, what am I doing?* Every time we kissed, I could not handle it. It felt so good.

I was still very involved in the ministry and enjoying life. Each week, Pastor would again begin talking about fleeing fornication. He said, "If you're dating, you should date to get married, and it should be with someone with whom you are equally yoked."

I was starting to feel convicted, because Jon was not someone I was marrying, and we certainly were not equally yoked. First Lady would look at me strangely at church. Her eyes said, "I know you are up to something." She would call to meet with me and ask me if I was dating someone. I answered, "No." I am not certain why I lied, but I knew if I answered affirmatively, she would ask me too many questions, and I was not ready to answer any questions.

Jon would always have an excuse as to why he could not attend church. He always had a business meeting or he was out of town. At that point, Jon and I were together every chance we had. I would drive to the valley when I got out of school at night, because I worked in the valley, and sometimes I would stop by Tammy's house who lived near my job. Often times, I would stay over his house during the week, but I never missed church on Sunday.

When Jon was in town, we would always go to the finest restaurants and shopping whenever we were both free. One day, Meagan called me and said, "I can hardly reach you. You and Jon must be enjoying yourselves." I said, "He's really cool, but my only issue is that he's not in the Word, and I don't want to backslide by being with him." Meagan said, "Girl, stop being a square and enjoy life. Jesus will forgive you." I said, "Square I am not, but you have no idea from my perspective how I must feel. We have so much fun, but I really want to live for God and do the right thing for a change." Meagan said, "Well, girl just see what happens and have fun."

"Do not be deceived: 'Bad company ruins good morals.'"

-1 Corinthians 15:33 ESV

I have always been a leader, and I firmly believe no one can make another person do anything. We all have our own free will and tend to make decisions we know are not right. Consequently, it is important to keep company with like-minded people who are capable of giving sound advice and will help you stay the course. As a believer, you should always surround yourself around other believers. Otherwise, you will have similar tendencies of those with whom you socialize. I knew all of these facts, but I continued to socialize with people who I knew were not beneficial for me.

A few months later, Jon invited me to a Mike Tyson boxing match in Las Vegas, NV. I thought it would be enjoyable, so I said,

"Yes, I would love to go. But, can we come back first thing Sunday morning, so I can make it to church?" Jon said, "Hun, how are we going to make it back that early? That means we would need to get up around seven a.m. and make to it to the airport." He hesitated and then continued, "Well, if it means that much to you I will schedule your flight to leave first thing Sunday morning, and I will come back later in the day." Jon had planned to see a few of his friends on Sunday for a business meeting. At least that is what he said.

We landed in Las Vegas, on a Friday evening. It was the beginning of the fall, and it was slightly windy outside. We stayed at the MGM hotel where the boxing match was being held. Everywhere we turned, Jon knew someone as usual, and that meant we were stopping every second to speak to someone. The fight was not until Saturday night, so we had planned to just relax Friday night and see a show.

When Jon opened a hotel suite door, I found the hotel suite was filled with red candles, thong lingerie set, and a fancy dress for me to wear to the fight. I was so amazed and overjoyed by his romantic nature. One of Jon's qualities was that he sure knew how to romance a woman. But, I asked him, "You really expect me to wear this thong around you?" He answered, "Why not?" I said, "Because that would only get you all excited." He said, "I can't wait." I laughed aloud and whispered, "Lord Jesus, help me."

I told Jon I had a gift for him. It was a nice shirt and card, to let him know I really appreciated how good he had been to me. He asked me if I loved him, and I said, "Yes." I really did not love him, but I did not want to hurt his feelings. I loved how he treated me. He was so spontaneous. He was what my girls and I call "The Good Time Charlie." It was not really love, but infatuation from everything he did for me. It was all very exciting. I could tell how he looked at me that he really loved me.

We met Meagan, Phil and two of his other friends and women for dinner that evening. Then, we all went to a magic show. It was a blast, and everyone was having a great time. After the show ended, we all left and went our separate ways.

Wrong Turn

We arrived back to our hotel suite, and Jon took a shower. While he was in the shower, I opened the door. Because the bathroom was so big, he could not see me turning on the water in the Jacuzzi bathtub next to the window with a nice view. I waited for him to come out of the bathroom. When he did, he said, "Beautiful, your bath is ready."

While in the bathtub and as I was soaking, I closed my eyes while the soft music was playing. After a few minutes, I opened my eyes, and Jon's face was right there ready to kiss me. He kissed my lips and proceeded to wash my back and body. Before I knew it, he had climbed into the bathtub with me. I said, "Jon, get out of this bathtub." As much as I tried to resist, he came closer and was not taking no for an answer. After a while, I just said forget it and thought about what Meagan said about Jesus forgiving me. That was all she wrote. The night was passionate, and he seemed like he was trying to take over my mind, body and soul.

The next morning, I felt awful, and when I opened my eyes, breakfast was waiting for me. I began to cry, and he said, "Monica, do not cry. I love you, and I will never leave you." I said, "It is not about you loving me or anything. It is about my commitment I made to Jesus, and I broke it." I told Jon I needed a moment to read my Bible. I confessed and repented of my sins and asked my Lord and Savior to forgive me.

Even after I repented of my sins, I could not rid the feeling of being dirty and disgusting from my mind. I knew it was the devil tormenting me, because Jesus does not remember your sins, once you repent.

> *"Repent ye therefore, and be converted, that your sins may be blotted out, when the times of refreshing shall come from the presence of the Lord; And he shall send Jesus Christ, which before was preached unto you."*
>
> -Acts 3:19-20 NIV

Jon wiped my tears away and assured me he really, really loved me and wanted to spend the rest of his life with me. I was about to say, "But I'm not sure if I want to spend the rest of my life with you, and I want to live my life for Christ." Before I could utter a word, he put his fingers across my lips and said, "Let's not spoil the weekend." We got dressed and headed out to the casino, so he could gamble. I was never a gambler and could not see losing my money that quickly.

Jon showed me how to play poker and craps. The games were fun, especially because I was playing with someone else's money. Despite winning $600, my spirits were still low. I felt like a failure even though I had repented. Jon just could not comprehend why I was being so hard on myself. For me, my commitment to God was rather important, but I finally started to feel better and enjoy the day.

Jon said he needed a belt, so we walked over to Neiman Marcus. While Jon looked for a belt, I surveyed the women's section. A very pleasant male salesperson came over to assist me. He was very flamboyant and amusing. He asked, "Is there anything in particular you're looking for today?" I said, "Not really. Just looking." Not taking no for an answer, he began to pull out a pair of classy jeans and a top and asked me to try them on.

I tried the outfit on and found it to be very appealing. I went to find Jon. He had found his belt. I showed him the outfit and asked, "What do you think about this?" He responded, "It looks great." I took his comment as consent, and I placed the outfit on the counter, alongside his belt. The salesman said, "Oh, honey. You need a belt as well." He walked away momentarily and returned with a $300 belt.

The man gave Jon the total: $1100. Jon looked at the man and said, "You made a quick sale." I realized I had not looked at the price of my top or jeans, but Jon really did not seem to care. With a smile, I said, "Thank you, love. That was so sweet of you, and I appreciate it." He said, "I told you I would do anything for you, Beautiful."

Jon said, "Come, wifee. Let's go get something to eat." As we were walking outside, I spotted a couple from my church that was in the ministry. My heart started beating and 'oh my goodness' was running through my mind. Jon was hugging me, and the couple spotted me, witnessing it all. The couple approached me and said, "Hey, Monica. What are you doing in Las Vegas?" I said, "This is my friend Jon, and we are going to the Mike Tyson fight tonight." They had a strange look on their faces, but they only said, "Sounds like fun." Then, they asked me if I was going to church the next day, and I said, "Yes."

The couple could not wait to get on the phone with Chris to tell him they just saw me in Las Vegas. They asked Chris if he knew who this friend was and told him he looked older than I. Neither had Chris nor my mom ever met Jon, so they did not know. Nor did they know I was in Las Vegas, but I was an adult.

My mom paged me, but I did not respond to the page. I finally returned her call when we returned to our suite. She asked me where was I. I said, "In Las Vegas. Didn't the Martins just tell you?" She ignored my rude remark and asked me, "Who is Jon?" I said, "A friend." She said, "Okay. Well, I will see you tomorrow at church." I said, "Okay." As I was speaking, I noticed Jon's eyes were filled with attitude. When I asked him what was wrong, he retorted, "Why are you telling everyone we are just friends?" I said, "Because I have not told anyone about you as of yet." Then I smiled, rubbed the side of his face, and continued, "Come on, sweetheart. Don't let this spoil our weekend." He said, "Okay, precious."

We went on to get dressed for the Mike Tyson fight, and we all had an exhilarating time that night. We went back to our suite, and Jon attempted to make love to me again, but I flatly refused saying, "I can't do this." I could tell he was disappointed, but he finally just went to bed.

I got up early the next day, kissed Jon on his cheek, and prepared to leave. He did not want me to leave, but I thanked him for everything and told him I would see him back in Los Angeles and left for my flight.

In Hot Water

When I arrived to church the next day, I was called into the office to meet with my first lady. She said, "So, I heard you were in Las Vegas this weekend with a guy. Who is this guy you were hanging with? I hear he appeared to be much older than you." I said, "Wow, why were the Martins in Las Vegas?" She said, "They are married and grown." I said, "I'm grown as well." She said, "That's true, but I think you're going down the wrong path and you're fornicating." I said, "I'm not fornicating." Just as quick as I said it, I had to repent for lying. First Lady said, "You're sat down from the ministry. As you know, you cannot indulge in any sexual sins and participate in any ministry. When you do that you block the financial blessings for yourself and the church." I shrugged it off and said, "Okay, no problem. I will sit down."

> *"Therefore, if anyone is in Christ, the new creation has come: The old has gone, the new is here!"*
>
> -2 Corinthians 5:17 NIV

Thereafter, I started to convert back to my old ways. Every opportunity Jon and I found, we were fornicating, and I was deep into sin. We were enjoying life, and I was sat down at church longer than expected. Finally, I introduced Jon to Chris and my mom. They did not dislike Jon, but I was unsure if they liked him at all. They asked me what he did for a living, and I said, "He's a real estate investor, among other businesses." The four of us never went out to dinner together, mainly because Jon was so busy.

With fornicating comes a love-hate relationship. Jon and I started to quarrel about the silliest things. Our disputes caused us to break up for a week. Then, we would get back together. When two people fornicate, they start to argue about any and everything. The arguing is a direct result of confused language. When you are in sexual sin, you are not going to have a harmonious relationship.

The Reveal

One day, while I was over Jon's house relaxing, he fell asleep. I noticed the black bag he would keep in his trunk lying on the floor, and I was curious what was in it. I opened the bag to find it filled with rolls of money. At the bottom of the bag was white powder in clear bags. There was more money in comparison to the powder. I knew what it was when I saw it. It was cocaine.

Instantly, I became perturbed. When Jon awakened, he noticed my demeanor and asked, "What's wrong with you, sexy?" At first, I lied and said, "Nothing." But wanting to know the truth, I asked, "Are you a drug dealer?" He yelled, "WHAT? Why would you ask me a stupid question like that?" I said, "Because I opened your black bag and saw money and some cocaine in there." He said, "For one, don't go in my stuff, and secondly, that's not mine. A friend of mine left that bag in my car, and I did not want to be driving around with it." I did not believe a word he was saying, so I replied, "Stop lying." Right at the moment, my pager went off several times. It was Dwayne, a friend of mine in the NFL who liked me. When Jon and I would break up, I would spend time with Dwayne, and he was really quite taken with me. I liked him too, and we were in the same age group and had a lot of fun when we were together. He was such a southern guy and never pressured me for sex.

Jon called the number back and asked the guy who he was. Dwayne said, "A friend of Monica's." Jon said, "Well, this is her man, so don't call anymore." Dwayne said, "Man, please. You're not her man, and she does not love you." Why in the world did Dwayne say that? Jon went ballistic and began calling me names saying I was just like all the other chicks. Then, when I demonstrated I could care less about his opinion, he started to get teary eyed and asked me not to leave. I told him, "I am sick of your mess and besides, now I find out you're a drug dealer." He said, "Monica, let me explain. That's just something I do on the side, but I do not touch drugs. I do invest in real estate and have my own business, but many people have a side hustle. I do not need to deal drugs, but it's in me and where I come from, so it's hard to kick. What you see in my bag is just a personal stash for friends. I'm not on drugs and do not take drugs." I stood to my feet and declared, "What? I don't deal with drug dealers, and besides I hear when you're not with me, you still mess around with your ex-girlfriend." He swore up and down he was not with her. Still refusing to believe what he was saying, I said, "Yeah right." I collected my belongings and left.

Afterward, I did not talk to Jon for a few weeks. He would call and page me, but I refused to answer. One night, he sat in front of my house and watched Meagan drop me off with two other guys. One of the guys was Dwayne who had come to visit me on his break. We had all gone to Disneyland. When I got in the house, Jon blew my phone up, and when I answered, all I heard was him screaming. I hung up in his face and did not want to speak with him ever again.

As much as I tried to get Jon out of my mind and body, I could not. I had created an unholy soul tie with him causing double-mindedness, and it was difficult to shake him loose, even though I knew he was not good for me.

"A double-minded man is unstable in all his ways. And is one with a divided soul."

-James 1:8 NIV

God's Hand on Me

Being young and dumb, I continued to date Jon, but I was deeply disturbed about my decision. The lovemaking was passionate and addicting, and we were connected. I was still sitting down from working in the ministry, but I would attend church and just listen to the Word. On one particular Sunday, I was sitting in church, and from time to time, Pastor would prophesy around the church the entire service. Most of the prophecies would be positive, but sometimes you may get a Word you would prefer to pass on.

That particular Sunday I was feeling like I wanted to get my life back on track and stop fornicating. Pastor walked around to me and said, "Daughter, God has a lot in store for you, and He wants you to live right, but trouble is going to come your way, and when it does, God said to call on Jesus. The purpose of this trouble is for you to know He really exists and to commit to His word, so you can receive all the blessings He has for you and depend on Him for everything. You can't even imagine what God has in store for you, but in order for Him to use you, this is the path He has to take you on."

As I listened intently to the words Pastor was sharing with me, I was saying to myself, *Okay, but all I'm doing is fornicating. What kind of trouble is going to come my way?* I started to cry, because I knew I had fallen and was not feeling good about it. Although Jesus will forgive me time and time again, at some point as a believer, I felt I needed to make a decision and stick to it. I always like to keep my word, so my lifestyle was really starting to bother me.

> *"Seek the Lord while he may be found; call on him while he is near. Let the wicked forsake their ways and the unrighteous their thoughts. Let them turn to the Lord, and he will have mercy on them, and to our God, for he will freely pardon."*
>
> -Isaiah 55:6-7 NIV

The Tragedy

Pastor would give everyone he prophesied to a cassette of the prophecy, so I listened to it when I got home and again on Monday. Monday night, I went over to Jon's house, and we talked. I shared the prophecy with him, but he could not relate and did not have much to say about it. I noticed he was acting weird and jittery, but I did not think anything of it.

When I spent the night at Jon's house, I would leave for work at six-thirty a.m. to make it to work by seven a.m.. Jon lived in a gated home community. The night before, both Jon and I parked our cars outside the gate, because the driveway was being remodeled and was filled with dirt, so no cars could be parked there. When I routinely walked to my car, with my mind focused on making my arrival to work, I was approached by three guys with hoods on their heads. As they approached me, I instantaneously recalled the prophecy Pastor had spoken two days before.

I started praying and repenting and asking Jesus to give me another chance. As I pleaded with Jesus, I said, "I promise I will do right." I could not see the guys' faces, but the tallest one came right next to me. I began to defend myself against him and said, "Just take the car." The perpetrator was very aggressive with me and was handling me very roughly. He told me to veil my eyes with my hands and to walk with him.

I was still attempting to fight him, so I could run away. To convince me to keep still, he placed a gun against my head. I began to pray more fervently. Meanwhile, one of the other guys grew apprehensive and said, "Man, let's go. Leave her alone." From what I could see, they had apparently put some tape on the gate, so it would not close all the way, and this would give them easy access back inside the gate.

I had wondered why that morning the gate had a little crack in it and was not completely secured. The guys escorted me to the front door of Jon's house and told me to knock on the door and tell Jon to open the door. I knocked and said, "Jon, open the door." Jon never opened the door and the Holy Spirit told me to tell the guys I was pregnant. I said, "Please, don't kill me. I'm pregnant." The guy grew angrier by the moment and said, "Ring the bell and ask him to open the door." He completely ignored what I had said.

By that time, Jon could hear them outside, and I thought for sure he would come out with guns blazing or call the police. The guy with the gun grew more frustrated, and the next thing I knew, he shot me in my side and the guys all ran. I ran around the back of the house, and saw Jon looking out the window. I yelled, "Call 911 and open the door! I have been shot!" My purse had fallen, and I did not think to open the door with my key in my purse. Apparently, the guys did not think to ask me to open the door with my key either. Praise God for that.

Jon opened the door. When he saw the condition I was in, he started to cry. He already had 911 on the phone, and they came right away. Jon called Chris and told him I had been shot. All I could hear was my mom screaming hysterically in the background. Chris asked, "Can Monica talk?" Jon answered, "Yes, she can." Jon placed the phone to my ear, and all I could say was, "It's burning." By then, the huge firemen and police had arrived. They cut off all my clothes and rushed me to the nearest hospital.

The firemen noticed the bullet did not pass through me and was therefore still in my body, so they knew the doctors had to act fast to remove it. The doctors transported me to another hospital. Before I was transported, Chris and my mom had arrived to Valley Hospital and were so glad I was alert. I was terrified, but they kept me calm. Chris asked Jon what happened, and he told him I was carjacked.

Chris prayed with me and said, "Everything is going to be fine." I was transported. When I arrived to the hospital, my aunts, uncles, cousins and many friends were waiting for me. When I was being wheeled into surgery, all of my family and friends kissed me on my cheek and were all crying.

My uncle Rollo was looking at Jon as though he was to blame. Men know a bad seed when they see one. Rollo and my cousins told Jon the shooting better not be his fault. My aunts had to calm them down. My mom informed me everyone prayed while I was in surgery, and when the surgery was complete, everyone was notified the surgery had gone well.

The next day, my godmother Mary Ann came to see me. When she arrived, she found me upset about my room. Before long, Mary Ann had notified the hospital administrator and a woman from my church who worked there about my dissatisfaction. With the two women collaborating together, I was moved to a private room. Pastor and First Lady came to see me, and Pastor had the more sympathetic personality, but First Lady went in for the gusto. She had no mercy on me. She said, "You know why this happened, right?" Innocently, I said, "No." She did not hesitate to alleviate my ignorance. She said, "Because you were living in sin, and when you live in sin, you do not have divine protection, unless you repent of your sins." Ultimately, when I was in sin, God showed me He is real and saved me from being destroyed by the enemy.

> *"No weapon that is formed against you shall prosper, and every tongue that rises against you in judgment, thou shall condemn. For this is the heritage of the servants of the*

> *Lord and their righteousness is of me saith the Lord."*
>
> -Isaiah 54:17 ESV

Pastor prayed with me and said he was so thankful I was doing well and God definitely has His hand on me. I reminded Pastor of the prophecy he gave me a few days before, and they started praising God, embraced me and departed. I was in the hospital for a week. During my stay, Jon stayed with me the entire time and slept on the couch in my room. Towards the end of the week, when I was healing, he squeezed in the bed with me. I was petrified and confused. Understandably, I was upset he had told people I was carjacked. He asked me if I wanted him to go to jail, if people found out the guys were trying to rob him, because of his drug dealings. I asked him if he knew who shot me, and he said, "No." That has always been his version of the truth. I was so scared and never told my mom or family what really happened, until now.

I was off work for one month, and during that time, I was trying to get away from Jon. The detectives called me and wanted to speak with me about the matter, and Jon kept saying, "Please, don't tell them what really happened. Tell them you were in an attempted carjacking." I met with several detectives, and when I told them about the carjacking, they did not believe me. They continued to inquire about Jon and told me my story did not make any sense. They told me when I was ready to tell the truth to pay them a visit.

I wanted to be alleviated of the entire matter and Jon. A few weeks after my incident, I finally acquired the nerve to ask Jon why he never opened the door. Jon said, "My princess, you're my angel. If I would have opened the door, we could have both been dead. You saved my life, and God saved yours." I told him his lifestyle was too risky for me to stay with him. I broke up with him after about a month. Jon had tears streaming down his face and declared he was so in love with me and could not be without me. Jon said he would do anything for me, if I would just stay. I said, "Sweetheart, I wish I could, but I cannot, and I'm so sorry. God has a plan for my life, and I need to get my life on track with Him. I cannot allow anyone to jeopardize my salvation. Do you understand, Jon, I almost lost my life? This is nothing to play with, and my life is more important than a few moments of pleasure. I love you, and I wish you well."

After that, I made a vow to God that I would be celibate and live for Him. I returned to the ministry and was about to graduate from graduate school. To this day, Jon will text me every now and again, and periodically, he will see me around town and text me. Because I sell real estate, he was able to retrieve my number from bench ads.

Jon has been married and divorced and has always told me he has never been in love with anyone else but me and no woman has been able to make him feel like me in all aspects of his life. Jon knows we can never be a couple and what we had a long time ago could never be. Yet, Jon calls me his angel.

Now, do not get me wrong. It was definitely a challenge for me to live a celibate lifestyle, and I realize it is a challenge many other men and women face. However, as a Christian, this is not an option. It is a requirement if you want to receive the ultimate reward of entering the kingdom and receiving all the blessings God has for you.

> *"Do you not know that your bodies are temples of the Holy Spirit, who is in you, whom you have received from God? You are not your own; you were bought at a price. Therefore, honor God with your body."*
>
> -1 Corinthians 6:19-20 NIV

Our God is so awesome that He even gives us many chances to experience His goodness, by allowing us to repent of our sins and by blotting our sins out.

> *"Repent therefore, and turn again, that your sins may be blotted out."*
>
> -Acts 3:19 ESV

> *"That if thou shalt confess with thy mouth the Lord Jesus, and shalt believe in thine heart that God hath raised him from the dead, thou shalt be saved."*
>
> -Romans 10:9 KJV

Unholy Soul Ties

Further, the misconception about fornication and adultery from many Christians is sexual sin is not a big deal. Either, they must test the goods before they get married or every man and woman is going to cheat at least once while they are married. This keeps the marriage fresh! Really? Well, did you know when you engage in fornication and adultery, you are creating unholy soul ties? We have no idea how promiscuity outside of marriage and adultery scatters one's soul and destroys his/her ability to commit to one partner. Often times a man or woman may have had a one night stand, and it could be years later and he/she is still thinking about that person, because an unholy soul tie has been created.

Most Christians do not understand the dangers of unholy soul ties and how it impacts their lives long term. Unholy soul ties can also be 'demonic bridges' between one person to the next. For example, if you were to have extra-marital sex or fornicate with somebody who has a spirit of suicide or depression, you could end up with the same kind of tormenting spirits that he/she has, although you may have never had a spirit of depression or suicide, before sleeping with this person. This is because you have opened yourself up to a curse for sexual sin, but also created an unholy soul tie with a person who is tormented by these demonic spirits.

When our strongest soul tie is to God, there is a divine covering and protection that will enable us to withstand forming ungodly soul ties. It is called the Holy Spirit!

As you can see, it is a dangerous game to have pre-marital sex and to commit adultery. This is why there are so many women whose minds are messed up, because they have given their prized possession away, and now they are tied to someone who had no intention of marrying them. Unfortunately, the only thing some men want to do is sample the treasure, and then he is ready to move on to the next woman. And, some women like to sample as well. However, rewards will be plentiful when you follow the word of God and adhere to His will for your life. Below is a great prayer that can help you to release your unholy soul ties by "brenda4prayer." However, renewing your mind day and night in the Word is imperative, in order to strengthen your walk with God.

Prayer to Release Soul Ties

Father, in the name of Jesus, I submit my soul, my desires and my emotions to your Spirit. I confess, as sin, all my promiscuous, premarital sexual relationships and all sexual relationships outside of marriage. I confess all my ungodly spirit, soul, and body ties as sin. I thank you for forgiving me and cleansing me right now!

Father, thank you for giving me the keys of your kingdom, the keys of spiritual authority. What I bind is bound and what I loose is loosed. In Jesus' name, I ask you to loose me from all unholy soul ties to past partners and ungodly relationships. Please uproot all the tentacles of sexual bondage, of emotional longings and dependencies, and enslaving thoughts. I bind, renounce and resist any evil spirits that have reinforced those soul ties or may have been transferred to me through evil associations.

Please cleanse my soul and help me to forget all illicit unions so that I am free to give my soul totally to my mate. Father, I receive your forgiveness for all past sexual sins. I believe I am totally forgiven. Thank you for remembering my sins no more. Thank you for cleansing me from all unrighteousness. I commit myself to you. By your grace, please keep me holy in my spirit, soul, and body. I praise you, in Jesus' name. AMEN!

Tips from Lessons Learned

1. Being flattered with gifts is not love. It is an allusion.
2. Get to know someone before you start trusting his/her every word.
3. God gave His people a spirit of discernment for a reason, so use it.
4. If something looks and smells like a rat, it is.
5. Once you see a negative characteristic in someone you are dating, ask God to reveal it and follow the Holy Spirit.
6. Share your experiences about someone you are dating with a like-minded person in Christ whom you trust to get his/her advice.
7. Do not create unholy soul ties by committing adultery or fornication.
8. Do not ignore God's signs to run from a bad situation.
9. Just because someone looks the part and says all the right things, does not mean that is who God has prepared for you.
10. Do not waste your time because you are bored with people with whom you are unequally yoked.

Chapter Seven
The Transition

> *"Repent, then, and turn to God, so that your sins may be wiped out, that times of refreshing may come from the Lord."*
>
> -Acts 3:19 NIV

I was thoroughly enjoying my life and was very appreciative to Jesus for preserving my life and effectuating a transition for me. From my experiences, I learned Jesus will give us ample opportunities to get our lives on track, but to continue to repent and repent is nothing to gamble with. Frequently, I have reflected on how my life would be if I did not have Pastor to administer the prophecy from God and tell me He loves me and has awesome things in store. My life could have been extinguished on that tragic day in my life.

I was really starting to enjoy the ministry much more, and one day, my friend Meagan called to tell me about a condo she found for me to purchase. I never wanted to rent an apartment, because that is a waste of money. My uncle Joe and aunt Maxine have been investing in real estate all their lives, and I remember them advising me to never rent but always to buy. I went to see the condo, and it was a hot mess. I have always had an entrepreneurial and strategic mind, and I knew that condo was not my dream home; nevertheless, I went through with the escrow process.

When the condo closed escrow, right away I had my contractor come in and redo my cabinets, bathrooms, paint, and replace all the fixtures. My furniture was dynamic and to remodel my house cost little to nothing. I had already purchased all my supplies, except the cabinets that I wanted my contractor to put glass in. To my surprise, he installed the cabinets complimentary. I am telling you, God is so good all the time.

When you remove sexual sins from your life, Jesus gives you favor, which is better than money. So, I was comfortable in my condo, and I had just been appointed to lead the Usher and Greeter ministry at church. I had no idea what I was in for leading a ministry and working with members of the church. Even though I was in this ministry as a worker, I thought leading the ministry would be a breeze. Was I in for a big surprise?

Leading a ministry could not have been further from my perception of what I would experience. Being younger than the ministry members was an issue in itself. Men and women who were all over forty-five years of age comprised my team, with the exception of two people who were slightly younger than I. From their perception, it was incomprehensible for Pastor to put a young woman in her twenties over such a large ministry. What they did not understand was my age was irrelevant. I was appointed, and it was an honor for me. For others, if they had been appointed, it would have been power for them. I did not petition for the role, but Pastor saw attributes in me that would be beneficial to his ministry, such as leadership, organizational, strategic, ability to build a collaborative team, and great relationship skills. Furthermore, he knew I would put structure into the ministry.

My ministry team met every second Sunday, for thirty minutes before church started. I created a mission statement and required everyone to memorize it. The parking lot, front door greeters and ushers were responsible for memorizing everyone's name that visited the church. This was all part of the church's hospitality plan.

No other ministry created a mission statement, and you are probably wondering if anyone in my ministry memorized the statement. The answer is only one person. As a reward, during one of our meetings, that one person received a gift. After that, everyone else wanted to memorize the mission statement, in hopes he/she would receive a gift. However, they were not as fortunate.

In the beginning, leading a ministry was exciting, rewarding and fun, but after a while it started to beat me down. Ever so often, First Lady would call all the ministry heads on a Friday or Saturday night unexpectedly and want to meet about any given topic. If you had something pre-planned, your evening or day was turned asunder. I really did not have a life, except for work and church. Also, I just graduated with my M.B.A., so at least that was a relief.

Most of my friends would visit my church from time to time, but some of them always felt my church was too strict about how a person should dress, etc. One of my friends came to visit one day, and her cleavage was showing, so one of the church ladies gave her a safety pin and asked her to pin her top. My friend never went back there. We would always give ladies lap cloths, if their skirts were too short. However, some visitors refused to place the cloth on their lap. We never forced anyone to do it, but I had been so accustomed to wearing a lap cloth, it did not bother me, but it surely was an issue for other visitors.

Dating had progressively slowed down for me, by choice of course, because I was focused on work and the ministry, but I was open to meeting someone new. I recently had an enormous thirtieth birthday celebration a few weeks prior, and I was ready for more entertainment.

Tall and Mighty Doctor

One sunny Saturday morning, I had just finished working out, and I went to the car wash. I was reading a magazine, and the next thing I know an older man approached me and inquired about what I was reading. I answered, "*Essence Magazine*." He asked me if I minded if he sat down next to me. I replied, "Certainly not." He asked my name, and I said, "Monica." He said his name was Dr. Scott Sand. Of course, he wanted me to know he was a doctor. I asked him what he specialized in, and he answered, "Cardiology." I said, "Oh, that's great you're a heart surgeon. You must be mighty intelligent." He boldly replied, "That's what they say."

He continued the conversation by asking what I did for a living, and I told him I was an HR professional at a Fortune 500 company. He said, "That's great and sounds like fun." Appraising his face, I could tell he was at least forty-seven to forty-nine years old; however, he was really fit to be an older man. He was six feet five, had smooth brown skin, and was handsome and clean cut. His accent was extremely sexy, and sure enough, he was from England. His ascent resembled that of Idris Elba, which is so sexy to me.

Dr. Sand and I were having great conversation, and he asked me if I would go to dinner with him. I responded, "Sure, next weekend may work." I would never meet someone the same day and then go out with him the same night. He called me that night, and we talked until after midnight about family, friends, dating, etc. It was a great conversation, and I could not believe he did not have a wife or a woman. He appreciated and loved the fact I was in the ministry and loved the Lord. He said because of his job, he is always at the hospital or his private practice and needed to make time to attend church.

Our first date was scheduled for the next Friday. That day he asked me to meet him at his house, because he was leaving his office late and needed to go home to get showered and dressed.

I went to his house, which is in Playa Del Rey a beach community in Southern CA. I pulled up to a five-story white beach house right off the water. It was something you would see in the movies.

I rang the doorbell, and he came to the door with a towel wrapped around his waist. I could not believe an older man had a well-sculpted body, and he stood over me like a giant. I said, "Oh, Lord. Help me." I had not seen a body like that in a long while. I pulled it together and regulated my mind, but based on our conversation on the phone, I knew he was not in the Word nor did he think living a Christian lifestyle was necessary. Scott was rich and was proud of his possessions. I was fully aware of all of this and still went out on a date with him. That was not wise at all and I thought, *Here we go again.*

> *"For all that is in the world—the desires of the flesh and the desires of the eyes and pride in possessions—is not from the Father but is from the world."*
>
> -1 John 2:16 ESV

Scott told me to make myself at home, offered me something to drink, and asked me to wait for him in the living room. Shortly thereafter, he gave me a tour around the house. From every room, you could see the water, and his master bedroom was exquisite. There was a balcony, with a telescope, off his master bedroom, and if the sliding glass door was open, you could hear the waves from the water. We walked around the wall to the master bathroom, which had his and her sinks, showers and a long infinity bathtub that was designed for his height. The fireplace in the bedroom had two sides, so you could be in the bathtub and continue to enjoy the warmth of the fireplace. I was in heaven and said to myself, *I could see myself living here.*

We went off to dinner to a nice restaurant called Javier's in Laguna Beach. We rode all the way there with the top down in his new Jaguar. At dinner, we were having great conversation, which was always the case. Even though he was about seventeen or eighteen years older than I, he had a younger spirit and was always amusing and entertaining. We remained until the restaurant closed for business, and we were not enthusiastic about leaving.

We finally headed back to his house. It felt so good to be in his presence and have intellectual conversation. When we arrived to his house, I said, "Well, thank you. I better get going. It's really late." He said, "How about you come in for a moment, and I'll make you some hot chocolate?" He was aware I did not drink. I knew my best decision would be to depart and head home, but I delayed my departure a little longer.

> *"Watch and pray that you may not enter into temptation. The spirit indeed is willing, but the flesh is weak."*
>
> -Matthew 26:41 ESV

Scott made popcorn for us, and we watched movies and had pillow fights. I kept my shoes on the entire time, because I did not want to give him any ideas from me getting too comfortable. Scott said, "Relax, and stay with me tonight. I can't let you drive home this late by yourself." Flabbergasted by his suggestion, I said, "Oh, no! That's okay. I have a lot to do tomorrow and need to get home." He then gently grabbed the back of my neck and pulled me closer to him with a big wet kiss. It felt so good, but I stayed alert and was not going any further. Scott tried to unbutton my shirt, but I said, "I can't do this. Besides, we just met." In disagreement, he asked, "What does that matter? I like you, and I know you like me, so what's the big deal?" I was thinking to myself, *Is this the dating scene now, where women are just laying up with men the first night they meet them?* In Scott's case, I was certain women dropped their panties quickly, due to his status, home and money. Little did he know, I was the prize, not him.

At that moment, I blurted out to Scott, "I'm celibate." He said, "You believe that old ancient stuff in the Bible that if you fornicate you will go to hell?" He told me I was brainwashed and I should not waste my youth with those types of beliefs, and no man will ever accept that, no matter how sexy I am. Politely, I stood up and said, "I respect your position, but no amount of money will make me change my mind." He said, "My plan may be to marry you, but I need to know if your sex is good first." I laughed and said, "Would you like to check my references?" He did not find my comment amusing, but I gave him a taste of my sarcastic side to let him know I may be celibate, but I was not inexperienced, square or stupid.

Scott began to apologize profusely and said he was going to follow me home to ensure I arrived safely. That was very gentlemanly of him, but the devil tormented my mind all night with the words Scott had spoken to me about my celibacy. I had met other men that said similar things to me, and the words were starting to bother me a great deal.

Meditating on the Word was always my focus, but I realized my reading was not consistent, and that was how I permitted the devil's entry into my daily life. Although the kisses and rubbing all felt so good, I had grown in the Word, and my salvation and blessings were not worth a few moments of pleasure.

> *"Keep this Book of the Law always on your lips; meditate on it day and night, so that you may be careful to do everything written in it. Then you will be prosperous and successful."*
>
> - Joshua 1:8 ESV

The next day, Scott called me and apologized again for his behavior and wanted to see me later. He stated he had something special for us to do. I did not have anything planned for that evening, so I went out with him against my own rule. I phoned Colette and asked her to pull my hair up for the night. It seemed as if we were going to an elegant affair, and I wanted to be astonishingly beautiful from head to toe. He asked me if I had a dress similar to a ball gown. Actually, I had the perfect dress I had worn to another event. Fashion was always my passion, and I believe a woman should always have a dress for every occasion.

He picked me up and said, "Wow, you look stunning!" We headed to the Dorothy Chandler Pavilion downtown to see an Italian Opera. I had only been to an opera once when I was with Cramer, but this one was different. It was passionate, and it was romantic. We had a wonderful evening, and it was so refreshing.

After Scott and I had been dating for about three months, he wanted to make dinner for my family. My aunt Lynn was visiting from out of town and wanted to meet him. So, my mom, Lynn and I went over to his home for dinner. He made Filet Mignon and asparagus, and we had delectable German chocolate cake. At the dinner table, he told my family he had a surprise for me in a few weeks. My family was very enthusiastic, thinking maybe it was a proposal. I had no idea what it was but could not wait for the day to come.

He told me later that night to take vacation in two weeks from work for four days and to pack a light bag for the beach. He said whatever I failed to bring, we would purchase wherever we went. Vivian took us to the airport and dropped us off at Hawaiian Airlines. We were going to Hawaii to the Annual Medical Conference.

When we arrived, it was every woman's dream to see all the eligible young handsome doctors in my age group all in one place. I was saying to myself, *Why would I travel to Hawaii knowing I will not be sleeping with this man?* That was a bad decision for me to place myself into a compromising situation. Also, I was still heading a ministry, and what I was doing would not appear favorable.

My self-control was stronger, and my mind was stayed on Jesus; therefore, going out of town was not going to temp me, and it did not, but my rationale was not right. In Hawaii, we had a great time, and the hotel was beautiful. The path from the front of the hotel led to the sand and water. The hotel had all the major designer stores: Tiffany & Co., Louis Vuitton, Salvatore Ferragamo, and many more. Every time we would go to the hotel lobby, he would say, "There go your fans." All the younger doctors would say hello to me, and we finally figured out some of them thought Scott was my father. One of the young doctors came up to him and said, "Dr. Sand, I did not know you had such a pretty daughter." He responded, "This is my lady, not my daughter." That was the joke of the weekend. While we were there, Scott tried to have sex with me, but I was not having it and reminded him he promised me he would be on his best behavior.

After flying back to Los Angeles, we continued to date. Scott was a little clingy, and said he desired to marry me one day, but he said, "We need to know if we have sexual chemistry before we get married, and if I were not going to marry you, I would not have met your mom." I told him pre-marital sex was never going to happen, so marriage was not happening for us. I was not going to jeopardize my life. In my spirit, I always knew God had a plan for me. Scott believed the Word was overrated and wondered who really lived that holy.

"Let marriage be held in honor among all, and let the marriage bed be undefiled, for

> *God will judge the sexually immoral and adulterous."*
>
> -Hebrews 13:4 ESV

Our relationship eventually faded, and I figured out he never wanted to get married or have children, unless it was on his terms. I felt really bad and was starting to question if a man could really abstain from fornication. Scott was everything a girl could want, but he was lacking spiritually and a little older than I really would have liked to marry. I did not want to be by myself and longed for the man God had for me.

Again, in the end, I wasted a little over a year with a man with whom I was unequally yoked again. Because I was not having sex with him, I am certain a silly woman was fulfilling his sexual pleasures, but it was not going to be me. We would always keep in touch, and he would leave me sweet messages from time to time. To this day, Scott is not married and does not have any children. He says he is waiting for me, but I cannot see myself marrying him.

Tips from Lessons Learned

1. Check out a person's righteous lifestyle, not his/her success.
2. Do not become romantically involved with unbelievers.
3. Do not put yourself in uncomfortable, pressured situations.
4. Get involved in a ministry at church.
5. Having an accountability partner is key, no matter your age.
6. No need to get frustrated if someone does not believe in the Word of God. Just ensure you continue to live as God would want you to.
7. Always ask God to guide you and give you wisdom.
8. Do not waste months with someone you know is not on the same page with you. Too many twelve-month dead-end relationships will cause delays in meeting whom God has prepared for you.
9. Never be intimidated by someone else's status that will cause you to give into his/her plan to deceive you.
10. When you get discouraged about your dating experiences, lean not unto your own understanding, but to God's.

Chapter Eight
Watching the Clock

> *"For my thoughts are not your thoughts, neither are your ways my ways declares the* LORD. *As the heavens are higher than the earth, so are my ways higher than your ways and my thoughts than your thoughts."*
>
> -Isaiah 55:8-9 ESV

After dissolving my relationship with Scott, I experienced a void in my life. I am unsure of what caused the void, but I do not necessarily credit it to his absence. I was developing in the Word and in the ministry, and my career was soaring upward. However, everything in my life was extremely repetitious, causing me to become so very bored with it all. I am a social butterfly, and I even got tired of hanging around the same people, because I was not feeling productive. I did not believe my only purpose in life was to work a job. At thirty years of age, I began to hear other women discuss how I should be married and having children. From my perspective, I was still young, and I had so much to explore and enjoy. When God was ready to bless me with my husband, He would. There is never any need, ladies and gentlemen, to "watch your clock." As scripture states above, the Lord's timing is not ours. He can change your life in a second, if you just keep your eyes on Him.

Pastor K.W. is one of the pastors on staff at Faithful Central Bible Church where I am presently a member, and she made a great point one day when she said, "When you watch your clock, you make desperate decisions, which leads to misery." This statement proves to be true for so many men and women, including myself.

On one warm summer Sunday after church, my friend Meagan called me and suggested, "Let's go to the Ritz Carlton in Marina Del Rey to listen to jazz, dance and have great food." I really did not want to go, because I was tired of meeting men who would challenge me about my celibacy, and I was starting to feel embarrassed about being celibate. My self-esteem has always been high, but when men were trying to conquer me, they would always try to make me feel less than when I told them I was celibate.

I knew what the Word says and how honorable celibacy is to God, but living a celibate lifestyle was becoming an on-going challenge.

Mr. Suavé

Reluctantly, I agreed to go with Meagan, and she came to pick me up from my house, and we ended up having so much fun, laughing and dancing and enjoying the ambiance. Meagan noticed a tall gentleman who continuously espied me. He was smoking a cigar. He and his friend eventually approached our table and inquired if they could sit with us. The cigar smoker introduced himself to me as Colby, and Meagan and I introduced ourselves as well. Meagan liked his friend Bill, because he looked to be in his fifties.

Colby was very charismatic and had a gift for gab; he claimed to own several beauty shops and was a hairstylist to the stars. Colby and Bill ordered drinks all night and told us to order whatever food we desired. Later, Tammy, Delania and a few of our other friends came to enjoy the ambiance. They were having a great time drinking, eating and dancing. Colby thought he was the man the entire night. He asked for my number and if I would allow him to take me out later that week.

Colby called me the next day and asked if I wanted to attend a concert with him on Saturday to see Mary J Blige, Frankie Beverly & Maze, and many more artists. I responded, "Let me get back to you tomorrow." I thought about it the next day and decided why not go out and enjoy myself.

Prior to our first date, we conversed on the phone about everything, and he asked me if forty-two years old was too old and out of my dating range. I said, "Not at all. I have always met men older than I am." He said, "You look to be about twenty-one years old, so I was not sure if you would talk to me." I said, "That's nice of you, but I'm thirty years old." He replied, "You look far younger than thirty."

I asked him if he attended church, and he stumbled on that question and named a church but forgot the pastor's name. My intent was to not take him seriously, based on many conversations we had. I thought it was strange at his age for him to have never been married and not have any children.

Celibate Fabulous & Fearless

On the following Saturday night, we went to the concert. I went for one reason and one reason only: to have fun. After enjoying the concert, he dropped me off at home. He asked me if I was going to invite him in. I said, "No, I have to get up early for church." The next day, my cousin Donna called me and said, "I heard you were at the concert with Colby." I said, "Yeah, how do you know him?" I forgot Donna worked at Elgin Charles Salon in Beverly Hills, and they were all in the hair business, so everyone knew Donna and Colby. Donna said, "Be careful. He's no good. All he does is use women and break their hearts. He even has one girl who works with me all crazy over him. I heard he gets women hooked with that good loving and then dogs them out." I said, "Well, not to worry, because Colby will be disappointed thinking he's going to put it down on me." Donna said, "Okay, just letting you know to beware." Then, Colette would later tell me the same thing about Colby and warn me to beware. Colette would always joke that Colby must have some good loving, because those women would go crazy over him. I told her I had never had any loving that made me go crazy, and I did not want any sex to take over my mind, unless it is with my husband.

> *"For such persons do not serve our Lord Christ, but their own appetites, and by smooth talk and flattery they deceive the hearts of the naive."*
>
> -Romans 16:18 ESV

I have never been naïve to the point where I did not know what I was getting myself into. Yes, I have made bad choices. One bad choice in particular was once I knew the truth about a man, I continued to date him. This is never wise, and it only wastes time. Time is something you can never get back. Colby called me quite often, and we continued to spend time together. I found him a lot of fun to be around. I questioned him about the rumors, and of course, he said, "The rumors are not true." After a few months, Colby proposed to me with a two-carat ring and silly me, I accepted. He was not my ideal man to marry, but at the time it was exciting and adventurous. Besides, my clock was ticking, so I thought. Colby knew I was celibate and did not bother me about sex. He tried once, and after I turned him down, he refrained from asking again.

The Reveal

Further into our engagement, I began to see the real Colby, and the truth began to reveal itself. Colby lived as a bachelor, in an apartment. Then, he informed me he wanted to save money, so he was going to reside in a trailer in front of his aunt's house to save money. I was thinking to myself: *If you are a celebrity hairstylist and have several beauty shops, why would you need to live in a trailer?* I saw a few of the beauty shops, and they were very nice. His decision to move into a trailer did not sit well with me, so I asked the Lord to reveal anything I needed to know that was not right about Colby, so I could get out of the engagement. I was very uncomfortable, to say the least.

"Deliver me, O Lord, from lying lips, from a deceitful tongue."

-Psalm 120:2 NIV

Later that week, I visited Colby at the one of the salons. When I entered, an older man was there. I asked, "Who is he?" Colby said, "He is the cleanup man." But, the same day I found out the man actually owned all the beauty salons. Colby had lied when he said he owned the salons. "Lord, help me get out of this engagement," is what I said all day.

While I was there, Colby asked me if I wanted a glass of lemonade, and I said, "Yes." Then, he asked Tina, one of the hairstylists, if she wanted lemonade as well. At the moment, there were approximately twenty women working in the salon, but he only chose to ask one other person, who was on the other side of the room, if she desired lemonade. My spirit would not rest, and I said, "Lord, something is not right with this picture." All the women in the shop would always greet me when I came to visit, but Tina would never say hello. I stayed at the shop all day, and she did not say one word to me and barely responded when I said hello to her. Colby, Tina and I were the last three in the shop that night.

We all exited the salon together, and that was the first time I saw Tina's old car. Colby had spoken so badly about Tina having four children and how she was a whore. My spirit was still on edge and said, "Something is not right with these two." As we were exiting the premises, Colby received a telephone call and said, "Oh, sexy," as he would always call me, "I need to take care of an emergency for my aunt. Can we have dinner tomorrow?" I said, "Okay, no problem." I went home, and the Lord woke me up at five a.m. The Spirit of the Lord was so heavy on me. He said to drive over to Colby's house. I was so tired at five a.m., and I could not budge, but the Lord would not let me rest. I called my best friend at the time Vivian and said, "Something is not right. I need you to drive over to Colby's house with me." Vivian came and picked me up to drive by Colby's trailer, and guess whose car we saw? It was Tina's car in front of his aunt's house. I started to praise God and curse at the same time. The Holy Spirit will always reveal things to you when your life is lined up with the Word and protect you from harm.

By then, it was about six-thirty a.m. We parked down the street and waited. I knew shortly Colby would be going to run at the park, so I called him and said, "Good morning. Are you jogging?" He said, "Yes, sexy. I'm at the Fox Hills Park." I said, "Well, I'm going to come join you." Colby's voice started to tremble, and he said he was almost done. I said, "Okay, call me before I leave for church. I want to make sure everything is okay with your aunt." Colby grew calm and said, "That's why I love you, sexy."

Vivian and I pulled in front of Colby's trailer. At approximately seven-thirty a.m., he and Tina came out the trailer, and they looked like they had a rough night. I rolled down my window and said, "Hello, Colby and Tina." You should have seen Colby's eyes; they were about to explode from his head, and Tina was smiling. I said in a very clear voice, "I knew something was going on. The wedding is off, and I wish you both all the best." Vivian and I drove off, and I refused to answer his calls. I was exhilarated, because the Lord saved me from what was going to be a disaster. God is good all the time!

The Islander

> *"A man who flattereth his neighbor spreads a net for his feet."*
>
> -Proverbs 29:5 KJV

When the Lord saved me from my last dilemma, you would have thought I learned my lesson, but my flesh was weak, and my clock was ticking. I needed someone to abate the heat that was threatening to rise within me. What made matters worse was the devil knew how to distract me-AGAIN.

I received a traffic ticket, and I needed to attend traffic school. So, along came Kayson. He was so handsome with curly hair, smooth caramel skin, a mustache and beard, with an accent but was a little on the short side. Kayson lived the majority of his life in Los Angeles, so it would be difficult for someone to know he was from Trinidad, unless he was trying to be a ladies' man, as he would say.

Traffic school was being held at the same office building my church at the time moved into years ago. Traffic school was breaking for lunch, and Kayson walked over to my car and knocked on my window. I looked at him with a look that said, "What do you want?" He said, "Can I take you to lunch?" I replied, "No, thank you." Then, he pleaded, "Please do not embarrass me in front of all these people." Everyone was watching to see how I would respond to his advance, and I did not want to appear contemptible, so I consented.

Kayson worked for Operating Engineers and made six figures, but he did not know how to manage his money. He was rough around the edges, and I am a woman of quality. We were like oil and water. Kayson's daughter Amber was one year old and such a gorgeous child, like a baby doll. I knew we were not compatible, but I let my flesh and my 'watching the clock' get in the way. Kayson was the first man I met in a long time that kept my flesh on fire. As with all the other men I had dated, I kept making the same mistake: being involved with men I was unequally yoked with. This formula has never worked, and I knew the Lord was asking, "When are you going to do it my way?" As God declared, He knew me before I was born; therefore, He knew all the mistakes I was going to make.

> *"Do not be unequally yoked with unbelievers. For what partnership has righteousness with lawlessness? Or what fellowship has light with darkness?"*
>
> -2 Corinthians 6:14 ESV

When a woman is watching her clock and is celibate, she may make stupidly desperate decisions. I knew with absolute certainty Kayson and I were not equally yoked, but my flesh was burning hot, and I needed to get married quickly. Kayson and I began dating, and he wanted to please me in every way possible. Kayson and I were the same age, so his energy level was equivalent with mine. We would rendezvous all the time at the beach, workout together, go to the mall or wherever we wanted.

We were one month into our relationship, and Kayson was moving in like a roadrunner. But, he had not waited until that point to place his claim on me. During our first week of dating, Kayson had claimed me as his woman. He had no idea I did not take him seriously.

Kayson came over to my house, and I prepared dinner. He was very enthusiastic and always complimented me about my hair, nails, cooking, physique and whatever he could think of. Kayson knew how to flatter me and pull me closer to him. I remember sitting on the couch, and Kayson rushed over and started to kiss me very passionately. As he touched me all over, he unbuttoned my pants and started kissing me all over. I was in heaven, but I had to say, "Stop! We cannot go any further. I'm celibate and cannot do this." Kayson said, "I just want to make you feel good. So, just lay back." My mouth failed to respond, but my body said, "My pleasure." Kayson was not physically fit, but at one time, he had been in the Marines, so his confidence was like Hercules. At that moment, I did not believe he actually was Hercules, but I knew I needed to flee from that situation.

> *"Flee fornication. Every sin that a man doeth is without the body; but he that committeth fornication sinneth against his own body."*
>
> -1 Corinthians 6:18 ESV

I was in hot water, and when the flesh gets in the way, you cannot think clearly. While engaging, I relied on my self-control. I did not think oral sex was a sin, but it is under the umbrella of sexual immorality. I was so focused on the promise I made to the Lord about not fornicating I actually thought everything else was fair game. All night, we were both in lust, not love. We continued to date and hang out with friends. Kayson started attending church with me. Attending church was not new for him, as he was raised in the church. His parents are definitely saved, but he always struggled with keeping God's commandments. That was a reason for me to run, but no- I stayed in lust.

My fellow congregants would often say, "Awe, you two look like brother and sister." The ladies really took a liking to Kayson. He was everyone's eye candy at church. He had caramel color skin, curly black hair and features of a model. Kayson met Chris and my mom. They did not say much about Kayson, but they seemed to like him, at least in the beginning.

Kayson joined the church and began to fellowship regularly with the men at church. He was really enjoying his life and felt renewed. After three months of dating, Kayson was ready to propose. We were at the beach playing volleyball and enjoying the sun. When we sat down to eat lunch, Kayson had the ring in the basket. He put his fingers on my chin and told me how much he was in love with me and appreciated me for all I had contributed to his life and asked me to be his wife. I said, "Yes." He was a nice guy but was not really the type of man I was accustomed to dating. I certainly was not in love with him nor did I love him. Rather, I was in lust and wanted to have sex. I thought maybe I would grow to fall in love with him.

We started pre-marital counseling with Pastor, and we talked about everything from children, sex, pornography, alcohol, family, work, church, staying attracted to one another and much more. We were married in 2003, within ten months of knowing one another, and we could not wait to consummate our marriage on our wedding day. Our wedding was beautiful and included a ceremony with white doves. Most of our friends and family were in attendance. Kayson and I had four bridesmaids and groomsmen. Unfortunately, for some strange reason, weddings tend to always break up friendships. After our wedding, a few of my friends and I discontinued speaking. My friend Tammy moved to New York City to manage her business for ten years, and I missed our friendship in her absence. As the years went by, my list of true friends dwindled down to a handful.

> *"Do not be misled. Bad company corrupts good character."*
>
> -1 Corinthians 15:33 NIV

A Turn for the Worst

As time progressed, everything was going well, and we were enjoying married life. Sex was definitely not an issue, and the passion was off the chart. About three months into the marriage, I started to see Kayson consume more alcohol than he admitted. He would have a drink every day, and when he drank, he would get angry, unlike others who are happy when they drink. Consuming alcohol caused anger and sadness within Kayson. We would argue about insignificant matters. When we would argue, Kayson would stay out very late.

One night, he came home at three a.m. He thought I was asleep, but I was not. I remained in bed, and I felt him trying not to awaken me. Little did he know, my eyes were fully open, and I saw the time on the clock. I even moved a little bit, and he began snoring as if he had been in the bed for a long time.

The next morning, I asked him what time he arrived home. He told me not to question him. I was very upset, and I said, "So, you mean to tell me, you can stay out until three a.m. with no explanation?" Kayson looked extremely puzzled, and I am sure he was wondering how I knew what time he arrived home. While he was trying to explain his lies, I was disgusted, so I got dressed and left.

As I was driving, I was thinking, *Lord, what did I get myself into?* This is what happens when you watch your 'clock' and marry because you want to have sex. You end up with a person God did not choose for you. I cried and wanted to get an annulment, but I was too embarrassed to do so. Failure was not an option for me. I have always been a high achiever, and that would have been a failure to me after ninety days.

All day, I dreaded returning home. Finally, I arrived home at nine p.m. Kayson heard the keys dangling, and he met me at the door. He yelled, "Where the hell have you been?" while still reeking of alcohol. I said, "None of your business!" This was not the right response, but I had lost respect for him very quickly.

Kayson became indignant and turned on the gas on the stove and was trying to find a match to blow up the house. I was upstairs and thought he was playing, until I went downstairs and my eyes started burning because of the gas. He was yelling, "You think you're smart. Well, we will see how smart you are once I burn this house down." He was so drunk. I guess he forgot we would be blown up with the house if he lit a match.

Kayson would not let me leave the house. I had my phone in my hand, so I called my mom. I was crying and telling her to come quickly. Then, I called 911. I was scared out of my mind. Kayson resembled the devil when he was drunk, and he became a person I did not know. His behavior was more than an addiction. He seemed as though he was mad at the world, and he hated me.

My mom came, turned off the gas, and inquired, "Kayson, what is your problem?" By that time, the police were there, and we were in our bedroom. The police pointed their huge guns at him, with the infrared beams on his back, telling him to turn around. Kayson would not turn around, and we were getting scared for him. Kayson finally turned around, and the officers forced him to the floor and put handcuffs on him. Kayson stayed the night in jail, and they released him the next day.

> *"Woe to those who rise early in the morning that they may run after strong drink, which tarry late into the evening, as wine inflames them!"*
>
> -Isaiah 5:11 ESV

Each day, I kicked myself for marrying Kayson. His behavior was new to me, and I could not believe I placed myself into that situation. Kayson was so apologetic to me and asked me to please forgive him, and I did. I asked him what was really going on with him, because he resembled the devil when he drank. He said he was going to speak with Pastor to get help with his alcohol addiction, because it was a problem. I said, "That's odd. You never told me you had an addiction." Then he changed the subject and said, "Monica, if I wanted to burn down the house I could have. Matches are in the kitchen drawer, so I was not that gone." I responded, "So, you were throwing a temper tantrum like a kid?" He laughed as if the matter was funny.

Deep Secret Revealed

Kayson met with Pastor, and the next week, Pastor wanted to meet with both of us. Pastor said, "Daughter, there is something you should know, and I am going to let Kayson explain it to you." Kayson started to cry and explained he drank a lot because he was molested as a child by his neighbor and he was still angry about it. He did not tell his parents until he got older, and he did not reveal it to us in premarital counseling. Pastor said if he had known that during our counseling sessions, he would not have married us. However, because we were married, Kayson needed to get some help.

Pastor said, "And you have to want it, Kayson. Do not only get help to be with Monica, but for yourself. You have to watch your drinking, because you're going to hurt someone or get hurt." Kayson then committed to getting help and counseling with Pastor.

> *"Give us help from trouble, for vain is the help of man. Through God we will do valiantly, for it is He who shall tread down our enemies."*
>
> -Psalm 60:11-12 KJV

Blended Family Chaos

Our marriage would remain calm for a few months, and then more drama would strike. The next time trouble arose, it was due to his daughter's mother. Raina had three children, including Amber, had no man and was miserable.

That was my first time dealing with a man's child's mother dissension. Raina was mad because we were married, and any involvement Amber had with us would always be a problem. Kayson made arrangements to keep Amber every other week, and we would meet Raina between our house and hers. She lived an hour away, and at first, I would be so excited to see Amber, but then it turned into an issue. Kayson would jump to Raina's every beat, because he did not want her to file child support and garnish his wages. Kayson would always pay child support, but Raina was still in love with Kayson, and her mission was to make our lives miserable.

One Saturday morning, Kayson was working, so he told Raina I would pick up Amber. Raina was an hour late to meet me, and when she arrived, my words to her were not pleasant. The Lord was still working on me, and she did not know what she had embarked upon. She returned to her car and left. Amber and I went to the nail shop, and we spent quality time together all day. Amber was the joy of my life and was a beautiful little girl.

As she got older, her mom would brainwash her and tell her negative things to say to me. Every time, Amber came to stay with us,

I would take her to the nail shop with me. One particular time when she was three years old, Amber said to me, "My mama said, 'No, I can't go with you.'" Kayson agreed and said, "She cannot go."

That made me feel horrible. I was trying to establish a relationship with his child, but he was agreeing with everything Raina said. He could never make a decision that did not line up with her demands. It was becoming a nightmare. If Amber had a school event, Kayson would tell me Raina did not want me to come, so he went alone. There were countless occasions where I felt like the outsider. I reflected back on how I treated Chris as my stepfather growing up and often wondered if that was karma.

I got so tired of Kayson allowing Raina to have power over him. Eventually, on the weekends when Kayson picked up Amber, I would always have something to do, because Kayson and I did not know how to handle blended family issues. Feeling like an outsider was not fun, and I felt deserted. Kayson began resenting the church, because he felt the elders did not support him, and he did not want to get counseling, so the issue never improved. If I would ask Amber to do something, she would say in public, "You're not my mother." Until one day, my mom heard her say that, and she had a talk with Amber. It was not Amber's fault she was confused by her mother placing negative thoughts in her mind about me. I promised myself if the marriage did not work out, I was not marrying anyone who makes me feel like an outsider against their child and child's mother.

In Too Deep

As it related to business, things were going well. We started a business: B&M Trucking and purchased our first Super 10 truck with cash. I never believed in having unnecessary debt. Kayson, on the other hand, had to have the latest fast and furious bike and truck. My BMW was paid off, and I only had my student loan as debt. Kayson managed the business, and we were doing well. Kayson encouraged me to get my Real Estate license, after we met a realtor who was trying to sell us a house.

We were ready to move and purchase a home together. Instead, we purchased a few investment properties and had planned to purchase more properties. The properties were in my name, because we would receive a lower interest rate with my high credit score.

The human resources department I worked in was shutting down; as a result, I was laid off. The layoff gave me the opportunity to focus my full attention on my real estate business. My real estate business had grown tremendously, and each month, I would close a minimum of five contracts.

I heard some single family homes were going to be built next to The Forum, in Inglewood, CA. I put our names on the list along with some of my clients and friends. We were called to purchase the home and select the floor plan. We were so excited, but the house would not be complete for ten months.

Kayson was growing tired of the church, because he did not want to be accountable to any men there. From time to time, we visited Faithful Central Bible Church (FCBC) and attended their New Year's Eve celebration. I really enjoyed the church, and the Word was awesome. FCBC is a larger church, and we were not accountable to anyone there, so Kayson felt free. We continued to stay at The Way, The Church, but Kayson would not attend church often. I did not want to leave, because I felt Kayson was not making sound decisions and not living by the Word. Further, I was not treating my husband according to the verse below. Despite his bad decisions, I should have won him with the word of God out of my mouth.

> *"Likewise, wives, be subject to your own husbands, so that even if some do not obey the word, they may be won without a word by the conduct of their wives."*
>
> -1 Peter 3:1 NIV

Also, I did not know how to handle Kayson's alcohol problem, and I was not sympathetic about him being molested. I felt at times he would use that experience as an excuse for his behavior, because he was not trying to get help for his alcohol or anger issues. He would attend anger management classes, but he would return home and repeat the same behavior. His anger was not dissipating, and it was becoming unhealthy and dangerous for us to remain together.

The Big Bite

Kayson was out one evening and returned home intoxicated, with alcohol emanating from his breath. I heard him come in the door, so I went to the stairs, and I knew trouble was coming. He proceeded to ascend the stairs, and I asked him to leave.

I knew with him being intoxicated, he would be ready to argue. I stood in front of him and said, "Kayson, you need to leave. I'm tired of going through this with you." I refused to grant him access to the upstairs bedroom. So, he shoved me out the way, and I slipped and hurt my back on the stairs. I then grabbed his foot to make him trip, but that was the wrong thing to do.

The next thing I knew, he stepped back, grabbed my face, and bit me under my eye like a monster. Kayson looked like the devil as he was biting me. The side of my face felt numb, and I did not know the extent of the bite. All I saw was blood running down onto my shirt. I scrambled down the stairs to the bathroom and shrieked when I saw my eye. Kayson had bitten a small portion of skin from under my eye, and the blood was being emitted with the flow of a waterfall.

Kayson came running downstairs, and I said, "Look what you did to my face!" Underneath my eye was a small hole. My eye was black and blue, and blood was everywhere. He looked stunned and immediately became nervous. I grabbed my keys and proceeded to the door, because I needed to get to the hospital. Kayson blocked the door and asked me if he could drive me to the hospital. He did not want me to tell the police what he had done. I said, "Okay." Once we descended down the stairs to the parking area, I hopped in my car, locked the door, and drove off to Cedar Sinai Hospital. This is where my doctors practice and the best hospital in L.A.

The doctor asked me what happened, and I said, "The medicine cabinet flew open and lacerated the under portion of my eye." The doctor stitched up the wound under my eye, and I headed back home. On my way home, I telephoned my play brother Riley and informed him of what happened. He told his friends, and they were ready to find Kayson. He told me to alert him if Kayson was still at the house when I returned.

Kayson was still there, lying on the couch asleep. He awakened when he heard the door open at two a.m. He ran over to me and started to apologize and asked me to forgive him. I was steaming and said, "Look what you did to my eye!" I had a black eye, and it was excruciatingly painful. I told him he was a monster and asked him why he was still there. He said, "I really need help and really want to get help now."

Riley has a wife and children, and his wife felt he was about to get himself in deep trouble. Riley was attempting to leave the gangster life behind, so his wife would not let him and his friends rip Kayson's head off. So, he called Pastor, because at that time he was a leader in our church and trying to live for God.

Pastor called about nine a.m., asking me what happened. He was furious. Pastor sent twelve guys over to my house, but by that time, Kayson had left, because he was scared Riley and his friends were coming. Riley had called him to let him know what he could expect from them. The men came and asked me to call Kayson on the phone and to encourage him to return home. They were going to make Kayson feel what I was feeling. I dreaded calling Chris and my mom, because I knew then my entire family would be involved, and it was going to be over for Kayson.

My mom came, because Chris was outraged and did not want to risk jail. When my mom arrived to my house, we called the police, and one of my cousins, who is a police officer, came to my house with his partner. They took pictures, and my cousin and his partner went looking for Kayson. I did not want anyone to jeopardize their family, jobs or livelihood as a result of doing something horrendous to Kayson. His actions could have gotten him badly hurt that day.

> *"He hath put forth his hands against such as be at peace with him: he hath broken his covenant. [The words] of his mouth were smoother than butter, but war [was] in his heart: his words were softer than oil, yet [were] they drawn swords."*
>
> -Psalm 55:20-21 KJV

A warrant was issued for Kayson's arrest, and he turned himself in a few weeks later. Kayson called me every day from jail, and I despised everything about him and wanted out of our marriage. He asked me to help him get out, and he would give me a divorce. I bailed him out, and he went to meet with Pastor. He told Pastor it was best that we divorce, because he did not want to hurt me any longer. Pastor told him to file, because biblically the woman should not file.

> *"It hath been said, Whosoever shall put away his wife, let him give her a writing of divorcement."*
>
> -Matthew 5:31 NIV

Kayson and I retained separate attorneys, and he filed for divorce. In regards to the house we were supposed to move into within nine months, I informed him I would still purchase the home. Kayson signed the grant deed to remove his name from the title, which allowed me to move forward with the house. Kayson started to listen to his friends, and before long, his attorney was asking me for $50,000. I told my attorney I did not owe him anything. Everything we had done, I had gone into my personal funds or retirement funds for B&M Trucking and purchasing any property. The condo was purchased before we married, and he was not getting anything from me.

By then, I was five months away from moving into my home. I checked my account one day, and Kayson had withdrawn $25,000 from my savings account, which was earmarked to use as part of a down payment for my home. I was furious! I called him, and he said he did not know what I was talking about. I filed a police report, and the bank had recorded the call for the transfer. Kayson had a woman pretend to be me. He had all my personal information, and he had the money wired to his account from my account. Due to our divorce proceedings, the bank did not refund my money and told my attorney we needed to resolve the matter through our divorce proceedings. I was sick to my stomach, but God is always faithful through your trials and tribulations. I said, "Devil, I'm still moving into my house."

Listening to the Holy Spirit

One day, very clearly, the Holy Spirit told me to increase my tithes. I always pay my tithes and give to others whenever the Lord tells me to. In response to His instruction, I said, "Lord, you know I'm trying to purchase my house and now you're asking me to give more." There is one thing everyone should be aware of: the devil will never tell you to pay your tithes or sow a seed to anyone. I was obedient to the Holy Spirit, and I did as I was instructed. The Lord told me to give $1000 to a couple at church I knew did not care for me. They were about twenty years older than I was, and it was very clear the spirit of jealousy was controlling them. I sowed a seed to them and kept praying to the Lord what He said in His Word.

> *"The point is this: whoever sows sparingly will also reap sparingly, and whoever sows bountifully will also reap bountifully."*
>
> -2 Corinthians 9:6 ESV

A few weeks afterward, real estate deals were flowing in abundance. I received several cash deals and refinances. The Lord blessed me with three times the amount of money Kayson purloined from my account. The deals closed three months before I was to take ownership of my house. I moved into my home in the summer and paid cash for all my upgrades and installed my cabinets, shutters on all the windows, molding on the ceilings, and upgraded my carpet. The landscaper even installed a waterfall in my backyard. When the Lord says He will give you an overflow, He certainly will!

I hired movers to help me move, as I do not remember anyone offering to help. I was extremely happy and excited about moving on from my terrible marriage. Every other week, my attorney would call and tell me what demands Kayson was making, and I always responded, "I'm not giving him a dime. If anything, he should be giving me money." The security officer called me and said Kayson was there to visit. Kayson unexpectedly arrived at my house. He had the address from when we initially were going to purchase the home. He said, "I want to work things out." I was not the least bit interested, but since we were still married, I used him for sex that day.

My behavior was certainly wrong, but at the time I really did not care. Afterward, he continued to make his presence known. That was during Christmas time when my family was visiting, so they did not know if we were together or not. Although Kayson stayed a few nights, we were still going through a divorce.

When Kayson realized I was not interested in rekindling our relationship, he became belligerent again and returned to making demands. That was the last straw, and he was getting on my nerves. Our divorce proceeding was an extensive two-year process. I told my attorney Kayson could have the investment properties we purchased while we were married, but he would be responsible for transferring them into his name. I was ready to press forward and was desirous of him signing the divorce papers, but he refused because he wanted more. Unfortunately, he was unable to transfer the properties into his name, due to a subpar credit score.

Resultantly, we prepared a written agreement stating he would be responsible if the tenants moved out, etc. Kayson agreed. But when the market fell, he did not pay one mortgage payment. He knew they were in my name and wanted to do everything in his heart to cause me agony and pain and to destroy everything for which I had worked so hard.

All three of my credit scores had always ranged from 780-800+; however, when I was unable to pay the mortgages any longer, I was forced to release them. I felt like a failure and asked myself, *How could I be so stupid?* My spirit and my credit scores were all lowered. For the next two years, I worked hard to increase my credit scores, and I was successful, but I felt lifeless and borderline depressed. I longed to return to the first day Kayson and I met and thought, *If only I had driven off and not gone to lunch with him during traffic school.*

Men and women, I reiterate- 'watching the clock' causes you to make "desperate" decisions. My decision caused a disaster, and I was miserable. By sharing my experiences, my goal is to help men and women stay the course of listening to the Lord and letting Him guide their lives. No amount of sex was worth what I endured, and to make matters worse, when we were mad at each other during our marriage, we did not even have sex. My regrettable decisions caused me many headaches, distractions, loss of finances, and to be in a verbally and physically abusive relationship. I was hard headed, and that was God's way of showing me He knows best and has prepared someone just for me, if I would just be patient.

> *"For I know the thoughts that I think toward you, saith the LORD, thoughts of peace, and not of evil, to give you an expected end."*

> -Jeremiah 29:11 KJV

The Divorce, Fasting and Praying

After two years, the divorce process was taking a toll on me. I had lost my fire and had no desire to sell real estate. I was consulting in human resources at a company to keep my household going. I should have been asking Kayson to pay me during the divorce, but I wanted out and did not want anything from him but to keep what was rightfully mine. He was determined to get whatever money he could, and he caused me misery during the entire process.

On our last court visit, I was so frustrated with my attorney, because Kayson kept asking me to give him $50,000, and when I declined, there was an additional delay, as the courts were inundated with divorces, which meant another court date had to be scheduled. On that particular court date, I asked the judge if I could speak for myself. I shared with him all that I had gone through in the marriage, and the judge told me I should have been an attorney, because of the way I presented my own case. The judge dismissed us, and said if we could not come to an agreement, he would make the final decision for us during our next scheduled court date.

I met with Pastor and First Lady and shared with them what was going on and how I desperately wanted out of the marriage. They told me to 'fast and pray' for three days as the scriptures says and watch the mountain of divorce be moved on my behalf.

> *"And Jesus said unto them, Because of your unbelief; for verily I say unto you, If ye have faith as a grain of mustard seed, ye shall say unto this mountain remove from hence to yonder place; and it shall remove and nothing shall be impossible unto you. Howbeit this kind goeth not out but by prayer and fasting."*
>
> -Matthew 17:20-21 KJV

I fasted for three days, having only water, and on the third day of my fast, Kayson called me right after New Year's Day and said he wanted to sign the divorce papers. I called my attorney and asked him if we could sign that day. Kayson was to meet me at my attorney's office. Kayson had hired a very expensive attorney, and he was no longer affordable. Due to non-payment, his attorney stopped returning his calls. That led to Kayson being willing to sign with my attorney.

After I signed, we hugged and said goodbye. I went to my car and started to cry. I praised God for His goodness and for releasing me from the situation. Divorce is ugly and not of the Lord. It drains the life out of you. The turbulent trial caused me to feel like I had failed. I continued to stay in the Word and get my faith and strength back.

Kayson called me around Christmas time the same year and apologized for the way he had treated me. He had joined a church he really liked and was getting his life back on track. I apologized to him for not being a supportive wife of the trauma he experienced as a child and not being more sympathetic about his addiction with alcohol. In any marriage or relationship, it takes two to make it work, and neither of us cared to understand how to manage the trials and tribulations we encountered during our marriage. He accepted my apology, and today, we are cordial, and he calls me from time to time to see how I am doing. That was a huge lesson for me.

Tips from Lessons Learned

1. Watching the clock may cause you to make desperate and regrettable decisions.
2. Patience is a virtue. Never be moved to act on what people say you should do in your life. God controls your destiny and has already prepared a mate for you.
3. Lust is only a fantasy and lasts but for a moment. Oral sex before marriage is also considered sexual immorality.
4. Women, just because a man says you are the one for him does not mean he is the one God prepared for you.
5. If your spouse has an addiction he/she struggles with, try to be gentle, supportive and understanding.
6. Do not sweep any kind of abuse under the rug, as it only gets worse.
7. Keep family and friends out of your business when you are married.
8. Marriage is sacred and should be treated very seriously. It is not a game or a temporary fix for lust.
9. Do not ignore signs the Holy Spirit gives you about anyone you are dating.
10. When you are married, you become one. You no longer have the mindset of this is yours and this is mine.
11. It is okay to ask uncomfortable and personal questions to someone you are dating. Never assume anything.

Chapter Nine
The Dating Scene

> *"I wrote to you in my letter not to associate with sexually immoral people."*
>
> -1 Corinthians 5:9 ESV

After my divorce, I was mentally, physically, and emotionally exhausted and felt as though I had wasted many great years in my life with drama. All that stemmed from not being with whom God prepared for me. As time progressed, I began to feel free and wondered what was next for me. However, the time was not a complete waste; I learned a lot about myself. My godmother always told me to never have regrets, but to learn from the experiences.

From my exhaustion, I asked Pastor if I could sit down from the ministry, because I had not taken time out for myself while I was going through a divorce. I needed a hiatus. I was exhausted with being in ministry as well.

Four months after my divorce, my friend Skylar called me. We conversed for a while. During our conversations, she would always try to get me out of the house. But, I was adamant about spending a lot of time meditating and remaining quiet to hear what the Lord had to say to me. She said, "Girl, you can't live your life just working, exercising and going home. You need to enjoy your life. You're beautiful, smart and have a lot of life to live." Eventually, I consented, and we went to a sports lounge to watch the game one Friday evening.

Six-Pack

As we were enjoying ourselves, an attractive thirty-five year old man with muscular abs came up to me and said, "Hi. What's your name?" He was scrumptious, and his name was Ashton. I said, "This is exactly why I need to keep my tail in the house." Skylar said, "He looks like Kayson." I could not see any resemblance. We talked all night, and I had men on the right and left of me trying to make conversation all night. Skylar was occupied with one of her friends, and we experienced a fun-filled evening.

I do not have 'a type' of man that I prefer. As long as he treats me well and has the qualities I like, looks are not important to me. You must have more than a six pack or good looks to satisfy me. When the evening came to a close, Ashton walked us outside. He gave me a hug, we exchanged cards, and we headed home.

He was an aspiring producer, and we began sharing our time together working out, going to movies, etc. I felt twenty years old again. He filled the void I was missing right after my divorce, but I knew he was not marriage material. Furthermore, we were not equally yoked, for he was a player and was not financially stable. He went to FCBC every now and again, but when he met me, he started to attend more often. I started to attend FCBC, because I needed a change. I sent Pastor and First Lady a letter requesting to be released from the church, because I felt I needed to move on. Pastor released me. It was not easy for them, because I had grown up in their church, and they were like parents to me. I appreciated Pastor and First Lady for giving me the foundation I needed to be able to join a large church like FCBC, whose senior pastor is Dr. Kenneth C. Ulmer (Bishop).

About four months after I met Ashton, we had sex. I was disappointed in myself because I had not even had sex prior to marrying my ex-husband. I knew it was wrong, but I needed to satisfy my flesh in some way, and I was still mentally drained from my divorce and weak. I repented and moved on. He knew I was celibate, and I told him afterwards I could not have a repeat. I had gotten over being embarrassed about being celibate and did not care who would mock or make fun of me. It is the Lord who would ultimately judge me, not the people.

He said he too felt guilty about the act, even though he was not celibate, but he understood my position. Ashton admired me for living a Christian lifestyle in this day and age and hoped one day he would be able to commit to God's word. He was still young and immature but had great talent. If he could just stay focused on accomplishing his goals, he would do very well in life. Like most young men and women, they have to get all the partying out of their system in order to accomplish their dreams. Some people are able to focus early in life, and some have to hit a few bumps in the road before they realize their potential. Our relationship eventually fizzled off and the truth is- being with Ashton was one of those rebound moments I experienced once in my life.

The Sports Agent

> *"The fool hath said in his heart, [There is] no God. They are corrupt, they have done abominable works, [there is] none that doeth good."*
>
> -Psalm 14:1 KJV

Eventually, my zeal returned, and I was ready to conquer the world. Cindy and I went to Las Vegas for the Mayweather boxing match. While eating lunch before the fight, a Caucasian guy approached me and asked if he could sit down with us. His name was Paul, and he had some swag and was very much in physical shape. With him was his African American friend, who came over to sit with us. Paul said, "Besides being attracted to everything about you, I could not stop looking at your beautiful eyes. Here's my card." Paul lived in Los Angeles, CA and was a sports agent and very nice to me.

Paul desired to spend time with me that evening after the fight, but I told him we would be going to the after party, so I would have to see him when we got back home. He was fine with my response and could not wait to call me Sunday night to ensure we made it home.

On our first date at a restaurant called Mastro's in Beverly Hills, he brought me a bouquet of red roses, and he was so nervous. He could not even get the door open to his Ferrari because his hands were shaking so much. As we continued to date, Paul would take me to the finest restaurants, and we would go swimming at his house, to events or whatever I desired. The time we spent together was enjoyable. Paul really liked me, but the chemistry was not there at all. I appreciated for once a guy was not always trying to put his hands all over my body or talk about sex without not even knowing my last name. Paul was really a gentleman at all times.

I would visit his office and meet his staff, and everyone knew about me. He was ready to move full speed ahead. You would have thought I was his wife already when I met his friends and family. Paul was very well to do, but I could not fake being with someone if the chemistry was not there. I have always met men with financial wealth but were spiritually broken throughout my entire life, but chemistry is something you cannot buy. My philosophy is their money is not my money, and at that stage in my life, I needed to have chemistry with the man whom God had for me.

Besides, I did not have any more time to waste. Either you have the chemistry with the person or you do not. No matter how much I tried to force myself to like him, it never worked out. Besides, I had grown and was continually growing in the Word, and I did not want to hurt his feelings.

Before we met for dinner one day, I asked the Lord to reveal what I should do. We were talking about church and celibacy. Instantly, Paul blurted out he was an atheist. I said, "Thank you, Lord for revealing to me how I should handle this matter." Then, I told Paul there was no way we could move forward with him being an atheist, besides the fact the chemistry was not there for me. Paul was so strong about his beliefs, and he said he would never convert to Christianity. I told him I wanted him to find the one for him, and I thought he was a really nice man, but we were unequally yoked, and I could not continue to date him. I offered to treat him to dinner, but he would never allow me to treat him. I broke his heart that night, and I did not want him to feel worse. Paul said he really appreciated me and was falling deeply in love with me. He kissed my cheek, and we parted ways. Paul continued to call me, but I would never return his call, so he eventually gave up.

The CEO

"For he that soweth to his flesh shall of the flesh reap corruption; but he that soweth to the Spirit shall of the Spirit reap life everlasting."

-Galatians 6:8 KJV

When I meditated day and night, I would say to the Lord, "I am tired of kissing these frogs." I truly started to stay focus on the Word and myself. It is so easy to go to church and speak in tongues, but the Lord really looks at what we do in the dark.

I attended an executive retreat, and I met the CEO and founder of a cutting-edge technology company. His name was Cory, and he stood out in the crowd. He was tall, dark, and handsome; he spoke very eloquently. He was definitely a catch. When I became aware of him approaching me, I moved around to another area. He finally caught up with me and asked, "Excuse me, what is your name?"

I told him my name; then, he asked me if I wanted to go up to his room and talk where there was peace and quiet. I was taken aback by his boldness. I looked him squarely in the eye and said, "No, not at all." So, we sat in the hotel restaurant.

Cory talked about church, his business and how he was looking for a great woman of God in his life. If you had met that executive, you would have thought he was the Lord's cousin. He knew all the right things to say. He saw me at FCBC one day, so he knew I attended church.

I would never tell a man I wanted to be married to him. If he asked me if I desired to be married, I would say, "Yes, one day I want to be married, but that doesn't mean to you." Ladies, remember men are hunters, and it is improper for you to choose them. It is expected for him to choose you.

It was getting late, so I went up to my room. The next day, he called me for breakfast before we were both scheduled to drive back home from Laguna Nigel. That week, he asked me to dinner, and I felt he was up to something, so I told him I would meet him at the restaurant. We met at Mr. Chows in Beverly Hills and had a nice dinner. Cory did not waste any time and began inquiring about which sexual positions I find most pleasurable. I looked at him with disgust and said, "Your line of questioning is disrespectful. You know nothing about me or my life, and you dive right into asking me about sex." He said, "Come on. We are adults, and there are many women who sleep with me on the first night. Let's just cut to the chase. I have to test the goods before I marry anyone." I said, "Well, I'm celibate, and we never talked about marriage." He said, "You're the only one in Los Angeles who is celibate, and you're going to end up by yourself. Come on, girl. I like you, and I know you will be my wife."

Cory proceeded to tell me how he wanted to make passionate love to me, and it would be nothing like I ever experienced. I wanted to cry at the table. I was so tired of meeting these fake Christians who like to play women. It hurts me more to know that women would fall for such men and feel so desperate that they give up God's precious gift to them the first night or any night. This is why some men feel like they can approach every woman that way. I was so hurt and wanted to let Cory know, even though I was not the norm, I am not desperate and will not be placed in rotation.

Cory was completely enthralled in the conversation, and he obviously was not taking no for an answer. I politely told Cory I needed to go to the ladies' room, and I took my purse and exited through the front door. I presented my ticket to the valet and asked him to please hurry to bring my car around. Tears started to fall down my face from frustration and disappointment. After about fifteen minutes, Cory called me on my cell and asked me if I was okay in the bathroom. I said, "Yes, I'm fine. But actually, I just left, because I do not socialize with men like you who degrade women and are so into themselves that they can't appreciate quality when they see it." Cory was so beside himself, and before he could call me a female canine, I disconnected the call.

I may have cried all the way home, but I was so thankful God had a hold on me and continued to have His hand on my life. Living a lifestyle of Christianity is not always easy and is not popular, but the rewards are great if you just wait on God.

The Pastor and Entrepreneur

> *"The saying is trustworthy: If anyone aspires to the office of overseer, he desires a noble task. Therefore an overseer must be above reproach, the husband of one wife, sober-minded, self-controlled, respectable, hospitable, able to teach, not a drunkard, not violent but gentle, not quarrelsome, not a lover of money. He must manage his own household well, with all dignity keeping his children submissive, for if someone does not know how to manage his own household, how will he care for God's church?"*
>
> -1 Timothy 3:1-7 ESV

Although I was never looking for a date, people were always trying to hook me up with their friend. I wanted a break, for my focus was on building my business, church, myself and trying to juggle corporate America.

My play big sister Diane, who owns Lady D. Skincare in Beverly Hills, and I have always been close. She has known me since I was nineteen years old. She always looked out for my well-being, and when she would give me chemical face peels, she would ask who I was dating and would give me sound advice.

On one particular occasion, she told me, "Oh, Monica, I have the perfect guy for you. My husband and I have known Ryan for many years, and I have always wanted you two to meet. Ryan is an ordained pastor." I refused by saying, "Diane, I do not want to date a pastor." Diane said, "Oh, no! He's not practicing, but he used to preach. Now, he's a successful entrepreneur. Ryan is chocolate, tall and successful just like we want for you." I said, "Diane, I'm so tired of meeting these knock offs. I don't know. Let me give it some thought." Diane kept on insisting I needed to meet Ryan and told me he would be back from Europe the following weekend. I consented for Diane to give Ryan my number, and he called me when he returned to plan a date.

Ryan was forty-five years old and seemed mature. He said all the right things over the phone. He did not have any children and had never been married. I thought, *Oh, wow! No children and never been married. What's this all about?* After my experience with Cory, I preferred to meet men at the restaurant until I got to know them, so if it did not work out I would be in my own car.

Ryan and I met in Manhattan Beach, CA for a nice dinner. He asked me a lot of questions about myself, my family, friends, and work. He seemed to be genuinely interested. I asked him why he had never been married or had children. He said he was always so busy and bringing children into the world before he was married was not an option. Also, he stated he had never been with someone who was worthy to be his wife. He had considered marriage at one time, but he found out his ex-girlfriend was stealing money from him, which resulted in the end of that relationship.

I did not tell him right away I was celibate, because I liked to see how the flow of our friendship was going first. Ryan has his Ph.D. and is very intelligent. He invited me to an R&B concert to see Kem the upcoming weekend. I agreed to go, and we had an awesome time. During the concert, he would grab for my hand, as he started to notice all the attention I was getting from other men.

The next week would be our fourth and last date, and I allowed him to pick me up. Ryan would always talk about how good God has been to him and his church. The Lord would soon reveal to me the true Ryan. We were on our way to workout at the beach, and Ryan asked me to travel to Miami with him the next weekend.

He said, "Make sure you bring something sexy, so we can get to know each other better." I asked him what he meant by getting to know each other better. I knew what he meant, but I did not want to assume or jump to conclusions.

Ryan said, "Hopefully, we can feel each other out, because there are some things I want to do to you that will make you go crazy." I immediately felt sick to my stomach. Finally, I said, "Well, Ryan, I'm celibate."

His head turned like the exorcist, and you would have thought I cursed him out. He yelled, "CELIBATE! I wish you would have told me that when we first met, because I wouldn't have been hanging out at concerts, etc." He was clearly upset. I asked him if he wanted me to give him the money back for the concerts and dinners that he sponsored. He glared at me and said, "Are you trying to be funny?" I calmly said, "Of course not, but you seem like you are mad that you spent money and are not getting any sex in return." He said, "Monica, no man is going to accept your celibacy. You can't take the Bible so literally. Some things were made for the old days, but this is year 2012. Everyone has sex before marriage." I said, "Ryan, I'm sorry. I don't agree with you. So if you are upset, you can take me home." He was furious and drove me home, and that was the end of our friendship.

After meeting Ryan, I was tired and wanted to take a break from dating. I would start to turn down every opportunity to meet someone's friend because of my experience with Ryan. The devil tried to play with my mind again about being celibate. He kept playing back in my mind over and over what Ryan had said, "No man would put up with that." But, I would soon experience true love, so I thought.

Tips from Lessons Learned

1. On the first date, ask questions about a person's Christian walk and their beliefs.
2. Do not be afraid to end a date if it is making you feel uncomfortable.
3. Be careful with judging a book by its cover by making assumptions (i.e. He's a pastor, so he must be righteous).
4. By the third date, inform the person you are celibate – you will know if they want you or sex.
5. Always handle yourself with dignity when things do not go the way you think they should.

Chapter Ten
Finally Mr. Right

> *"Then the Lord God said, "It is not good that the man should be alone; I will make him a helper fit for him."*
>
> -Genesis 2:18 ESV

In summer of 2012, I celebrated my forty-first birthday with an extravagant party. Everything was going well, and I was yet focused on my real estate business, working out with my trainer Reggie "The Machine" a few times a week and on my own in the evenings, and being employed in corporate as a human resources executive. As the summer came to a close, Layla, one of my friends at the time, met a guy named Josh at a biker event. When I met him, he presented himself as a gentleman. He was well connected but was very loquacious. He resided in Arizona.

I did not enjoy going to biker events, as that was not how I preferred to spend my free time. The one time I relented, I grew acutely aware the biker scene was not the crowd for me. Layla was getting closer to Josh, and she was desirous for their relationship to develop further.

One evening, after I finished working out, Layla called me and said Josh was at her house. She had made enchiladas and invited me to stop by. As usual, Josh talked the entire time. He said he wanted to introduce me to one of his friends. Josh began scrolling through his phone naming one man after the other, while providing a description of the man. If I frowned with a look of disinterest, he continued his search. Finally he said, "Oh, I know the perfect man for you: Blake, but he lives in Houston, TX. You and Blake are both picky. He's an entrepreneur like you prefer and a home builder." As Josh continued with his description, he said, "Blake is a different type of dude and a hard nut to crack." I inquired, "What do you mean by that?" He said, "You will see, but Blake is a good guy and is all about his business." Josh called Blake around ten p.m. Houston time, which is a two-hour difference from Los Angeles, and he left a voicemail. I went home, and the next day at five a.m., Josh called me with Blake on the line to introduce us. Josh is an early riser, so five a.m. to him was like nine a.m. Blake's voice was extremely deep like I love, and he asked me to write his number down, and he would call me later.

Josh said he told Blake he needed to come meet me that week, because although I was forty-one years old, I put those twenty-one year olds to sleep. Blake called me later that day, and we talked for a while. He seemed rather pleasant over the phone. He told me that day was his forty-fourth birthday, and he was contemplating visiting Los Angeles that week, so he would come see me Friday. He asked me where I wanted to go for dinner Friday, and I told him it was his decision. He asked, "What about my favorite restaurant Crustaceans?" I said, "That's my favorite restaurant as well." He said, "Okay, so make reservations for us around six p.m." I was really impressed Blake would come to see me for a few hours from 3,000 miles away.

The next day when Blake and I talked, he told me one of his employees passed away, but he would still come to see me, because he already promised he would. But, he would need to leave the same night on a red-eye to attend the funeral on Saturday. I suggested a postponement, and he said he would still come because he likes to keep his word. I thought that was very nice of him to make a sacrifice and still come to see me, despite his loss. That made for a great first impression.

Our First Date

Blake told me it was his birthday the first day we talked, so even though I did not know him, I wanted to do something special for him for taking the time to travel to visit me for a few hours. I purchased him a small cake from Hansen's Cakes in Beverly Hills. Blake was at my house at six p.m. precisely on Friday evening. I was very nervous, but my expectations were not high. I thought at the least if there was not a connection, we could be friends.

When I opened the door, Blake was about six feet tall, chocolate, very handsome and dressed very causally with jeans and a button-down shirt. He gave me a hug, and I said, "I have a surprise for you." He looked on my kitchen island, and there was his cake. His eyes lit up, but he failed to show any emotion. However, I could tell he appreciated it. Blake is definitely an introvert, and I was unsure by me being an extrovert how we would get along.

As we departed for dinner, Blake was such a gentleman. He opened my car door and the venue door, which is always a must for me.

We arrived to Crustaceans, and the conversation was a sigh of relief. We had a fabulous time. Blake asked me so many questions about my career, church and family, which I loved about him. He seemed more interested in me than sex, which was so refreshing. I asked him if he was saved, and he answered affirmatively. I was exhilarated and explained to him that is important to me, but what mattered to me more was how strong his walk with God is. He told me the name of the church at which he fellowshipped in Houston. I then asked him if he was happy he had come to see me, and he said, "Of course." I said in a sarcastic manner, "You sure don't act like it." We both laughed. Blake was a man of few words and did not show any emotions, but I knew how to pull out the best in him in a short period of time.

I picked up my Blackberry cell phone, and Blake asked, "You still have a Blackberry?" I said, "Yes. I don't care about technology. As long as I can text, make calls and use the calendar, I'm fine." He said, "I'm going to have to buy you an iPhone." He had just upgraded his phone a few months ago. We both laughed, and I said, "Whatever makes you happy, since you can't be seen with this Blackberry." I asked him about his family, and he told me his parents were pastors, and he had two children: a son Jamie, who was twenty-two years old, and a daughter London, who would be nine in a few months. Also, he had two brothers and two sisters. Blake is the oldest of all his siblings. I asked him if he had any drama with his children's mother, because I really did not want to date anyone who had any drama with his ex. He said his child's mother and he have a great relationship. Blake said he had been divorced from her for ten years and had dated several women since his divorce. He had married his son's mother when they were twenty-one years old, but she left him when Jamie was a baby. So, he raised his son as a single dad, and at the time, they were not on speaking terms.

He said he had not met anyone he wanted to marry, and at the time, he was just seeing someone, but she was not his girlfriend and he was free to date other women. That meant he was a typical bachelor who would sleep with several women, but he would not be seen at a concert or public functions with any of the women, as he later stated. I told him I had been divorced for two years and had not met anyone with whom I was equally yoked, nor did I have any children. He asked me if I wanted children. I answered, "With the right person. I love children, and if God blesses me, I will be happy. If not, I will accept it." I told him I wanted to have a child when I was married before, but after the chaos started in my marriage I was scared to have a baby by my ex-husband, in fear that I would be his child's mother and have to interact with him for a lifetime. I told him I love children, but as a stepmother, I have always felt like the outsider, and I did not enjoy that feeling.

I have only seen one man, who is my friend Khloe's husband Brett, handle a blended family situation well. He sat down with Khloe and his children and ensured the children knew Khloe was going to be his wife and his love for her is different and does not change his love for them. At the same time, he informed them she would not be disrespected at any time. In the Word, God says family order is God, spouse and then children. When a man sits with a blended family to be, he removes the illusion that his wife is competing with his children.

No woman can compete with any child. When the man sits everyone down to have the conversation, everyone knows the stepmother's role, so the children do not feel jealous or as though another woman is taking their biological mother's place. Brett said these types of relationships take time for everyone to grow accustomed to one another, and he has always been the referee to protect everyone. It is not something that happens overnight, so the man really has to be a leader, a true man of God, have patience and be mature enough to make a blended family work. Brett said most men could not do this, because they idolize their children, but the Bible says one should not idolize anything. Men usually want to be their children's friends. Sometimes, men feel as though they owe their children for the mistakes they made with their mothers. Brett said he learned this through marriage counseling, and he went back to his ex-wife to apologize for the wrong he had done to her, so he would not compromise his relationship with Khloe, by showing more favor to his ex-wife.

Brett said also Khloe shared with him she always felt like the outsider in her previous relationship, so he wanted to ensure he protected her and made her feel like the queen she is at all times. The unconditional love he showered upon Khloe, she put into his children. Brett never made her bow down to his children or if she said something to them, he would not interfere but let her handle it. It was a win-win situation.

I told Blake when Brett and Khloe told me that story, it made me have hope that there are men out there who knew how to welcome the new wife into the family. Brett did say it took time for Khloe and his children to adjust to each other. Khloe cried many nights, because children can be cruel at times, but he always supported Khloe and never made her feel inferior. Now after a year or more, his daughters and Khloe are inseparable. Blake said, "Well, my kids would never disrespect you, so never worry about that."

> *"Train up a child in the way he should go; even when he is old he will not depart from it."*
>
> -Proverbs 22:6 ESV

At Crustaceans, we both ordered our favorite garlic noodles and crab legs. While we were waiting for our food, Josh called Blake. I then excused myself to the ladies' room. When I returned to the table, I asked Blake what Josh said because Josh had called my phone as well. Blake said, "He was just checking on us, and I told him this date was terrible." I responded with, "Yeah, right." He said, "I am just joking. I told him everything he said was correct, and I am enjoying myself." Then, Blake said he asked Josh again, "Man, you sure she's not dating anyone?" Josh said, "Not that I know of. I never hear Layla say anything about another man, and she always says nice things about Monica."

Blake complimented me on my hair, and I told him I had a weave, but most of my hair was left out at the top, and it was just convenient, because I worked out a lot. I said, "My hair is down my back. It's as long as this weave." I showed him a picture and said, "So, don't get it twisted thinking I'm a chicken head." He said, "I can tell you're not a chicken head, and I don't care about hair, but I had told my sister before I didn't like weaves, but yours look natural. I am interested in more than just your hair. As long as you're happy with your hair, I'm happy." I said, "Great." We laughed a lot, and Blake asked me if I had ever thought about relocating to Houston. I responded, "Oh, no. I used to visit Houston every summer, and after a while, I would probably be bored." He said, "Well, I can always relocate to Los Angeles." I said, "You sure can!" It was the best date I had been on in a while.

We left Crustaceans, and Blake wanted to stop by The Cork, a lounge in Los Angeles. Blake was very familiar with Los Angeles, because he used to visit often when one of his ex-girlfriends relocated from Houston. He openly shared he had several women friends in Los Angeles.

We listened to music, while he had a drink and I had my signature Shirley Temple. The owner came by and complimented us as being a nice couple. Even though we were not a couple, we complimented one another very well. The men there were trying to approach me, and they did not even care that I was with Blake.

On the way back to my house, Blake said the next Friday he would fly back out to see me, and we could spend the weekend together. I told Blake next Friday I had plans already, but I could see him on Saturday. He agreed, and we planned to attend Josh's biker event on that Saturday during the day.

After dinner, we relaxed at my house for about thirty minutes; then, he headed back out to the airport. His flight was full, and Josh called me and said, "Your man is stuck here due to the plane being overbooked." Blake did not want him to bother me, so he stayed at the Radisson Hotel and took the first flight out the next morning, which was very considerate and really the way it should be.

> *"Look not every man on his own things, but every man also on the things of others."*
>
> *-Philippians 2:4 KJV*

Blake called me when he landed and told me what happened. I told him he could have called me, and I would have come to get him, but he said he did not want to bother me after having a long workday.

During the week, Blake and I talked and text one another. He told me when he left my house, he called his friends and told them he was happy he met me. I, of course, blushed. I did not like Blake as much as he liked me at first when I met him, and I figured we would need to hang out again for me to get to know him. It takes a few dates for me to even know if the chemistry is there. Also, he lived in Houston, and I was concerned how our dating experience would play out. I was not for any games, nor was he, as he made that very clear during one of our phone conversations. We were always transparent with one another. Blake told me we could do whatever I wanted on the next

Saturday night, and I told him there was an R. Kelly concert we could go to.

Blake asked me to check on the tickets, and he would do the same. He called his ticket person, and he had the fifth row from the stage, but my contact had the better seats in the third row from the stage. Blake preferred the better seats, so I gave him the ticket man's contact information, and he purchased the tickets.

The Next Weekend

Blake called me before the plane took off Friday and after he landed. He went to the hotel where Josh was staying, and they went to Josh's event. Blake did not really want to stay at the event, so he left and went back to the hotel. He text me and said he could not wait to see me the next day, and I said, "Yeah. Why?" in a joking manner. He said, "Because I really enjoyed our short time together last Friday."

After my morning workout, I picked Blake up around nine a.m. from the hotel. We went to breakfast at the Serving Spoon in Inglewood, CA and back to my house for a few hours.

We conversed further about life, goals and anything you could imagine. Blake's facial expressions were always so serious, and he was not affectionate, but the words he spoke I knew were genuine.

From his appearance, Blake was my type of man. He was casual, not flashy, wore Chucks, jeans and tee-shirts. He is a homebuilder and entrepreneur of other businesses, which required him to drive around town most of the day and did not require him to wear a suit every day. When he met me, he said he was just starting to buy tailored suits to wear to church and other functions.

Neither one of us really wanted to attend Josh's biker event, as that was not our interest, but we went for a few hours, because Blake told him we would attend. Josh and Layla greeted us, and we walked around the Harley Davidson shop, and men again were trying to talk to me. One guy apologized to Blake, because he did not know we were together. I think by then Blake knew a man finding me was not a problem. Josh kept walking by telling me to take care of his friend, and I would respond, "You don't have to worry, but what about your friend taking care of me?" Blake said, "Babe, don't worry about that. I got you."

We left the event and went back to my house to get ready for the R. Kelly concert. I told Blake he could sleep in the other bedroom, as

I have three bedrooms. With a sarcastic tone, he said, "No problem." I put on a fabulous dress, and when Blake came downstairs for us to leave he said, "Wow, you look like a bag of money." I said, "And, you look handsome yourself." Blake had on a pair of jeans and a sports coat. I love simple and clean, and Blake is all that and more, but I needed him to loosen up a little. He seemed to be so detached, as though he had a lot clogged up in his mind.

We had a great time at the concert, and at one time, Blake said I needed to calm down, because R. Kelly was lightening up the stage, and I was dancing and enjoying myself. At one point, Blake went to purchase nachos for me, and when I sat them on my lap to eat, he was so scared that I would spill the cheese on my lap. He told me to put the napkin across my dress. I said sarcastically to him, "Do I look like your eight-year-old daughter?" We both laughed, and I said, "Babe, I got this." By our second date, we had started to call each other 'babe,' but I was still trying to figure out what he was all about. I could tell he was really into me. The mere fact he flew out two weeks in a row to see me said a great deal about his interest.

The next day, we went to my church at FCBC. He really enjoyed it, and then we went to brunch at the Four Seasons Hotel in Beverly Hills. Blake looked so serious but quite dapper and handsome in his suit I must say. I was looking fabulous in my black and red suit with my black Christian Louboutin stilettos. He asked me when I was going to visit him in Houston. I informed him I needed to check my schedule but would let him know that week.

He told me while we were eating that I was the one for him, and I asked him what he meant. He said, "You are my wife." I was so nervous that I dropped my fork on the floor. He asked, "Are you okay?" I said, "Yes, but God has to tell me you're the one." He said, "I'm sure in due time He will reveal that to you." I asked him if we could take it slow, and he said, "We can take it as fast or slow as you want, but I am still moving full speed ahead." Blake said he was starting to think something was wrong with him, because he had not met his wife, and although he did not know exactly how God would package his wife for him, he knew the foundation he wanted his wife to have, such as being a Christian and loving the Lord.

He said, "You definitely have all of that and more, besides being a beautiful young woman. I know what I want, and God blessed me with more than I could ever ask for. Monica, you're God fearing, intelligent, beautiful, have a nice figure, but it is more than your figure that attracted me. I'm coming on strong, so be ready." I said,

"But, there's something you should know. I don't date men who date other women, and when we met you said you were hanging out with someone that was not your woman. I believe if you're dating several women, you can't possibly focus on me who you say is your wife to be."

He said he was going to end that relationship and not to worry, because it did not mean anything to him. I did not know what to think, because I did not have that total chemistry yet with Blake. But, God's word is true in the scripture below. This is the natural order of how God made it for your husband to find you, but these days, women are telling men they are the one for them.

> *"He who finds a wife finds a good thing, and obtains favor from the Lord."*
>
> -Proverbs 18:22 KJV

Blake said he loved that I was not the type to tell him he was the one for me and that I wanted to marry him. He said most women he met are the aggressors. He also loved that I allowed him to be the man and take the lead. He left that Sunday evening and from that day forward Blake would call me every day between six-thirty a.m. and seven a.m. PST, and we would text and chat during the day and talk to one another each night. Later that week, I told him I could visit him in Houston within the next two weeks. He responded, "So, I have to wait for two weeks to see you." I answered, "I guess so, babe." He said, "Okay, babe. I can't wait to see you, and when you come, we will go to my church, so make sure you bring attire for church."

Houston, Texas Visit

I was on my way to Houston on a Friday afternoon. Before the plane took off, Blake called me and said he could not wait to see me, and he would be at the airport with bells on. I did not know what to expect for the weekend, but I was going to just have fun and enjoy. Blake picked me up from the airport, and we went to eat. He was in his work truck and had his work boots on. One thing about Houston, I remembered there was always great food, and the crab enchiladas would become my favorite dish. We went to his house, and yes, as Christians we should not have been staying at one another's homes, but I felt I had self-control, and I was not having sex with him period. Also, a mutual friend who knew him introduced us, so I felt safe. We arrived at Blake's house, and he gave me a tour of his very nice home.

Shortly thereafter, he invited me to make myself at home. He showered and changed his clothes from a hard day of work. We watched *Shark Tank* on TV and relaxed for the evening. I had decided against wearing anything sexy, so when I came out of the shower I had on a silk jumper. Blake's face dropped to the floor, and his facial expressions said, "What does she have on?" He expected something a little sexier, but I was not trying to entice or tease him.

We stayed at home Friday night and chatted, getting to know one another. As we were watching T.V., apparently he turned his ringer off on his home phone, but the caller ID kept showing up on his T.V. screen. I could tell he was becoming uncomfortable when the women's names would reflect on the TV. I just laughed inside. I also was thinking, *I hope he's not some playboy, because I do not have time for this.*

> "But put on the Lord Jesus Christ, and make no provision for the flesh, to gratify its desires."
>
> -Romans 13:14 ESV

All of a sudden, Blake was on top of me, trying to take my jumper off, but that was not happening too easily. He could not figure out how to get it off, so we kissed, and I said, "Wait a minute! Wait a minute! Good things do not come that easily." He played it off, and said, "I just wanted to see what you were about." Meaning, he wanted to know if I was the type of woman that would have sex with him so soon. I had not told him I was celibate yet, but it was coming. We laughed about his thought about what I had on. He admitted, "I was saying to myself, 'She is not getting in my bed with that jumper on.'"

I told him, "I know you are used to getting what you want, but I am an image of God, and His precious cargo is not something that's easy to conquer." He told me there had been times in the past he would not even touch a woman if they slept in the same bed, even when the women wanted him to. His behavior caused the women to think he was not interested in them or something was wrong with him. We cuddled all night as we slept, and it felt so good to have that chocolate handsome man keep me warm.

The next morning, we got up and went jogging. Even though I worked out at least four to five times a week, I hated to jog, but that was what Blake loved to do, so I went with him. When I would slow down, Blake would say, "Come on, babe," and encouraged me to pick up my speed. Afterward, we went to breakfast. When we arrived, the line was around the corner. Of course Blake knew the owner, so we were seated immediately. He was proving to be my type of man: first class. The Breakfast Klub is popular for their waffles with powdered sugar, and boy were they delicious. We had great conversation, and Blake looked into my eyes the entire time. Blake already knew I liked to eat and was not shy about taking down food.

Blake told me he loved my infectious personality and sarcastic ways. He had started to loosen up and would hold my hand when we were out and showed more affection. He told me he never would show any public affection with the women he dated, but he would try his best to do better with me.

Blake had been telling all his friends about me, and I soon inherited a nickname: "California Love." We went to the famous Frank's Ice Cream Parlor, and one of his friends Steve called and said he was going to meet us there to see who Blake was so in love with.

Steve is the ticket man and was very boisterous. He did not care whom he was talking to or if he knew you or not. Steve pulled up a chair and said, "Let me see your eyes. What did you do to my friend?" I said, "Nothing." He said, "You better treat my friend right." I responded, "What about how he treats me?" Steve said, "You're in good hands with Blake, and he will treat you right for a life time." We ate ice cream and laughed. Blake told him he was moving to Los Angeles, but Steve said he could not go and leave his friends there in Houston. I told him they could visit anytime.

We soon left the ice cream parlor, and Blake took me around with him while he was working. Later that evening, he took me to his lounge to meet his best friend Kyle, who manages the lounge. I walked into the lounge, and Blake introduced me to Kyle and he said, "We have been looking for you, Monica." I met his son Jamie and his fiancée, and they were both very nice. His friend Carl said, "Man, who did you bring from Los Angeles, Beyoncé?" We all laughed, and the men and women in the lounge were making advances towards me.

Blake saw all the action I was getting and came over to me and suggested, "Why don't you come over here and sit down." I agreed, but it was clear he did not appreciate the men socializing with me. Blake did not know I was telling my admirers I was with him, and I did not want to be rude and cut people off abruptly. I am an extrovert, and I can adjust to any environment and socialize at all levels. I am not a flirt by any means and would never disrespect Blake. The music was great. We stayed for a while; then, we left and headed home.

While driving back to Blake's house, he held my hand, kissed my hand and whatever I wanted to do he was in agreement. Our conversation was so refreshing, and he never talked about sex. Instead, he focused his attention on getting to know me. He did try to have sex with me my first night in Houston, but when I shut him down, it was not the topic of our conversation going forward. He seemed to really be into me. After spending that weekend with Blake, I was starting to like him a little more. He always rolled out the red carpet for me, and going forward, he treated me like a woman of God.

I am Celibate

The next day, we went to church, and the service was great. The sermon was about Christians living by all the principles of the Bible, such as not fornicating or committing adultery, etc. During church service, I noticed Blake kept holding his head down to pray.

After church when I asked if he was okay, because of what I had noticed, he said, "Yes, during church, Monica, when my head was down, I was thanking God for you because I am so thankful you are in my life." I said, "Awe, babe. Thank you so much, and I am starting to feel the same way." His puppy-like eyes looked so genuine and sincere, and his words touched my heart. We headed to brunch, and it was delicious. He shared with me he did not speak to his parents often, and they knew not to bother him about anything. Blake did not have a close relationship with his father because he said they treated him badly when he was growing up. I figured that caused him to be distant and unable to show affection, because he was never given any affection as a child. I did not think much about it and just wanted to be supportive and lend a listening ear to him.

We went back to his house until it was time for me to fly back home. I shared with Blake I had a breast reduction in April earlier in the year, and my doctor was going to fix my scar in a few weeks. He asked me who was going to take care of me after the surgery, and I answered, "My mom or a friend."

He said, "Well, I'm going to take you to your surgery and take care of you when you get home. Then, I will leave the next day, because it will be Thanksgiving." I told him he did not have to fly back just for my surgery, because I did not want him to waste any money for a few days. He said, "Monica, I'm coming to take care of you, babe, so let's stop talking about it. Besides, I fly free. My uncle has been with the airlines for over thirty years, and I'm one of his companions and can fly anywhere in world for free, but of course on standby." His demeanor was a huge plus because I really like a man who takes charge. I accepted what he said and replied, "Okay, sounds good to me babe, and I really appreciate the sacrifices you're making for me!"

On our way to the airport, I asked him if he believed all the principles in the Bible his pastor preached about in service that day, and he said, "Yes." I queried, "Really?" He asked, "Which ones are you speaking about?" I said, "Like not fornicating." He said, "So, are you saying you are celibate and not having sex until you get married?" I replied, "That's correct." I asked Blake if he had a problem with that, and he said, "No, not at all." I told him I was not proclaiming I was marrying him, but I am celibate and living a righteous lifestyle and I wanted whom God has already prepared for me as a husband. I told him, "If God or my parents do not approve of my husband, I will not marry him."

Blake said he had been praying for a wife who was saved and celibate. He also said, at times he would abstain from sex for a few months or so, but it was not consistent. I left refreshed and let out a sigh of relief. He asked me to be his woman and said he really respects the way I live my life. I asked him how we were going to manage a long-distance relationship, because that had not worked out well for couples I knew. Blake assured me he would be committed to me, and he was all in and not to worry. We arrived at the terminal, and he gave me a kiss and big hug. I could see in his eyes that he was falling in love with me.

On the plane, I prayed and said, "Lord, if he is the one for me, please reveal it to me. I do not want to waste any time with a man who is not for me."

> *"But I would have you without carefulness. He that is unmarried careth for the things that belong to the Lord, how he may please the Lord."*
>
> -1 Corinthians 7:32 KJV

I had not disembarked from the plane before Josh called me to see how my trip went. I told him we had fun. He asked, "Did he try to have sex with you, because women have said in the past they have been with him and he did not try anything, so they thought something was wrong with him." I said, "He tried, and he did share those rumors with me." I told him Blake was a very nice guy, and we would see what would transpire in the future. Josh is a gossiper, so I certainly did not want to tell him everything that went on. Josh asked me what I did to Blake, because he was in love with me already. I said, "I am just being me, and he is being himself." I shared with Josh, "Blake and I were very transparent with one another, and I believe that is the best policy." Josh said, "Okay, well keep me posted, and I'm happy everything is working out."

I called Blake to let him know I landed, and I told him Josh had called. He said, "Yeah, he just called me too." Blake told me he missed me so much already and could not wait to see me in about seven days to take care of me. He told me we would never go more than seven days without seeing one another. I told him I could not wait to see him again as well. I thanked him for everything and told him I had a great time.

Blake and I talked every morning, and he led our prayer. We text and talked most of the day. There was not a day that passed when he did not get me on the phone at seven a.m. or he did not answer the phone when I called him. If we were both busy, we would always acknowledge each other and say, "Babe, can I call you right back?" Or, we would text one another saying we would call each other right back if we were in meetings. Blake would give me a rundown of his schedule each day; in case, I needed him, and I would do the same. We did not discuss that ahead of time or make any rules about how we would communicate with one another. A woman should not be required to operate in such a manner, because if a man knows what he wants and is pursuing her, he will do everything in his power to please and respect her.

My Surgery

Blake flew out to visit me and take care of me pre and post-surgery. When he arrived, he brought a huge bag of clothes, shoes, underwear, tee-shirts and his personal items to hang in the closet. He said that would make it easier when he visited me; he would then only be required to bring his iPad and paperwork.

He said when he got back home, he was going to ship one of his cars, a Jeep Wrangler, so he would have a car to drive when he was here. Blake never wanted to use my car, and I loved how he was such a God-fearing man and leader.

The night before my surgery, we prayed together, as we would always do each morning and evening. I felt so secure when Blake came to take care of me, but I always made sure he felt like a king when he would come as well. His dinner was made, towels were laid out for his shower, and whatever he needed was available. I would always ask him what he wanted from the store and, of course, he would never like for me to buy much and always said when he came to Los Angeles, we would go to the store together.

During that particular visit, Blake did not want me to do anything. His focus was on taking care of me in every aspect. We again cuddled all night and spoke 'sweet nothings' to each other. The next morning at six a.m., Blake drove me to my surgical appointment and met Dr. Stuart A. Linder, a renowned plastic surgeon in Beverly Hills, who is like a brother to me and had reconstructed my scar when I got shot. He told Blake to make sure he treats me as a woman should be treated at all times, and Blake smiled and told him he had everything covered.

When I awakened after the surgery, Blake was present. The nurses dressed me and wheeled me out, while Blake went to get the car. Blake drove me home and carried me into the house. I was in heaven and really appreciated my babe being there for me.

He kissed me gently on my forehead and told me to sleep off the anesthesia, while he worked. A few hours later, I woke up, and Blake was right by my side. As I lifted my eyes, I heard his deep sexy voice say, "Hey, babe." He then asked me if I wanted some soup. Very softly, I said, "Yes, I'm so hungry, babe." He made the soup and brought it to me. I looked at him and said, "Babe, you have no idea how much I appreciate you coming to take care of me from 3,000 miles away. I know all the businesses you juggle each day, but you still came here to take care of me. That lets me know that you're quite special." Blake rarely smiled. However, my comment caused him to have a big smile on his face. He grinned and said, "It is what I'm supposed to do, babe."

I was sitting up on the bed, while he lay next to me. I felt him looking intently at me, so I said, "You're looking at me like you're in love with me." He said, "I am, babe." His look communicated, "I need you in my life. You're mine." His eyes looked like those of a little puppy. His utterance was so sweet. Although I was in much pain, hearing him say, "I'm in love with you," made me forget about the pain.

Even though we had only known each other for thirty days, it was evident to me when a man knows what he wants, he will conquer her. We watched movies and relaxed the entire day, while he worked throughout the day as well. Blake was heading back to Houston in the morning. He refused to allow me to drop him off to the airport, but we both wanted to spend every bit of time together.

Blake would always text me when he landed and called me when he got in the car. He would always leave his work truck at the airport, so he could go straight to work after returning from Los Angeles.

Thanksgiving Day

Blake called me on Thanksgiving Day at seven a.m. and asked me how I was feeling. I said, "A little sore, but much better." He thanked me for the lovely text message I sent him the night before thanking him again for coming to take care of me and letting him know how much I appreciated it. Blake told me to call him if I needed anything, and he would figure it out.

He then asked me what my Christmas plans were, and I told him I would be flying to St. Louis to see my family. Blake said he would like for me to meet his parents and asked if I could meet him in New Orleans, LA the day after Christmas, since I had never been to New Orleans. A few days later, we would drive to Baton Rouge, LA, to visit his parents. After our visit, we would drive back to Houston, and spend New Year's Eve at church. I said, "That sounds great. I would love to meet your parents." He said, "I have been telling my parents about you." I said, "Oh, really? What did you tell them?" He said, "Well, I told them we were getting married, but I didn't want to say anything to you, because we had not talked about a date or anything." Sarcastically, I said, "Really! I didn't say I was marrying you." He said, "I have not taken anyone to meet my parents since my daughter's mom." I said, "This sounds like fun, and we would spend almost ten days together, because I don't have to go back to work until January 7, 2013." He said, "Okay, I will book your flights." The excitement grew within the both of us.

He said he had never wanted to spend more than two days with anyone he was dating, so our time together would prove if we could stand to be around one another for a long period of time. I said, "For sure, babe."

He said he was going to pick up a pie one of his lady friends made for him. I noticed Blake would be very transparent about his lady friends, and most of them he had slept with in the past. I appreciated the transparency; however, I did not want him to think we and his lady friends would be one big happy family. If you are a God-fearing man dating me and you want to marry me one day, I knew for certain I was not accepting those women friends lingering around. He told me he had made a fried turkey for one of his lady friends. Her husband threw it in the trash and thought it was disrespectful for her to accept a turkey from Blake, as they had dated in the past.

Apparently, Blake did not see anything wrong with it, which I thought was weird. I gathered when Blake told me he was not treated right from his parents when he was younger, these women friends filled that void of love that he longed for. It seemed to have made him feel good about having many women friends to talk with, and he would give them advice on their relationships and vice versa. It is definitely inappropriate when you are married to discuss your relationship with the opposite sex, which could turn into adultery, as the other person fulfills your emotional needs.

> *"For by means of a whorish woman a man is brought to a piece of bread: and the adulteress will hunt for the precious life."*
>
> -Proverbs 6:26 KJV

Blake had shared with me one of his lady friends would need to stick around, because she is very resourceful. Well, I am very resourceful, and that comment deeply concerned me, not to mention, it hurt my feelings. Because we were both so transparent with one another, I felt comfortable to share how I felt about that comment to Blake, and instantly, he realized maybe he should not have said that. With regret, he apologized. God will supply all we need, and certainly no Jezebel would be any type of resource to my husband.

My viewpoint was different, and it showed in my actions. As I committed to Blake, the male friends I had were on notice that I was dating Blake with the intent to marry him. I informed them I could only deal with them on business terms. Often times, when I would talk to my male friends, they would try to discuss inappropriate things, and I would always cut them off. I certainly did not want to disrespect Blake. Blake was everything I had written down that I wanted in my husband, and I would only accept children if he did not have any drama with their mothers. He would need to know how to balance a wife and the children, so that I would not feel as the outsider. I kept praying on the matter and asking God to guide me in the right direction and reveal to me anything I needed to know that was not pleasing to Him.

Who is This Mystery Man?

Between Thanksgiving and Christmas, Blake flew to Los Angeles a few times, and I flew back to Houston once for us to spend time together. I told Vivian about Blake. Because she had never heard me speak about anyone as I did when I spoke of Blake, when he came to visit, she was determined to meet him. Vivian came over on a Saturday, and I was making a banana pudding. Vivian said, "Blake has you cooking; he must be special." We all laughed, and Vivian told Blake she just had to meet him, because she could hear in my voice that he was special.

Blake told Vivian, "Monica is very special to me, and I have never been in love with anyone like I am with Monica. She means a lot to me, and she is going to be my wife." Vivian said, "Wife? You two are getting married? Monica never told me this news." Blake said, "Nothing is planned yet, but I already told her she is my wife." Vivian was a little tipsy, so she was quite jovial and said, "Let's drink to this great news. I'm so happy for you both."

Then, she directed her attention to Blake and said, "Monica is my girl, so please treat her right." He said, "Don't worry. I got this. You just take care of her when I'm not here." Vivian said, "Deal." Vivian left, and Blake said, "She seems nice." I said, "Yeah, we have been friends since grade school."

Blake and I talked about our holiday plans, and we were so excited. He was telling me all about New Orleans and the restaurants at which we would eat. Blake said he held back from traveling so much, because he wanted to experience it with his wife.

He loved the fact I had not traveled all around the world as of yet. We certainly had a lot to enjoy together for a lifetime. Even though

Blake and I were not engaged, for some reason I believed him when he said I would be his wife. He was so sincere, and I was the apple of his eye. He would tell me he was relocating to Los Angeles, and all of his friends were upset that he was saying he wanted to relocate.

Blake said he was tired of Houston and had been there for twenty years. He said the only thing in Houston was his children, and they could always come to visit and we could visit them in Houston also. I said, "Of course, we could always travel back and forth."

Chris and my mom were very desirous to meet Blake and to see whom I was visiting in Houston. So, the next day after church, I planned to take Blake to meet Chris and my mom. Chris barbequed and was getting to know Blake. Both my mom and Chris asked Blake what he did for a living, where he grew up, how he liked Houston, his children, etc. Everything went well, and they could tell Blake was really into me. Blake told them he really liked me, as he did not want to make them think he was coming on to strong with saying he was in love with me.

When we left, my mom text me and said Blake seemed to be a nice man and how he kept staring at me every time I talked. She joked and said, "He has his nose wide open, huh?" We went back to my house.

Later that evening, who other than Josh would call Blake? Josh teased Blake because he seemed to be so in love with me. Blake was not offended nor did he deny his feelings. Instead, he told Josh he owed him a nice gift for introducing him to me. Josh would always say he wished us the best and said we better come to his biker event in March 2013, in Arizona. Blake told him we would. As much as we disliked the biker scene, we wanted to support Josh's event.

I took Blake to the airport, which is the part we dreaded, for we disliked being apart from one another. We were always looking forward to seeing each other again. Even though Blake was a man of a few words, he would always tell me things like, "You are the best thing that ever happened to me" and "I have no desire to be with another woman."

Those words melted my heart, and I was getting so nervous, because I had encountered several fakes, but our relationship would only get better and better each day.

"Love is patient, love is kind. It does not envy, it does not boast, it is not proud. It is not rude, it is not self-seeking, it is not easily

angered, and it keeps no record of wrongs. Love does not delight in evil but rejoices with the truth. It always protects, always trusts, always hopes, always perseveres. Love never fails."

-1 Corinthians 13:4-8 ESV

Best Holiday Ever

It was time for me to head out to the "Show Me State" a few days before Christmas to spend time with my family. Before I boarded the plane, Blake and I did not want to hang up the phone from one another. I finally landed in St. Louis, and my first stop would be White Castle burgers. I love White Castle, and then I went to my grandmother Jean's house.

My grandmother Jean has a big Christmas Eve dinner where family from several states comes, and we have great food. It is an entire week event with many festivities.

The days could not go by fast enough for me to arrive in New Orleans, the day after Christmas. Blake and I talked every morning and night, as we would do when I was in Cali. Blake still called every morning at seven a.m. My grandmother Jean said, "You two must be tied to the hip." We just could not get enough of one another and were counting down the days until I would arrive in New Orleans.

We enjoyed Christmas Eve with family and friends, with delicious food, dessert and card games flowing all night. On Christmas day, we ate more, played games and visited other friends and family homes. When Blake called me that morning, he told me he really liked his gift. I mailed his gift before I left, because there was absolutely no room in my suitcase. Blake's gift included a pair of soft all black men's loungewear, with a V-neck collar, and Warren Buffet's new book about being a billionaire.

Blake liked to read a lot, so what better book to get him. He was so appreciative and said, "Thank you so much, babe, for my gift." I like to see my man in fresh nice loungewear. I think that is so sexy.

Blake drove from Houston to Baton Rouge to see his family. We talked part of the way while he was on the road. He sent me a 'selfie' of himself, letting me know he missed his baby doll. Blake arrived safely to his parents' house, and we text each other all day and talked in anticipation of the next day. Blake said his family could not wait to meet me in the next few days, and I was excited to meet them as well.

New Orleans, Louisiana Here I Come

December 26, 2012 finally arrived, and I boarded the six a.m. plane off to New Orleans. My flight was delayed an hour, and I could not get to my babe fast enough. The plane landed, and Blake was waiting for me at the baggage claim. He called me and asked, "Babe, where are you?" I told him I was walking his way and dragging my luggage, due to the zipper being busted from the cold weather. I snuck up behind my babe, and we gave each other a big hug and kiss. I could tell Blake was thrilled to see me. As we were driving to the hotel, I was so excited to see the scenery. As we drove, he told me all about the history in New Orleans and showed me some great restaurants we were going to later that day.

We planned to stay two days in New Orleans and then drive to visit his parents for a few hours. We freshened up and Blake said, "Babe, here are my Christmas gifts to you." He gave me a lovely Christmas card, a white iPad, Coco Chanel lotion and perfume, and when we arrived in Houston, he would take me to buy me the iPhone I wanted.

The Christmas Card

He told me to open the card last, and when I opened it, my heart just filled with love. The card read: *"People always say when you find "the one" you'll just know." I knew. (Still do).* Then to my surprise, Blake, the man of a few words, actually wrote quite a bit, and it read: *Babe, this card is so me for you. It's straight and to the point. I don't know if you noticed, but I'm a man of a few words and expressions☺. All I can say is that I knew from the moment I saw you, I wanted to spend the rest of my life with you. On my way back to Houston after meeting you, I was so thankful to God for the blessing He had given me in you. My life has new meaning with you in it. I wanted you to know that I love you with all my heart and that there isn't anything I would not do for you. I love you! Blake*

I thought, *Okay, God. Every time I pray for the reveal, it gets better, so this must be the one.* I continued to pray for God's direction, because Blake was all in, and I wanted to be as well and give him my heart, but I was scared and wanted to believe everything he was saying. His actions were so genuine, and no one would ever think otherwise that his intentions were nothing but authentic for me.

> *"But whoever keeps his word, in him truly the love of God is perfected. By this we may know that we are in him."*
>
> -1 John 2:5 ESV

I was so excited that I jumped on his chest and said, "Thank you, babe cakes." "Babe Cakes" would be his new nickname from me, and when I called him that, he would smile.

That evening Blake and I went to a nice seafood restaurant and had intimate conversation. Blake would initiate the talk about our future together and family business plans. We stared into each other's eyes all night, and for Blake not to be a touchy feely person, he would always compliment me on my hair or the outfit I had on and my eyes. Blake loved my eyes and said they were hypnotizing and beautiful.

We walked around New Orleans, and I thought the place was beautiful and compact where you did not have to drive far for anything. We went back to the hotel because we were both exhausted, then his mother called. Blake put the phone on speaker, and she told me the family could not wait to meet me. I said, "Likewise." I took a hot bath, and we both just relaxed. I ordered dessert from room service. I was starting to feel so secure with Blake and was on top of the world.

Open and Honest

It was approaching eight p.m., and we were both enjoying each other's company and conversation. Blake started to open up and share with me his childhood experiences and how he grew up. He and his dad really did not have a relationship and rarely talked, but when they did it was always cordial. He said his mom was not always nice, but they spoke periodically. His younger brothers are twins, had just turned twenty-one years old, and were finally getting their own townhouse. His two sisters were both in their thirties and married with children.

Blake had spent some time in the Air Force, but he quickly got out, because he did not want to be sent to war. Blake said raising Jamie as a single dad was not easy, but he did not let that stop him. He knew Jamie was his full responsibility. Blake was hired by UPS where he worked as a driver for a few years. He said he used to love UPS, and it was a great place to work as a young man in his twenties.

He said at times during his youth, he lived in his car, because times were tough and money was low. Shortly after working at UPS, Blake met a guy who showed him the way of the street life, and he hustled for some years when he moved to Houston twenty years ago. It was not the life he wanted, but money was rolling in fast, and that was his way of life to take care of himself and Jamie.

Blake met his second wife when he was about twenty-seven years old in Houston, and they divorced after six years. When Blake finally decided to leave the marriage, his wife was pregnant with London. Blake admitted he still proceeded to leave his wife even after he found out she was pregnant. Blake admitted to committing infidelity during his marriage, but said he would always spend holidays with his wife. I asked, "So, I guess you thought that made it right?" We both had to laugh, because we were acutely aware the answer was no.

At some point, Blake stopped being a hustler and turned his money into businesses. As a result, he became an entrepreneur. At times, business was good. While at other times, business could have been better. Blake said a few years before we met, his money was tight with the real estate market taking a dive, but now things were starting to pick up. I was so appreciative how Blake was so open about his past. I was not there to judge him, because everyone has a past. What intrigued me was his motivation to live for God, to be married and enjoy his family.

Blake and I had already talked about my family and about my biological dad being ill. I shared with Blake the shooting I experienced, but I told him it was a carjacking, as I had told everyone else, including my family.

I was not going to share the real story with Blake until we were married, because that was a life-and-death situation and not something to be shared with a boyfriend. Because the guys were never arrested and I did not know who knew who, I did not want my story being told to anyone. However, I knew I was going to write a book about my life, celibacy and meeting Mr. Right, so everyone would know then.

I shared with him about my marriage and how I had to give up two properties, because my ex-husband agreed to take responsibility for them but failed to pay the notes. Paying the notes was a burden left on me. When I was unable to bear it, I had to make a decision to walk away from the properties. That was the hardest decision for me, and then to see my credit score decrease from eight hundred was even more treacherous. But as time progressed, my score eventually began to rise. I had two credit cards I was still paying on from my ex-husband along with my student loans.

That was the only debt I had, and it was manageable. Blake told me he really appreciated how I was so transparent, and he loved that about me. He said his credit score had also fallen in the past, but it was rising as well.

> *"Do not lie to one another, seeing that you have put off the old self with its practices."*

> -Colossians 3:9 ESV

It is very important when discussing a potential marriage to disclose everything. As one man told Blake, there are fifty-two cards in a deck, and you must place all fifty-two cards on the table for discussion, but not everyone does that. I asked Blake if there was anyone from his past who had his heart, and he said, "No, only you, and you are here in the present." He asked me the same thing, and I said, "There is no one besides you that will have my heart, babe." The long-distance relationship was a new experience for me, and I did not want anyone coming around later that had his heart and would tempt him.

As we continued our back-and-forth questioning, I asked Blake if he ever had any gay encounters, and he said, "No." He returned the question, and I responded, "No way." I asked him what his imperfections were, and he said, "If I sensed a woman was playing games or made me mad in the past, I would shut down for a few days, because I have zero tolerance for games or when a woman made me mad. Also, I can be direct at times, and some people may take it the wrong way." I had witnessed that for myself. For example, when he would be around the daycare or Jamie and others, they did not question or attempt to try anything with him. He asked me about my imperfections, and I told him, "When I am stressed, I wear my emotions on my shoulders, and everyone around me feels it. Intense stress and pressure causes me to be demanding. However, God is still working on me."

He said, "Babe, like I told you, there isn't anything we can't ever work through." We are both perfectionist, but Blake was more tolerable with less-skilled people, and I only want the best and smartest on my team. This of course, depends on the type of business one has. Blake did teach me how to have more patience with people of a slower pace, because in my field of human resources, it is cut throat. I have always had to be on top of my game. Some of my mentors were hard on me, which made me a great student of any business.

We talked so late into the night our eyes were burning, but we really learned a lot about each other. We discussed everything from what made us tick to things we liked or did not like and intimacy. Blake told me he did not expect me to be perfect, and he was there to support me.

At the end of our lengthy conversation, he said, "If you need anything, I want you to tell me." I agreed, "Okay." He said, "Monica, promise you will tell me, because I want to take care of you and there isn't anything I will not do for you." At that point, I could have melted in his arms, and he looked as if he could have melted in my arms with such love and happiness in his eyes.

Kissing Passionately

Blake told me I turned him on very much. Then, he began kissing me on my neck. I stopped him and said, "Come on, Blake. We can't do this." He said, "Just lay back. I just want to show you how much I love you."

I was in deep water, but my self-control was not going to let it go too far although our passion for one another was nothing like either one of us had ever experienced. Slowly, we stopped kissing, because he said he did not want to disrespect me, as he really appreciated my celibacy and was so blessed he had found me. We talked the rest of the night, and my heart felt so wonderful.

When a couple is not sexually intimate, the man and woman have more intimate conversation, not necessarily about sex, but romance and getting to know one another. When you are not having sex, it forces you to engage in conversation more often. Blake said our discourse was the best type of conversation he had in a long time. We spooned all night, and it felt so wonderful to be in each other's arms.

Now granted if you are celibate, you really should not tempt one another and spend nights with each other in the same bed. This is not something I would advise, but my mind was made up. I did not care how good the kissing was. Nothing was going to make me go against the Lord's word. Blake did not try to cross the line, since the first time he was rejected. Also, we had a long-distance relationship, so any time we spent together was special.

> *"No temptation has overtaken you that are not common to man. God is faithful, and he will not let you be tempted beyond your ability, but with the temptation he will also provide the way of escape, that you may be able to endure it."*
>
> -1 Corinthians 10:13 ESV

New Orleans: Day Two

On our second day in New Orleans, we went to a few shops, ate, and explored the casino. It was not much more to do. Blake just wanted to ensure I saw New Orleans and that we spent time together. The weather was a little cool, but as we walked, we kept each other warm. I kept seeing signs for Beignets, so I asked, "Babe, what's a Beignet?" He countered, "You never had one?" I said, "No, I haven't."

To show me rather than explain, we went to a spot that was famous for them, but they were little too mushy. Next door to that venue was another Beignet spot, and theirs were crunchy with powdered sugar. After tasting it, I whined, "Babe, why did you turn me on to these? You know sweets are my weakness."

You better believe we took a box home for me. Also, my mom had asked Blake to bring her a box of Beignets before we left, because she loved them. But, we were both tired of eating at that point.

I learned it is true when you are crazy in love, you want to eat everything together. After sharing the tasty treats, we walked around and took pictures. Blake was not really a picture taker, but I wanted to capture the moment, so we took many pictures.

We also went to his favorite place to eat: Gina's Po Boy Sandwich. I never had a po boy sandwich, but when Blake ordered a hot link sandwich, I tasted it. Boy was it delicious. I had never seen Blake eat something so quickly and enjoy it the way he enjoyed that sandwich. We hung out all night walking around the French Quarter and finally returned to the hotel. We were driving to Baton Rouge in the morning, so we wanted to get some rest. While Blake and I were together, we would read our Word day and night and Blake would lead the prayer. That is another thing I loved about Blake: he took the time for us to read the Word together and pray. I never leave home without my Bible. Wherever I go, it will be in my suitcase.

Meet the Southern Family

The next morning, we had breakfast and then got on the road headed to meet his parents. On our way, I reminded Blake to stop at the mall, because I wanted to ensure I purchased his parents a little gift for welcoming me into their home. I did not want to buy anything in Los Angeles, because I barely had room in my suitcase, so that was the original plan. We stopped at Macy's, and I chose a set of nice drinking glasses, which Blake wanted to pay for. I told him it would not be appropriate for him to pay for something I was purchasing for his parents. His eyes lit up, and he said he was again so grateful to have me in his life.

We arrived at Blake's parents' home, and I was, of course, nervous and did not know how his parents would act towards me, based on what Blake shared with me about them. To my surprise, his dad Blake Sr. and mom Becky welcomed me and very much appreciated the gift. Becky complimented me on my boots, and we all just talked. Blake did not really say too much, and the interactions with his parents were minimal. He talked mostly with his siblings. Becky asked me how I liked New Orleans, and we talked about my family, Christmas and had basic everyday conversation.

Blake and his brothers were in the kitchen, and Blake asked me if I wanted something to eat. Refusing, I explained I was tired of eating, because Blake had me eating so much. His brother Brandon mumbled in the kitchen, "Look like she had been eating in Los Angeles before she got to New Orleans." Blake and Brandon thought that was so funny, and they just kept laughing. Finally, after I asked what was so funny, they shared the joke, and we all laughed. I was a little thicker than I wanted to be, but I was in heaven.

Only his sister Rachael was there with her children and husband; the other sister Stacy did not make it. Peter, the twin brother, had stayed briefly, then left for his date. It was a great visit. Then, his parents had to get dressed for a dinner they were going to. Blake and I left shortly after that.

Back to Houston, Texas

Driving back to Houston was a three-hour excursion. Before embarking upon our journey, we could not leave Baton Rouge without getting some Beignets for the road. We laughed and joked all the way back to Houston. Before we drove out of Baton Rouge, Blake showed me where he had lived as a kid, his high school and childhood memory areas.

I never really liked road trips until I met Blake. While driving, I asked him relationship questions, and he would ask me the same. That was our way of getting to know each other, and we had fun doing it. I would kiss Blake on his cheek while he was driving and told him how much I really appreciated him taking the time from his businesses to spend the holiday with me, and Blake thanked me for doing the same. I knew how hard he worked, so I wanted to make sure he knew I had a great time, and I enjoyed New Orleans.

When we made it to Blake's house, we relaxed next to one another from the long drive. Blake came closer to me and whispered in my ear that he had never been in love like he was and so into a woman. He said he could not get enough of me. At that time, it was our third day together. Generally, that would be his breaking point where he would have grown tired of the woman. Blake said he never got tired of me.

The next day, Blake and I engaged in our workout regimen at the track. Then, I rode along while he completed his work during the day. Before returning home, we purchased my white iPhone, and I was both excited and appreciative of my Christmas gifts from Blake.

Each day, I felt more love for Blake, but I was really trying to pinpoint why I was falling in love with him, so I continued to pray about it. It certainly was not the Christmas gifts; it was something deeper than anything a man could do monetarily for a woman. I asked

God to allow me to be "in love" with a man, because I had never been in love before. God would soon reveal to me why I was falling for Blake.

Returning to Blake's, I began arranging my facial products and personal items. Blake told me to use any drawer I desired to house my items. As I opened a drawer to place my items inside, I discovered scarves and other women's items. I said sarcastically, "Babe cakes, my stuff can't fit in here, because there are items in this drawer." You should have seen Blake's face. He said, "Oh, babe, just throw it in the trash. That stuff is old." He was so nervous. I laughed so hard, and he said, "Ha ha. You're too funny," as he smiled while looking at me with so much love in his eyes.

That evening, Blake and I decided to go to a comedy show to see John Witherspoon, and it was actually funny. At first, I did not think he would be funny, but Blake and I laughed all night. We loved being in one another's presence, and it was as if we had known each other for years. Neither one of us had ever felt the chemistry we had with one another with another person.

When we returned to the house, we enjoyed ice cream and watched movies. I said, "Babe, I'm going to purchase additional sets of sheets, because I like my sheets to have at least six hundred thread count, and we all know how bachelors live." Blake agreed, "Go ahead, babe. Be my guest." After I purchased new sheets, I would then purchase white towels, because I like everything white, especially my towels. Even though Blake had a housekeeper, I always made sure the house was clean when I visited, including the bathtub, shower, bathroom, etc. Both Blake and I appreciate a clean house.

The next morning, I prepared breakfast. Blake never wanted me to work too hard, but I preferred cooking instead of eating out every day. Blake cooked for me also. While eating, we sat at the table and played footsies, while discussing New Year's Eve, which was the next day. We had planned to go to church and dinner. Kyle and his wife Crystal were going to meet us at church, which was abnormal for Kyle. Blake reasoned Kyle's behavior changed because he served as an example for him. After all, they were best friends. Kyle is a hot mess, so I was elated knowing he wanted to come to accompany us to church. Crystal is such a sweet woman, and as I became more familiar with both of them, I began to pray their relationship would improve.

On Saturday, Blake took me for a tour around Houston. Although I had visited Houston every summer during my youth, much had changed. During our tour, we went to see my uncle Richard, who owns a barbershop, but he was not there. Afterward, we went to a birthday party for one of Blake's friends. There, I met many of his friends, which was wonderful.

New Year's Eve

On Sunday, we attended morning worship at Blake's church. After the service, we enjoyed a delectable brunch. As we ate, Blake shared with me what Jamie had said to him: "Dad, at least Ms. Monica has a few more years, so you can enjoy her." He meant, Blake usually dated much younger women than me, and because I was forty-one years old, my sexual energy would last until I am forty-five. I laughed so hard and said, "I know Jamie is accustomed to seeing you date younger women, but like Josh told you, I'm putting those twenty-one year olds to sleep, and you have no idea what's going to hit you if we get married. You may not be able to keep up and may break a few bones." I was thinking, *Whoowee you have no idea how you're going to get it with all the frustration built up in me*. We laughed, and he said, "I just love your smart and sarcastic remarks, and I love the fact we can have fun with one another and not be so serious." We finished dining and conversing; then, we headed back to his house.

We thought it would be wise to relax because later in the evening would be the New Year's Eve church service. Jamie came by to wish us a happy new year. He was always so nice and respectful. Jamie called me Ms. Monica, which made me feel fifty years old, so I asked him to call me Monica. I was tempted to ask and joke with him about the comment he made about me to let him know his dad would need more praying for than I, but I let him slide on that one.

Jamie ran errands, managed the car lot and worked at the daycare for Blake. Jamie desires to be a CEO one day like his dad, and I always spoke positive words to him encouraging him that he can become anything he wants to.

Blake would get frustrated with Jamie at times, but I would always ask Blake if we could pray about it, instead of him always speaking to him as if he were disgusted. Blake said he appreciated my honesty and feedback on how to handle his son. The relationship between the two of them improved, and Jamie confided in me one day saying Blake had been nicer since he met me. I was happy to know I had become a light in Blake's life that would shine onto others.

I had not met London at that point and remembered Blake saying he would only introduce London to someone he was going to marry, so I knew if we got engaged, we would meet then. When Blake and London would be in the car before I came for the holidays, he would ask London to say hello to Ms. Monica, and she would always be very sweet. Blake would text me pictures of both of them out and about, and I always appreciated him sharing special moments with me.

Blake and I headed to church for New Year's Eve and called our friends and families on the way to wish them a happy new year. We were inseparable, and in Blake's eyes, I could not do any wrong. Kyle and Crystal arrived to church before we did. While Blake parked the car, I stood at the door waiting. Once Blake entered, we greeted Kyle and Crystal with hugs and sat down for service. The service was awesome. Kyle enjoyed the service so much that he stood often and clapped his hands.

After service, we all spoke for a short while and walked to the car. I called Blake "babe cakes," and you would have thought the sun came down. Kyle and Crystal started laughing and said, "Blake, that's your new name? Boy, you must be in love to let Monica call you 'babe cakes.'" Kyle thought Blake's nickname was soft, but little did he know when a man is in love, there is nothing a woman can say that is not music to his ears.

Blake and I headed out for a quick meal. As we dined, he openly professed his love for me. Blake told me I was the love of his life, he could never envision being without me, I brought new meaning in his life, and nothing would ever break us a part. Hearing his heartfelt words, I wanted to weep. I then honestly told Blake I had not been sure about us at first, but each day we talked and spent time together, I learned more about him and loved the fact even though he was not accustomed to holding hands and showing affection, I appreciated him making the effort and sacrifice to please me, because we had talked about one another's love languages and 'physical touch' is one of mine.

I also asked him what was going to keep him faithful to me, seeing how in the past he dated multiple women at once. He said many women long to be with him. I knew when he made that statement he just wanted to make me jealous. That is what my friends and I call the "older man" syndrome: when they bring up other women to get a reaction out of you. But, I am very secure in my skin and not intimidated by other woman, regardless of beauty or status.

God only creates the best, and every woman is unique in her own way. Blake assured me no one could take my place, and he was so far from that lifestyle that he had no desire to be with anyone else. I asked him if he had cut off the woman he was seeing. He answered affirmatively, saying, "Yes, I told her I was moving to Los Angeles, and she said she would come with me, but I told her that wasn't going to work." He never told her the truth, which I found weird because according to him she was not relevant.

In my spirit, I was a little apprehensive about Blake not being honest with his lady friend, but I said to myself, *For once in my lifetime, I'm going to step out on faith in this relationship and not hold back my feelings.* One mistake I made was not trusting God to lead me. Instead, I put all my trust in Blake's every word, for he was my prince who had found his princess.

> *"It is better to take refuge in the Lord than to trust in man. It is better to take refuge in the Lord than to put confidence in princes."*
>
> -Psalm 118:8-9 KJV

Blake said he was moving fast with us and as he had said before, "I see you as my wife and plan to spend the rest of my life with you." Blake asked me how I felt about him. I said, "I'm all in, babe, and I would like to spend the rest of my life with you." Blake said, "I love you so much, Monica, and again I appreciate how you allow me to be the man." I said, "You are the man, babe!"

We kissed at dinner, and I could feel his heart beating against my chest with love. He held me so tightly, as though he never wanted to let me go. His passion was overtaking me, and it was like nothing I had ever felt in any past relationship. To myself, I said, "Lord, this must be my time."

When we returned to Blake's, I ran upstairs very quickly while he was in the kitchen. I lit my candles and placed a card on his pillow. I never wanted to go overboard. I am a very romantic and spontaneous person, but I did not want to turn him on. However, I wanted to do something to give him some excitement for New Year's Eve. I took Blake's jacket, and he sat on the bed and opened the card. My card thanked him for the awesome holiday time we spent together. I told him I had never felt so good about a relationship and how I really loved everything about him. I told him he is a phenomenal man, and I look forward to what God had in store for us.

Blake's eyes began to tear up, and he grabbed me and gave me a big hug and kiss. He yelled, "Man, I love you so much. You just make me feel so good, and I want to conquer the world for you." A tear ran down my eyes as I reminded him I was precious cargo, to handle my heart with care, and to please not ever break it. He said, "Never, babe. You're stuck with me for life." We cuddled and went to sleep. That was the best New Year's Eve I ever had with a man.

New Year's Day

We woke up the next morning, and Blake made breakfast and was preparing his favorite black-eyed peas for later that day. I said, "Hey, babe, I'm going to hate to leave you tomorrow." He inquired, "Tomorrow?" I answered, "Yes, my reservations are for Wednesday, January 2, 2013 to fly back to Los Angeles." He said, "You don't go back to work until next Monday, January 7. So, are you trying to leave me earlier, babe?" I said, "Of course not, babe. Maybe you weren't sure how our time together was going to go, so you made the flight for January 2." We both found my statement humorous. Blake asked, "Babe, can you stay until the day before you go back to work?" I smiled and said, "Of course babe." We changed my reservations to the upcoming Sunday.

All that week, we spent time together, cooking, hanging out and getting to know each other better. Kyle called one day and said, "Man, you and 'California Love' been hanging, huh?" Blake said, "Yes, that's my baby doll." Kyle said, "Man, you not getting any bootie from nobody?" Blake responded, "No." Kyle was amazed, because Blake apparently was usually with several women, and Kyle could not imagine him not cheating on me.

"He who walks with the wise grows wise, but a companion of fools suffers harm."

-Proverbs 13:20 NIV

Back to Los Angeles

The day of my departure arrived, and it was time for me to fly back to Cali. We were both reticent to discuss the fact we did not want to be apart from one another. On the ride to the airport, Blake and I held hands tightly all the way, never wanting to let go. Blake reminded me, "Babe, now call me if you need anything. Don't ever hesitate to call me, and I will see you next weekend." I said, "Oh, babe cakes. I'm so happy you're coming to see me." He said, "Of course. I told you we are never going more than seven days without seeing one another."

That time, Blake parked his car and walked me to the ticket area. Generally, he dropped me off at the front. I felt my emotions overtaking me, and as we walked to the security area, he said, "Are you okay?" All I could muster up was, "Yes." I continued hugging him as we walked. He did not want to let go, and I did not either.

He said, "Okay, babe. I love you. Call me when you land." I said, "Okay." Blake was trying not to cry in front of me, and I grabbed his jacket and said, "I don't want to go, babe." He said, "Well stay." I said, "You know I have to work tomorrow, babe." He said, "Soon enough, we will never be apart, except when you or I are traveling for business." We kissed again, and Kyle was blowing up his phone. Blake answered and said, "I'm at the airport with my babe." Kyle was teasing Blake, saying, "Man, I don't know what "California Love" did to you." Blake said, "Man, I will call you right back." I said, "Bye, babe cakes." Then, I watched his tall, dark, sexy and handsome self walk out the door.

As soon as he walked out, I broke down in tears. He called me and said, "Are you okay, babe?" I paused, and he asked, "Babe, what's wrong?" I said, "I don't want to go home." He heard the cry in my voice. He said, "Awe, babe. I feel the same way. Don't worry. We just have to sacrifice for now, until we can be together for a lifetime." I said, "Okay, babe cakes. I will call you when I arrive." I did not even reach the gate before he called back.

We talked until my plane was ready to take off. He told me he felt empty without me by his side, and my presence was definitely missed. We were both head over heels for one another. I still did not know yet what exactly it was that made me feel that way about Blake.

While on the plane, a man next to me asked me if I was okay, and I said, "I miss my babe." He said, "It's nothing in the world like true love, and if you experience it once in a lifetime you're blessed." He wished us the best. I was in heaven and slept the entire plane ride. Once I landed in Los Angeles, Blake and I talked until I got home.

Sacrifice is the Ultimate Love

Before I went to bed, I meditated on the Word as I always do. Further, I slept well as though I was on cloud nine. The next morning, Blake called me as usual between six a.m. and seven a.m. We prayed and conversed for a moment.

On my way to work, the Holy Spirit came to me so clearly and answered my prayers, providing an answer to why I was in love with Blake. I was 'in love' with Blake because of the 'sacrifices' he made for me. I had never been 'in love' with anyone, but I was 'in love' with him. Yes, I had told people I 'love' them, but I never was 'in love.' I had even lied to men saying I loved them although I knew I did not. This feeling was nothing like I have ever felt before. Many of us have thought we loved someone, but the love of 'sacrifice' is the ultimate love. Blake sacrificed his time, resources and not to mention flying back and forth to Los Angeles and sending for me to fly to Houston. It did not matter if he flew free. His time and the sacrifices he made for me were priceless. We each have a different reason why we fall 'in love' with someone, and for me, sacrifice outweighs everything.

Anyone can give you money or sex, but when you take the time to go out your way for someone and do it when you are tired and it is an inconvenience to you, that is true love. The beauty of 'sacrifice' is the person does not have to do it, but he/she does it because he/she is 'in love' and possesses a desire to please.

Planning for the Future

When I arrived to work, everyone said I was glowing and must be in love. They were certainly right. The first thing I did was call the nearest Edible Arrangements next to Blake's office in Houston and requested a 'Thank You' basket to be delivered the same day. When Blake received it, he was ecstatic and told me he really loves that I appreciate him. I said, "No doubt. You are everything I ever wanted in my life, and God has truly blessed me." Blake said, "God has blessed me more, babe."

That Friday, Blake came to visit me, and we rode around in his Jeep and went sightseeing around town. In January 2013, we continued our routine. If he were not in Los Angeles, I would be in Houston, over the weekend.

We discussed purchasing a home in Bel Air Crest, which is a wealthy area in Los Angeles and purchasing a home in River Oaks, which is the Beverly Hills of Houston. We had already identified a distressed home in the area, and because Blake is a contractor, we could rebuild it. I composed a letter and sent it to the owner; however, they failed to respond. We believed if it were meant to be, we would purchase it one day. Blake planned to expand his business to Los Angeles, so we created a California corporation, and we were on our way to doing awesome things together. At first, Blake was going to relocate, but we decided we would live both in Los Angeles and Houston for the moment, owning homes in both cities. I was not sure when we would be engaged and never asked him about it. I figured when he was ready, he would propose.

> *"Do not be anxious about anything, but in everything by prayer and supplication with thanksgiving let your requests be made known to God."*
>
> -Philippians 4:6 ESV

One weekend in January, when I was in Houston, Blake drove me to jewelry store and asked me if I were to pick a ring, what would it resemble. I told him I was not overly concerned about the ring size. For my previous marriage, I had a three-carat round diamond ring, and our marriage was a mess, so a ring was not even important. The man I was going to marry is what is most critical.

He said, "Just show me." I admitted the sales woman's ring was nice. It had one stone, with diamonds around the stone; it was flawless. He did not like the diamonds around the stone; he said it looked like costume jewelry. So, I said, "Whatever you think you want me to have is fine, babe, because I'm in love with you." Blake looked around for a moment, and then we left. He said Josh had provided him with the name of a jeweler in Los Angeles who makes rings for NBA players, so he would see what the jeweler had to offer one day. We left and enjoyed our weekend.

When I returned to Los Angeles, during that week, Blake called and asked me if I wanted a destination or local wedding when we got married. I said, "A destination wedding would be great, but I wouldn't want to travel with my entire luggage on a plane and be inconvenienced by having to constantly carry everything around. When we renew our vows one day, it would be romantic for us to have a destination wedding. For now, if you are okay with it, we could find a hotel in Los Angeles to have the ceremony and wedding. What about you, babe?"

He answered, "Whatever my babe wants, because I will just write the checks until I tell you that's enough." We both laughed. The next weekend when Blake came, he told me one of his friends was visiting Los Angeles and they were going to get together, so he went off and visited with his friend on Saturday. When we met up later in the day, I noticed he was very excited when he came back to the house and was extremely lovable. He could not stop kissing me on my cheeks, and I was wondering what got into him.

The Proposal

The weekend before Valentine's Day, Blake said he was going to come to Los Angeles that Friday, so I said, "Okay, babe, but you know I'm coming next weekend for the NBA All Star Game." I did not want him to leave his business affairs and be exhausted from flying when he could relax for that one weekend. He said, "No, babe. That will be more than seven days of us seeing each other, and that's too long." I was happy, of course, and always loved to see my babe.

On Friday, I had begun to cough, and my stomach was upset. I feared I was getting sick. The last thing I wanted was to be sick when my babe was coming to see me. I did not desire for us to be required to stay inside due to illness.

Plus, Blake had said he wanted us to have dinner on Saturday. When he arrived Saturday morning, I said, "Babe, I don't feel well." He said, "I know. I can see it in your face." As I lay on the bed, Blake said, "Babe, I want to take you to Crustaceans for dinner tonight." He knew that is my favorite restaurant, and he knew I would get out of my bed.

However, I said, "Babe, I don't feel well, and I don't even feel like getting dressed." He said, "You must be really sick if you don't want to go to Crustaceans." I intently viewed Blake's face, and he looked so disappointed, and he really wanted to dine at Crustaceans. I said, "Okay, babe. I will do it for you." His face lit up, and he said, "That's why I love you, babe. You are selfless and always accommodate me. I can't wait to be your husband. You make me so proud." I got up and slipped on a pair of jeans. People who know me know I rarely wear jeans. I would normally wear a dress and look great if we are going to dinner. On that night, I did not wear hardly any makeup, just a little mascara and lip gloss.

We headed out, and Blake was blasting the music. He was so excited, and I felt so bad that I was not in the mood. We arrived to Crustaceans, and I noticed Blake was going back and forth to the bathroom. The lady seated us and said, "Hey, Monica. Good to see you." She was extra excited. They seated us upstairs, which I never like, because it is so congested. We saw one of Blake's friends whom he had hung out with in Los Angeles a few weeks prior.

When Blake and I sat down, he was texting on his phone. Then, he said he needed to go wash his hands again. I thought that was weird, but I was too sick to even think about it. I leaned a little bit on the rail. Before long, Blake came back to the table and stood in front of me. As I looked up, I heard my mom's voice behind me; she and Chris were there. My mom was just smiling and about to burst into tears. I said, "Hey, you guys just happened to be here?" They just smiled.

Then, Blake took a case out of his pocket and said, "Babe, you mean everything to me." He opened the box, which held a flawless four-carat princess cut diamond with diamonds totaling one carat on the sides creating a five-carat ring and said, "Will you marry me?" My ring was so flawless and crystal clear; you could cut ice with it. I said, "OMG! Yes, yes, babe. I will marry you." He was so nervous. He put the ring on my finger, and we hugged and kissed. Everyone on the top floor started to clap and congratulate us. We then proceeded to go down stairs, because he only had us sit upstairs, so I would not see Chris and my mom walk in until our table was ready. That was the most amazing night of my life. He had called my mom earlier and asked her and Chris for my hand in marriage and asked them to come to Crustaceans.

We sat at the table, and I text a picture of my ring to my friends to let them know I had become engaged. I was so excited, and it was such a surprise to me. I had no idea he would propose to me that night. I figured at least by March 2013, since he said he was coming on strong, and he confirmed with me on New Year's Eve that he wanted to spend the rest of his life with me, and so did I. My mom blurted out, "So, when are the kids coming?" Blake said, "Hey, Ms. Vicki, not so fast. We need to plan the wedding first. We did talk about having a child, but most likely one year after we have been married, so we can enjoy one another." She said, "Okay." We all were full of joy and enjoyed dinner.

I thought it was so wonderful he would invite Chris and my mom to share that special moment with us. That exemplified the values from our grandparents' way of loving a woman; that was a real turn on for me. I could tell Blake was excited and ready to be one in marriage.

We left Crustaceans, and in the car, he said, "Okay, when we get home, let's set a date and plan to see at least three locations for the wedding before I leave Monday or Tuesday and get them to hold the date. I don't want to waste any time." I agreed because I did not want to waste any time either.

Before we could start planning the wedding that evening, my friend Linda, who lived around the corner from me, pulled into my driveway to congratulate us. At least that is what she said. Linda is very messy and does not have a filter. She walked into the house with her neighbor Sherry. That was her first time meeting Blake, because I had not seen her in a while. She said, "Oh, I'm so happy for you, Monica, and nice to meet you, Blake." Next, she asked, "Blake where do you live?" Blake said, "Houston." She said, "Houston? You're mighty handsome. You don't have a woman in Houston?" Blake just smiled and said, "No." I said, "Linda, that's going too far."

I knew she could be direct, and I knew Blake would not like her attitude and would read her if he needed to. Then, Linda leaned over to me and slightly whispered, "Does Blake know?" I said, "Does he know what?" Blake and Sherry had a look on their faces that asked, "What is she about to say?" I was not sure what she was talking about. Linda then said out loud, "Monica, did you tell him you got shot?" Linda did not know the truth about me getting shot. She knew what everyone else was told: it was a carjacking.

Blake said, "Yes, I do know about her tragedy." I said, "Linda, that's not cool or your place to share with anyone." Unemotionally, she said, "I just wanted to see if he knew." I was thinking to myself *What if I had not told him? That is my personal business and who does that to someone's new fiancé?* Linda thought it was funny. I told her we had some work to do, so they left.

After Linda left, Blake was surprised someone would blurt out something so sensitive, not knowing if he knew or not. Nevertheless, Blake and I commenced to planning our wedding, and he gave me a budget for the entire wedding, which included my dress, décor and the location of the wedding. We decided on a date in August to have our wedding.

I wanted a particular place in Palos Verdes, but when I called that evening, I learned Donald Trump had purchased the land to build single family homes and a golf course. Blake and I started to brainstorm on other locations.

The next morning, Linda called me at work and said, "Something is up with Blake. I don't know what it is, but you better watch him." I said, "Linda, the Lord will protect me from whatever it is. I was just about to call you as well, because I didn't appreciate you bringing up the tragedy about me getting shot. That life event was very serious for me, and it's not something you get to deliver to anyone. I had already told him, but what if I wasn't ready to tell him? That's not your place, and you were out of line." She said, "Oh, please. He lives in Houston, TX, and you'll see when it doesn't work out. Don't call me crying." Abruptly, she hung up the phone. It hurt me to see the haters start to come out and show themselves, but Linda and I had disagreements before, but not on that level. Linda can be a nice person, so in the past I ignored her antics, for she was like a big sister to me. Her last set of theatrics was the last straw, and I felt we needed to end our friendship. I knew if she did not think her behavior was wrong, there would be a problem, and there was no telling what she would do in the future. That would be my last time speaking with Linda.

I'm Scared

Taking a break really quick from deciding on what hotels we would visit by Tuesday, I shared with Blake how happy I was to be engaged to such a phenomenal man. He said he was more excited to become my husband and thanked me for accepting his hand in marriage. I shared with Blake I was scared that he had my heart, because I had never given any man all of me. I played the song "Getting Late" by Floetry. The song talks about how she was scared he would hurt her. I asked him how he was going to abstain from sex from February through August, when we were to get married, if he had not done so for a long period of time before.

I know when I first started living a celibate lifestyle, it was hard for me, and I am a woman. I said, "We have this long-distance engagement, and you always share with me how all these women in Houston are after you. I'm not worried about any women, because I'm fabulous, but I want to know how you will handle your commitment to me, even when we may have a healthy debate, and the devil tries to temp you with sex."

Before he could answer, I continued, "Some of your friends, who are married, cheat on their wives, and some of those friends you speak highly of." He said, "Hopefully, we will be an example to them, and besides, I'm the leader, and I don't do what my friends do." Even though men do not bond through sex, souls are tied, and the devil is always busy. Blake told me, "Babe, I don't want anyone but you, and I will never hurt you. You have my word."

I asked him what "unconditional love" means to him. He said, "God says I should love you like Christ loves the church and lay my life down for you." He said the last part in a laughing manner. I said, "Yes, that's true, babe. God also says in 1 Corinthians 13:4, *"unconditional love" is patient, not irritable, not resentful or hold grudges, does not keep track of wrong doings, not envious, does not insist in its own way, endures/bears/believes all things and never fails.*" I shared with him, "I have always measured my relationships (personal/business) not by when everything is going well and everyone is agreeing on everything. But, you and I will know in our relationship if we truly have unconditional love for one another if we ever disagree on a matter or decision and how our relationship is after the disagreements. In my experience, when everything is going well between two people and either person is agreeing with everything or there is no tension, the unconditional love is there. But, as soon as the man or woman does not do what the others want or disagrees, it becomes conditional. My love is unconditional for you, and I need to know that's what you have for me."

I wanted us to be like "Bonnie and Clyde," not robbing anyone (LOL), but being there for one another- no matter what. It is like the John Legend song "All of Me." He loves her with all of her perfections and imperfections, and she loves him the same. He said, "Babe, I got you, and like I said, there isn't anything we can't ever workout." I said, "Okay, babe. I'm excited, and I'm trusting in you."

After our talk, we agreed on two hotels, and I made two reservations for the next day. One was the Ritz Carlton, in Marina Del

Rey, CA and the other was the Four Seasons, in Beverly Hills. The Ritz Carlton was the first stop. When we arrived, we both agreed that would be the place. We met with the director of events Cindy, and she was very pleasant. She gave us a tour and sat down with us to review the price. I love quality, but I am frugal and never pay full-price for anything. So, of course, I negotiated the price down ten thousand lower than the original price. Blake and I both do not like to spend frivolously, which is important in marriage.

Cindy gave us five days to sign, and we told her we would make a decision the next day, and I would get back to her. In the car, we both said at the same time, "This is the place, babe." I asked Blake if he still wanted to go over to the Four Seasons, knowing we like the Ritz Carlton. He said, "Let's just go to see what they have to offer." Right when we walked in, we both agreed it was too modern and old school. When the director came out to meet with us, she was nice, and we went through the entire process, but we knew where we wanted our wedding. We thanked her, and Blake told me to call Cindy to hold the date in August. I called Cindy right away and told her we would fax the contract over that evening. Blake put the deposit down, and we were on our way.

While Blake was driving either in Los Angeles or Houston he would text me songs he wanted to play at the wedding. I thought that was very special. His love for me was overtaking every aspect of me.

NBA All-Star Weekend

That Friday, on Valentine's Day, I flew to Houston for the NBA All-Star Game. I sent Blake's Valentine's gift overnight to arrive on Valentine's Day. It was a navy blue Italian suit, including a shirt and tie. Blake said, "Thank you so much, babe. This suit is so nice." He loved that suit and could not wait to get it tailored. I must say, Blake looked spectacular and handsome in the suit. I knew he wanted to increase his suit wardrobe, and I wanted to do something special for him.

Blake, I, Jamie and his fiancée Mimi went to Shaq's All-Star Comedy Show. The show was mediocre, and Blake was not happy, but it was a nice outing. My ring was a little big and needed to be sized. While we were watching the show, I clapped my hands, and my ring flew off my finger. I was so scared. Blake asked, "What's wrong, babe?" I said, "OMG. I dropped my ring, babe."

I got on my knees with my dress and boots on and began crawling on the floor. I was praying, "Oh please, Lord. Don't let someone take my ring." There were three women sitting in back of us, and I asked them if they saw a ring, and they said, "No." I was moving their feet around; then, they started looking around for my ring, and I started to wonder if they had already picked it up. By that time, everyone was wondering what was going on. Blake and Jamie were looking for it as well.

We were two rows from the stage, so I completely distracted the entire show. I was in the aisle on my knees asking people to move their feet, because I dropped something. I was sweating, and I thought *Blake is going to be livid*. My next move was to call the security guard to search everyone. I was such in a panic and did not hear Blake call my name, "Monica, Monica." I said, "Yes, babe?" He said, "I found the ring in your cup holder." Jamie, Blake and Mimi were laughing so hard, saying I was mooning everyone, but I did not care what anybody thought. I was so relieved, and then Blake said, "Babe, if you would have lost the ring, we would have just reported it to our insurance." Blake had added my ring to the insurance policy.

I said, "Oh, babe, I didn't want to disappoint you, and that was so careless of me." Jamie said, "Ms. Monica, you should put that ring in your purse, because you can't lose that rock." I said, "I know, Jaime." I immediately put the ring in my purse. Nonetheless, I was the joke of the whole weekend, and Blake had to tell everyone about my ordeal. Blake love to throw shade, but it was all in fun.

I asked Blake if London was going to be a junior bridesmaid, and he said she did not need to be in the wedding and may not even come. I said, "Okay, babe." I thought it would have been great for her to participate, but it was his decision. On Saturday, we planned to take London, his nephew Bailey and sister Tara to the NBA All-Star Dunk Contest. That would be my first time meeting Tara who lived in Houston. She had been trying to meet me when I was there for many weekends, but she could never catch up with us.

Blake went to pick up London, and when I met her, she gave me a big hug. She was so sweet. We talked and laughed, and she seemed to be clinging to me quickly. Tara was nice, and Bailey was spoiled.

I noticed with London present, Blake was not as close with me as he generally would be. It was as though he did not want to show any closeness towards me around London. London nor his ex-wife Sarah knew we were engaged at that time. Blake and Tara were talking in codes around London about the engagement, and I was not sure what that was about, but I just went along and enjoyed my day. If I went to hold Blake's hand, London would definitely not approve and come in between us or she would go on the other side and hold his hand. I ignored it and just said to myself, *In his own time, he will share the news with London.* In London's mind, I was just Ms. Monica, her dad's friend, and she had no idea I would be her stepmother soon.

Everyone had a blast the entire day, and it was time to take pictures. Tara and Bailey went to get in line; then, Blake and London went to take a picture with the "NBA All-Star Game" sign. I sat on the side and waited for them. After Blake and London took a picture, Blake looked at me and realized he and I had not taken a picture together.

So, Blake called me over to take a picture, and then London came running up and got in the middle of us. We all took a picture, which was nice, and then Blake asked London to sit down while he took a picture with Ms. Monica. London looked puzzled again. Her look said, "I thought this lady was your friend, looks like more to me." I understand a daddy's little girl and how she may have been feeling, but that is why it is so important to sit down with children to let them know what is going on, so there is no ambiguity with the child.

Arriving back to Blake's house, I was holding all the mugs and gifts Blake purchased for Kyle and others. Within the bag was a mug London purchased for her mom. I dropped the bag by mistake, and everyone looked as though the end of the world had occurred. I opened the bag, and London said, "That's my mom's mug." I felt so bad, and Blake looked like he was going to faint. He said, "Don't worry about it, London. We will buy your mom another mug." I said, "I'm so sorry, London. I truly did not mean to drop any of the mugs and especially your mom's." London looked sad, and we all went into the house. My feet were a little sore, because I wore my high heel boots, as I do not like to wear tennis shoes unless I am working out. I went to take a quick nap, and Blake said he was taking London to the store.

When they returned, I was still lying down, and they both came in the room. London said, "Ms. Monica, are you sleep?" I said, "Hey, London. Did you get another mug?" She said, "Yes." I said, "I really want you to know I didn't mean to break your mom's mug. Will you forgive me, because I love you, okay?" London said, "Okay, Ms. Monica. I forgive you, and I love you too." I gave her a big hug and kiss, and she wanted to play some games. Blake watched the entire interaction and thanked me for being so nice to London and being the bigger person, which I would not have had it any other way.

It was time for London to go to bed, and Blake and I were relaxing. Blake said, "Babe, thank you for being you today. I love you so much." I responded, "I love you too, babe." Then, I asked Blake if he had told London we were engaged, and he said he had not because he was waiting for the right time. He also stated London had just met me, and he did not want her to think we just met and got engaged. He said, "Sarah knows I have a girlfriend, but I didn't tell her we were engaged yet for the same reasons. She didn't know we were dating." I said, "Babe, that's fine. I trust your judgment, but my motto is to always be honest with people, because we want God to bless everything we do and besides, honesty is the best policy, babe." He said, "I know, babe. Don't worry; everything will work out."

His responses made me wonder in my spirit if it was Blake's practice to be deceitful and not be honest about the smallest things. We left that topic and went on to another. In the morning, before Blake and I went to church, we dropped London off at home. We never missed church in Houston or Los Angeles, unless we were traveling elsewhere.

> *"For nothing is hidden that will not be made manifest, nor is anything secret that will not be known and come to light."*
>
> -Luke 8:17 ESV

The next month, it was Easter weekend. I traveled to Houston to attend London's theatrical play at church. I bought her a nice sundress and hat to wear. She really appreciated the outfit, and I was pleased she did. That day, I would meet Sarah for the first time because on another occasion, she was not dressed and said she would meet me another time.

Blake had mentioned to me previously Sarah was looking forward to meeting me and would like to take me to dinner and formally introduce me to London. By that time, Sarah was aware we were engaged. I agreed thinking it was a nice gesture.

When we arrived to the church, I was expecting to be greeted by an equally excited Sarah as Blake had told me. Blake introduced us, and I gave Sarah a hug and said it was very nice to meet her. Sarah, on the other hand, did not seem to have the excitement Blake said she would have.

Later, when we were in the car, I mentioned, "Babe, it didn't seem like Sarah was looking forward to meeting me." He replied, "Babe, you know she probably had some emotions she was going through. I have never introduced her to any other woman in ten years, and you're about to me my wife." I said, "Oh, okay." But I thought to myself, *I'm all alone out here. One could imagine the emotions I'm feeling, because most people in that church was her family and friends.* The church was very small, and my personality is infectious. I always had a smile on my face. It did not matter how people were staring at me and probably wondering, *Who is this woman Blake has brought to church?* I was looking fabulous as usual. I still maintained a great attitude. Some of the ladies were very nice to me, as I walked around and introduced myself to people. I was already feeling awkward, so I wanted to loosen the atmosphere.

Blake introduced me to a few people, but it was not the same as when we were at his church when he would hold my hand. I could tell he felt uncomfortable. Blake told me he vowed to never make London feel uncomfortable, and in my spirit, I felt he still was holding the guilt from leaving Sarah when she was pregnant, while they were going through a divorce. Not that he wanted to be with Sarah, but London, I am sure, wondered why he was not with her mother. Because of the words I would always hear Blake tell me about how I am everything to him, I thought he would have understood the emotions I was feeling and asked me how I was feeling about everything. I think because I am so confident in myself and act like nothing ever bothers me, some people believe I do not need any comforting. Needless to say, a woman of God loves for her man to treat her like the apple of his eye at all times, no matter who is around.

Blake's Encouragement

"Commit to the Lord whatever you do, and he will establish your plans."

-Proverbs 16:3 NIV

Working in Corporate America, I have always felt in my spirit God had something bigger for me. As I began to develop and grow in my career, getting promoted always seemed to be a struggle for me although I was smarter than or just as smart as many of my peers. I had been promoted in the past; however, in some cases, I was required to ask, prove and get feedback from clients I worked with to justify my promotion. With some of my peers though, it seemed easy to get a promotion, and I never understood why, until God matured me more in the Word. Despite not being promoted to the same level of the people who were being hired over me, I always maintained stellar performance and knew God had a monumental plan for my life. I wanted to be obedient with what He had blessed me with, despite my disappointments in the corporate world.

I have had a number of great executives support me and envision me much further in human resources than where my prior promotions had situated me. I would always outperform everyone, and people never understood how I managed my workload, but I knew it was only God who paved the way. Even with my high self-esteem, I sometimes felt as though I was not good enough when I was provided explanations from my boss as to why I was not ready for a promotion. The devil was really tormenting my mind. Each time those thoughts invaded my mind, God sent an angel to my job to lift up my spirits and to bless me. At one of the companies for which I worked, even though I was not promoted at the level some executives thought I should have been promoted to, when the head of human resources came on board, he recognized my hard work and compensated me with perks and high performing stock grants, which was greatly appreciated.

When I had met Blake, he saw how stressed I was and how hard I was working at the company I had been with for about seven years. A headhunter had been calling me for three months to interview me for an executive role at a network. I really was not interested in working for another company, because my goal was to resign from my job within a year to work on our real estate business, and I did not want another job. I shared the information regarding the calls I was receiving from the headhunter with Blake, and he said, "Babe, it doesn't hurt to talk to them, and if it is a promotion and they are going to give you an increase in pay, why not check it out?" I really did not want to, but because I trusted Blake to lead our family, and he supported me, I said, "Okay, babe. I will check it out." I felt on top of the world with my babe's support, as he cheered for me along the way. I phoned the headhunter and scheduled a phone interview for the upcoming week.

The headhunter told me she had been trying to fill the role for one year, and they were looking for someone replete with my talents. Our conversation went well, and the next step was to fly to New York City (NYC) to meet the team and the C.E.O.

While in NYC, I called Blake from my hotel room and said, "Babe, this role has a lot of potential, and it sounds great, but if it turns out I will be relocating to Houston, I wouldn't want to waste their time, knowing I would not be employed with them long." Blake said, "Babe, great job. Just keep going through the process, and let's see how things work out. Besides, they may be flexible and let you work from Houston sometimes, as you do now. And who knows, we just might live in both Los Angeles and Houston for starters. God will work everything out, babe. Don't worry." The interviews went well, and on the third round, I met with the executives in Los Angeles who would be my clients. I participated in videoconference interviews with the Washington, D.C. team and the President of Human Resources.

I Landed the Job

The following week, the headhunter said the network wanted to make an offer. I informed her a few times a month on Thursday evenings, I fly to Houston. I asked if it would be acceptable to work remotely from there. She said, "Let me ask the Network and get back to you." She called me back and said, "They are fine with that, and they really like you." She made the offer, and I ran it by Blake to see if he was amenable to it, and he said, "Yes, accept it, babe." I resigned from my present position, and many of the executives I worked with were disappointed I was leaving, but were so happy for me, because they felt I should have been promoted long ago. However, they were not happy the company let such great talent leave.

I felt God was ready for me to move on, and my mission was complete there. Additionally, I would be able to help enhance other people's careers in the next season, which is my passion. My last day at the company was extremely difficult. The teams and executives I worked with gave me iPads and parties. It was really hard to leave so many great people I had worked with for so long. That evening, I flew to Houston, because Blake and I had plans before I started my new gig the following week. When I arrived to the Houston airport, I ran into Blake's arms. He kept telling me how proud he was of me and congratulations on landing the new job. It is icing on the cake when your man tells you how proud he is of you.

I thanked him as well for always being in my corner and encouraging me to go for the job, because if it had not been for him, I would not have interviewed for the position. When we arrived to the house, I went upstairs to change from my work clothes. Blake said, "Babe, you didn't see what's on the bed?" I looked and said, "Oh my goodness! You got me a gift! You're so sweet." On the bed was a nice card from Blake that said how proud he was of me, how smart I am and how much he loves me. Then, I opened the box, and it was a pair of Christian Louboutin shoes, which he knows I love.

He said he wanted me to look great on my first day of work. I jumped up and down and gave him a big hug and kiss and told him how much I really appreciated him being such a great leader and how I felt so secure with him leading our family. Blake told me I deserved it and more and thanked me for trusting him to lead and for loving him unconditionally. We were both crazy in love and in heaven.

> *"But I would have you know, that the head of every man is Christ; and the head of the woman [is] the man; and the head of Christ [is] God."*
>
> -1 Corinthians 11:3 KJV

Marriage Counseling and Planning the Wedding

Blake agreed to Bishop Ulmer officiating our wedding ceremony. But, in order for that to occur, we had to go through the church's eleven week pre-marital counseling session starting April 20, 2013 and continuing every Friday thereafter until mid-July.

We had every intent to participate in pre-marital counseling, so we never viewed it as an option, but as a must. I asked Blake how he was going to attend counseling every week, and he said he would figure it out.

The next Friday, we attended our first marriage counseling session. There were fifteen couples at the first meeting. Most of the sessions began in a large group; then, we would separate into groups of four. That was very exciting, and with one of the pastors and his wife teaching the class, we were provided an overview of what we would be discussing, such as finances, sex, blended families, communication, in-laws, how a husband and wife should love one another, expectations of one another, and open sessions to discuss any topics from the couples. Blake and I had discussed a lot of these topics already, except in detail about the blended families. We discussed our debt, sex, communication, love languages, family, having children, our imperfections and much more.

> *"All scripture is inspired by God and is useful to teach us what is true and to make us realize what is wrong in our lives. It corrects us when we are wrong and teaches us to do what is right. God uses it to prepare and equip his people to do every good work."*
>
> -1Timothy 3:16-17 NLTB

The last part of that scripture is key that God's Holy Word should be applied in preparing our hearts and minds for the good work of marriage, which He instituted.

Blake would fly to Los Angeles on Friday mornings or if he missed his flight, he would come later in the afternoon. A few times, he arrived to Los Angeles thirty minutes before our class was to start. We were enjoying the sessions and even though Blake was an introvert, he would ask questions and make jokes, which he loved to do.

We had a lot going on at that time and I was planning all the details of the wedding. Even though I hired a coordinator named Bela, I knew where to get all the décor, so I was not going to pay her to do it. Bela's job was to put all my details together. Once I identified the vendors and décor, she would administer the rehearsal dinner and wedding day. I coordinate extravagant events from time to time and just needed a little help, but actually I wish I had hired someone else to plan our wedding, because trying to save money for us was not worth the stress and many late nights staying up and not getting any rest. I realized it was the worst decision for a bride to plan her own wedding. Plus, my family and some friends were stressing me out.

I asked Vivian, my maid of honor, to help find the bridesmaids' dresses. I showed her the style and color, and she was to locate a seamstress, because we could not find a dress in the store. Of course, she waited until June to identify someone, and the lady could not start on the dresses until the first week of August, but she assured me she understood the design I wanted from our initial meeting. This would prove later to be wrong.

Then, there was an issue with one of the bridesmaids, because I asked them to style their hair a certain way, because our wedding was an elegant affair, not a birthday party. It was becoming stressful because I did not have assistance with anything pertaining to my wedding. The two weddings I had ever been in were organized. One bride gave us a checklist of things to do, such as how to wear our hair, items she needed each one of us to take care of for her, and the type of accessories and shoes to purchase.

When I was in my friend Nicole's wedding, I helped her every weekend for one month, as all the bridesmaids had appointed times to assist and all the bridesmaids were very supportive. The day of the wedding, we barely had time to get dressed, which was fine with all of us, because our priority was the bride, helping her get dressed. We were all so excited for her big day. The wedding is all about the bride and groom. I do not think bridesmaids realize it is an honor to be a bridesmaid. It is all about the bride, not the bridesmaids.

I have truly learned from experience to never allow anyone to stress me out or affect my daily interaction with others, especially for any of my special events. If people do not want to do what you require for your event, then they have the option to not participate. No longer will I feel obligated to include anyone who does not have my best interest. Life is too short to be bothered with chaos, and your loves ones should want your big day to be non-chaotic for you, not a drama-filled disaster. Sometimes, God has to take you through situations in order for you to grow in certain areas.

Blake and I continued our marriage counseling, and he was there every Friday. That caused me to fall deeper in love and even more so for all of the sacrifices he was making for the success of our marriage. When we started to talk about the blended family section in marriage counseling, the pastor said if any couple was going into a blended family, the man should sit down with everyone (children and wife-to-be) and discuss the roles and his love for them and his fiancé. Blake did not seem interested in doing that, but I remembered Brett saying the process helped his family, and it was imperative to go through the process. When we talked about the matter at home, Blake said, "We have no issues with my kids, babe, and I love how you are with London and Jamie." I did not think much of it, unaware we would never sit down as a family with the children to discuss anything, as we were informed to do in marriage counseling.

One weekend in May, while Blake was in Los Angeles for our marriage counseling, he noticed I was stressed with everything that was going on and gave me words of encouragement. He went to the car wash, and when he came back, he gave me a card that said: *"You are my once in a lifetime," and once in your life, someone comes into your life that you really connect with heart to heart…soul to soul. A friendship develops and love follows. With all my being, I know that you are my "once in a lifetime," and each time I think of you, I realize how lucky I am to have found you. Thank you for all your love…Thank you for all that you are….Thank you for being a part of my life each and every day! I love you!!!! Blake*

Blake always knew how to make me smile and make my day. It felt so wonderful to have someone who loved me so much to be by my side when I was stressed and feeling discouraged. I was honestly looking forward to getting married and leaving Los Angeles for a while and getting away from everyone. Even though we would be traveling back and forth, I was ready for Blake and our family to start enjoying each other, traveling and working on our future goals.

In May, an executive asked me if we wanted to attend the Mayweather boxing match in Las Vegas, and Blake said, "Sure. Let's go." I treated him that weekend, because that was the least I could do for all he had done for me without regret. I wanted him to know how much I appreciated him. We had a fantastic time, and we both were looking stunning as always. While I was standing in the concession area, while Blake ordered food for us, different men would come over and talk to me. Blake said, "I can't ever leave you alone for one second I see." We would always laugh at each other's sarcasm, as we were so in love with one another. That evening, even some of the executives kept telling me I had an amazing glow on my face and Blake must be a very special guy for me to fall head over hills for him. I said, "Yes, he is that and more." Blake said he really loves how I always show him how much I appreciate him. Blake never wanted me to pay for anything, but my babe was working so hard for our family, making major sacrifices for us, and I wanted him to rest for a change.

> *"And He said to them, 'Come away by yourselves to a lonely place and rest a while.' For there were many people coming and going, and they did not even have time to eat."*
>
> -Mark 6:31 NASV

The next weekend, I went to Houston, because we did not have marriage counseling that particular Friday, and the stress was piling on with my new job, getting all the details together for the wedding, and allowing people to affect me negatively.

At Blake's, I noticed the cards I gave him were not visible in his house. Generally, they would be on his nightstand. Although it was dumb on my part, I asked him on Saturday morning where the cards were I bought him. When I am stressed, everything irritates me.

He said, "Babe, what you want me to leave them on the dresser forever?" I said, "I don't have any presence in the house." He had old cards on the mantel from other family members, and I thought for sure the one he loved, his once in a lifetime, mine would be posted somewhere. I was not yelling, but my tone was one of irritation. Blake could have taken the high road, knowing I was stressed, and consoled me by saying, "Babe, I know you're stressed, but I got you and will gladly put your cards up." Or, he could have said any of those kind words he generally told me that always melted my heart. Let's face it, as silly as it sounds, the matter at hand was really only about cards. But, he instantly shut down and went to the drawer and put my cards on his nightstand. Blake was not the same the entire weekend. He was really hard and cold, and I had not seen that side of him, and he had not seen me get irritated with him, but when you love someone unconditionally, you talk about the issue and move on. From his coldness, you would have thought I cheated on him.

Blake did not like to deal with any issues. No one does, but it is imperative to discuss issues. Otherwise, you let things build up and then you explode one day. Communication is key in any relationship. Regardless of either one of our mistakes, I always relied on Blake's promise to me that there was not anything we could not work out, and he always expressed his unconditional love for me. I thought for sure we could move past the silly matter, but actually his love was "conditional." I apologized to him right after it happened and told him how childish my actions were, and he said he accepted my apology.

Moreover, my hormones were acting up with frustration if you know what I mean, and I am certain his were too. My personality is such that if we have a disagreement or healthy debate, once we apologize to one another, I can hug and move forward and say, "Let's go to the movies." Conversely, it takes Blake time to resume his positive composure. Later that evening, we discussed what the Word says about not being on one accord when we get married. This is where the devil can come in and takes our blessings, and we could not afford that.

> *"The thief comes only to steal and kill and destroy. I came that they may have life and have it abundantly."*
>
> -John 10:10 ESV

The beauty of relationships is when a couple can withstand any trial and tribulation with which the devil attempts to blindside them. The devil does not want couples to get married or stay married, and he knows their weak spots to keep them divided. That is why it is important for the man to recognize when the devil is attacking and not go against his mate, thereby appeasing the devil.

My flesh could have been overwrought with an attitude as well as a counteraction to his attitude, but that is childish, and if we are images of God, unconditional love is patient. Thankfully, God had already worked on me with having patience.

> *"Be humble and gentle. Be patient with each other, making allowances for each other's faults because of your love."*
>
> -Ephesians 4:2 ESV

I had always been patient with Blake when he would make comments about his women friends and their conversations. Blake would always say I needed to trust him and as long as he tells me about the innocent conversations, I should just be okay with it.

I shared with Blake, "I trust you, but I don't know your women friends, and I don't think it's wise for a man that's about to be married to have these women friends lingering around and giving them advice about their relationships, especially because some of these women are ex-girlfriends." I would eventually share with him I could not be with him if he was going to continue to have relationships with women he had been intimate with in the past. It took him a few months to understand where I was coming from. As I continued to pray about the matter, God confirmed what I was saying to him through a word at church one Sunday about other women lingering around and during one of our marriage counseling sessions. All I could do was smile to God for answering my prayer.

> *"Love the LORD, because He hears My voice and my supplications. Because He has inclined His ear to me, Therefore I shall call upon Him as long as I live."*
>
> -Psalm 116:1-2 KJV

Blake's Heart Turned

A few weekends later, I traveled to Houston in June. When I arrived, we went to dinner and relaxed that Friday evening. I noticed Blake was not acting like himself, and he was not lovable as he used to be with me. Generally, when I would be in Houston on Saturdays, he would take me with him while he was working. That time, however, he said, "I will be back. I need to make some runs." He came back to get me a few hours later. While we were driving, I asked him if everything was fine, and he said, "Yes, babe."

We went to the court sale to bid on a few tax properties, and I met one of his other friends Tony. Tony kept telling me, "You better treat my man right." I just laughed and said, "No need for you to worry about that. This is my babe cakes." Later on, Blake told me Tony said, "She seems nice, but I hope she doesn't break your heart, man." I could never break Blake's heart and still be able to look myself in the mirror each day.

The following weekend, it was my birthday, and because we were both running around and juggling so many tasks, I told Blake we did not have to do anything special for my birthday. Blake came that Friday, and he bought me a piece of Louis Vuitton luggage, and we remained at home for the evening. I was so appreciative of my gift and thanked him profusely. The next day, he said, "We need to attend counseling on communication." A friend of his had told him about the next class, which was to be held in July for three days. I asked, "Oh, is this because of the card incident?" He replied, "I just want us to have great communication when we're married."

I thought to myself, *Now he will rip someone's head off quickly and tell him/her where to go.* So, at first, I was a little taken aback, due to the manner in which he spoke. I could not believe he was still fixated on that matter. He acted as though he had been robbed or cheated on. I did not say what was on my mind. Instead, I said, "Sounds good to me."

I had been looking forward to learning new communication techniques, because I was certain holding grudges and not communicating with your mate are not two of God's principles. I was excited for us to attend the class. Blake signed us up for the session and told me he really loves me and thanked me for agreeing to attend and submitting to his lead.

My spirit was out of sorts, and I was in a low mood. I felt something was awry. That night, we attended our counseling session, and the men and women were separated from one another. That afforded the women an opportunity to discuss their issues with men with the female pastors, while the men discussed their issues with women with the male pastors. I mentioned the card incident and told them I believe that was the reason he desired for us to go to communication counseling. The pastors responded, "Girl, please. Did you hold a grudge about the concerns you had about other women? Don't worry about that, young lady. You're a great catch. Just know, the first year in any relationship there are growing pains. So, I hope he lays off a little bit and does not treat you like you're in boot camp. He definitely holds grudges." A few of them said, they would not have agreed to going to the counseling. I said, "I agreed to it because I know it would be an eye opener for him too." One of the pastors said, "By you two not being intimate and following God's word, the devil is really going to try and cause confusion in your relationship, and I think it's great that you two have a balance and not both of you are pouting at the same time." They told me not to worry; it would all work out if God wants it to.

One of the pastors said, "This is why the man, who is the head of the household, has to know the Word and know when the devil is coming against the family. He must pray against the devil and not follow his plan to destroy the relationship. It took my husband a long time to figure this out, but when he did, he stopped entertaining my mood swings and prayed against the devil." We could hear the men in the next room laughing loud and agreeing on everything. We just laughed ourselves. After class, Blake said he mentioned the card incident, and the men all said, "Yeah, women be tripping sometimes, and you have to ignore their hormones." We laughed it off. Then, he gave me a big kiss.

The next day, we headed to the tasting for our wedding at the Ritz Carlton. All the food was great. I noticed Blake kept leaving the room, while talking on the phone. He walked down the hall and out the door.

At one time, my wedding coordinator's husband went to find him, because we needed to know what choices of food he wanted. I always allowed him to be the man and make the final decision. At times though, he would ask me to make the decision, which I appreciated. Blake came back to the table, and we agreed on all the food. We enjoyed each other's company for the rest of the day, and his mood seemed to be getting better.

The next morning was Sunday, and we had planned to attend my church. However, Blake said he was not feeling well and was going to stay home. I asked if he was okay and if he needed anything; he said he was fine. I told Blake I would miss him and see him when I returned home and gave him a big hug. Ten minutes before I left, Blake rose and said he felt better and would meet me at church.

That made my morning, so I said, "Great babe. See you there." Thirty minutes after church started, Blake still had not yet arrived. I sent him a text and asked if he was still planning to attend. Two minutes later, he walked down the aisle. He said, "I went to get something to eat." At church, he seemed to be a bit more exuberant, and we enjoyed the service.

After the service, we entered our separate vehicles and headed to the house. Blake asked me what else needed to be done for the wedding, and we checked off a few more boxes and made more deposits, which was our regular wedding check-in when he came to Los Angeles. Later that evening, Blake was scheduled to return to Houston. Blake and I would always talk at the gate while he was waiting, but he did not call me. Finally, he called me right when the plane was leaving and said he loved me. I asked him how he was feeling and he said, "Much better." Once again, in my spirit I knew something was not right.

> *"This people honors me with their lips, but their heart is far from me."*
>
> -Matthew 15:8 ESV

The next Friday, when Blake came to Los Angeles, for our marriage counseling, all the couples were in the room together for the first hour. Right before we were to go into our breakout sessions, Blake said he needed to go to the car very quickly. Again, I found his behavior disturbingly weird, but I continued to pray about it. In the midst of Blake's unexplainable behavior, on a daily basis he continued to send me song choices for the wedding. The messages he was sending me were very much mixed. That is why I continued to pray for the reveal.

That weekend was Father's Day, and I knew Blake wanted to spend time with London, so he left Saturday traveling back to Houston. Blake kept saying he really appreciated my understanding him having to be in Houston for Father's Day. My weekends were consumed with wedding planning anyway, so I kept busy. I gave him a nice outfit for Father's Day and white tee-shirts and underwear, which I always did. Giving to one another was never an issue, and Blake loved the fact I was not selfish and cared about his well-being.

Essence Festival

On July 4, we planned to attend the Essence Festival in New Orleans. When I stepped off the plane in Houston on July 3, Blake seemed to be his old self and was so happy to see me. He gave me a big hug and told me he loved me and missed me. I had on a nice flowing Tiffany blue sundress and looked sweet as a lollypop. It was like old times. The next day, we drove to New Orleans.

On the way, we engaged in great conversation and asked each other marriage questions and talked about our future. I shared with him how my spirit was feeling lately, as though he was cheating on me. He responded, "Of course not, babe. I only want you and can't wait to make you my wife and be your husband." He asked me where I wanted to go for our honeymoon, and I answered, "It doesn't matter. I know after the wedding I want to sleep for a few days from all the stress of planning the wedding." He said, "Well, I know there will not be much sleeping, but we will play it by ear." I said, "That's for sure," and we both laughed. We hung out, and our trip was very romantic.

I noticed Blake had started to turn his phone face down all the time and would take it with him everywhere, including the bathroom while he was showering. His behavior was not customary; it was a definite change from before. As women, we notice everything and men do as well. We both had the codes to one another's phone, but I was not about to go snooping. I always prayed to the Lord, "If this is indeed my husband, let us be one." If it were not to be, I knew the Lord would not honor it.

While in New Orleans, we went to concerts and saw many of Blake's friends. One of his younger brothers came with his girlfriend, and we had dinner one night. We drove back to Houston on Sunday, and the following day, Blake drove me to the airport. My flight left Houston around nine p.m., and I was scheduled to land in Los Angeles close to one a.m. Houston time.

Each time I landed, when returning home, I always text Blake to let him know I made it safely and followed up with a call when I got in the car. That particular time, Blake left me a voicemail from his car playing music in the background right before I landed. He sounded very chipper and asked me if I landed yet and said he could not wait to hear from his babe. When I called him, I said, "Hey, babe. I just landed." He said, "Great, babe. I miss you so much. I'm glad you called, because I was knocked out, babe." He tried to sound as though he had been asleep. I said, "Babe, you fell asleep fast, huh?" He stumbled and said, "Oh, yeah. I did, babe." I just shook my head, because I knew he had just made it home.

For the past nine months, I had never known him to be out at one a.m., but it was fine if he did. It is just not good practice to lie about one's whereabouts. If he went anywhere, as common courtesy, he would say, "Hey, babe, I will be here or there if you need me." I would always do the same. Like I mentioned earlier, we never made any rules, but it was a known fact that we would let one another know where we were going. It was just common courtesy. One thing I know for sure, I better not have tried to sneak out any night without him knowing. He would not have trusted me anymore and would have ended the relationship quickly, because he told me he had zero tolerance for games.

I continued to pray and had too much on my mind to worry about insignificant matters. I know God sees all things done in secret, and I knew He would alert me to anything I needed to be aware of.

> *"Can any hide himself in secret places that I shall not see him? Saith the Lord. Do not I fill heaven and earth?"*
>
> -Jeremiah 23:4 NKJV

The next weekend was the last weekend of our eleven-week counseling sessions. I wanted to thank Blake for making the sacrifice to fly out to Los Angeles each week. We were permitted to miss two sessions, and the two times he missed were because he was flying standby and could not make it. He did purchase tickets on a few occasions, when the flights were booked, so everything worked out.

On Saturday, I informed him we were going for a drive. We went to Malibu and walked on the beach. Blake was very surprised and expressed his love for me. He said he could not wait for our wedding day, because he was going to tear me up. I said, "Yeah, right. You better get your oxygen tank out." We just laughed, as we walked in the water and let the waves hit our feet. I felt as though I was in high school all over again. Afterward, we went to Geoffrey's in Malibu for dinner. Blake had never been there, so he found it to be a real treat.

After dinner, I had the waitress tell Blake the dessert was for him, because he was so phenomenal. He looked like he wanted to tear up. He said the spontaneous romantic person I am made him love me even more. I said, "Oh, babe. This is nothing. Just wait 'til we get married. The fire will be burning all the time." We laughed as we watched the sunset. While we were driving down the coast, we called my mom to say hello. Blake told my mom, "Your daughter makes me so happy." That night felt like when we first met, and he made me blush.

During the next week before I arrived in Houston, Blake told London he had a surprise for her at his house and when they arrived, she said, "I thought Ms. Monica was the surprise." London loved to be around me, and we always had a lot of fun. One night, we put whip cream on Blake's face, and London had a wonderful time.

Blake would tell me about one of his friends who was recently married and how his wife does not help with his children. Blake would always say he told his friend, "I am blessed, because Monica is so good with London, and I do not have those issues." I felt so blessed that he would say great things about me to his friends.

Communication Counseling Session

The next week it was July 16, and I flew to Houston for our communications class. There were fourteen other couples in the class that had already been married for seven plus years. We did not have any issues similar to those of the other couples. Before the class started, most of the couples were not even talking to one another; however, we were laughing throughout the class and enjoying ourselves. The class was breathtaking and was based on God's word. The men had a lot of responsibility as to how they should treat their wives. The parts of the class we both felt most beneficial were "Communication Plan Structure" and "Top 12 Commonly Identified Needs." The twelve needs were affirmation, respect, acceptance, admonition, attention, comfort, support, security, encouragement, affection, appreciation and instruction.

Often times as couples, your mate may vent about something, such as when I vented about the cards. My stress did not actually emanate from the absence of the cards. Rather, I was stressed from all sides about family, friends, and wedding planning. I needed more 'emotional support' from Blake. He could have easily relieved some of my stress by saying, "Babe, I know you're stressed. Besides replacing those cards, what can I do to support you?"

Another example, one day, we were in Los Angeles at church, and Bishop Ulmer was preaching on parents not being so hard on their children. That resonated for Blake, because he had been hard on Jamie. Bishop had an altar call, and I asked Blake if he wanted me to go up with him. Blake said at the time he did not prefer me asking him if he wanted me to go to the altar with him, and he wondered why he felt that way. He realized that during our class and explained he did not need an alter call; he just wanted me to meet his need of support. That revelation was powerful.

Additionally, the instructor asked the men to schedule weekly meetings with their wife or wife-to-be to learn if any of her needs had not been met during the week or to give accolades for her meeting certain needs of his. All of the disseminated information was very helpful, and it was clear since God made the man the head, he was responsible for keeping the relationship in order, and I was glad he suggested we attend these sessions.

During the session breaks, Blake would go outside to talk on the phone when there was a break area wide enough for everyone to make calls, only he would make his downstairs. I continued to enjoy the class and continued to pray about what I was feeling. On the third day, when the class was over, we both shared the same sentiment that we enjoyed the class. That evening Blake took me to a nice dinner to show me how much he appreciated me. Blake said he was excited our wedding was in six weeks, and I said I was as well. Blake would still send me loving texts and call me every day by seven a.m., when we were apart. He would tell me all his friends and family were looking forward to our wedding day and about fifty guests were flying to Los Angeles. We had a total of 120 people attending the wedding.

At times, Blake's friends were so surprised he was getting married and could not wait to meet me on the big day. Blake was very persnickety and said he was a big time player in his days, so people desperately wanted to see who was slowing him down. I remember one guy called Blake on his cell, and his phone was on speaker. Blake told him he was getting married, and the guy said, "To which one man, because I know you an old time player?" Blake seemed to be flattered when people would mention his player stats. Blake told me, "You know all my women were bad, and some of the women would look great on paper, but I didn't see them being my wife." I said, "Yeah, but I'm the baddest you ever been with, babe cakes, regardless of how much money or success any of them had. It is obvious if you wanted to be with one of them, you would have proposed." He said, "You got it all, babe."

Those types of comments from his friends never moved me, because I am not an insecure person, and I sensed he was trying to get a response out of me. My focus was on us moving onward and upward and getting excited about our big day.

Four Weeks before the Wedding

Four weeks before the wedding, I still had much to accomplish. Blake continued to send me texts about how he could not wait for me to become Mrs. Blake Carey on August 24. He said, "It is about to be on and popping." Not long afterward, Blake called me and said, "London wants to be in the wedding. Maybe she can walk down the aisle with my mom and sit with her." I said, "Well, ask London if she would like to walk down the aisle and sit with her grandma or if she would like to walk down the aisle and stand next to me at the altar." He asked London, and she decided she would like to stand next to me. That meant I had to quickly find her a dress.

The following weekend, I identified one dress and texted it to Blake. The dress looked like it was for a Disney princess in a movie. I treated London like she was my own daughter and wanted nothing but the best for her. Later, I found another all-white princess dress, and we decided that was the perfect dress. He asked London which one she liked, and she liked the white one as well. At that time, I had not purchased my lingerie or my honeymoon wardrobe, and I was stressed beyond belief, so that was my last weekend looking for a dress for London. I said to Blake, "Well, even if she didn't like the dresses, she would wear what we decided on." Sarcastically, he said, "I know, babe. I just wanted to get her opinion on the dresses."

The next week, I traveled to Houston one last time until after the wedding. Blake dropped London and me off at the nail shop. While at the nail shop, I asked her if she was excited about being in the wedding. Excitedly, she said, "Yes, Ms. Monica. But, my mom said I have to leave my braids in my hair for the wedding." I said, "Oh, I was thinking your hair would be in one of these nice hairstyles on my phone." I commenced to showing her the pictures and asked her if she liked any of them, and she said, "Yes," with her eyes beaming full of excitement about the hairstyles.

I told her, "Your mom probably wants your hair to be braided for when you start school that following Monday after the wedding. If that is the case, don't worry. I will talk to Blake about it, and we can discuss it with your mom."

Blake would return and sit in the car most of the time on the phone and then came inside when we were done. When we got home, I shared with him my conversation with London and asked him if we could get her hair done in Los Angeles, then pay for her hair to be re-braided. He said he would talk to Sarah and yes, we would get her hair done in Los Angeles, not to worry about it.

For a few weeks, I noticed Blake would add to our morning prayer that he prays no one comes between our relationship. He had never prayed anything like that, but I was so consumed with the wedding planning and could not focus on that matter. He would still send me nice texts daily about our wedding day, saying he was so excited about our wedding. I felt in my spirit a woman in Houston caught Blake at a weak moment a few months before our wedding, and he was conflicted with what to do.

Blake's father had told him a month before our wedding, and earlier in the year, to make sure when he gets to the altar he does not have any other women lingering around. His parents know their son, and as pastors, I am sure they had a sense of what was going on. One thing I knew for sure, God sees everything and had my best interest.

> *"But every man is tempted, when he is drawn away of his own lust, and enticed."*
>
> -James 1:14 KJV

Bridal Shower

Vivian asked my mom if she wanted to help out for my bridal shower, and she assented. My mom said when she would get together with the bridesmaids, there was not any real planning going on and all Vivian would say is that they were on a budget and did not have it like Monica. I always asked Vivian if she needed any financial help to let me know and I would contribute, because I wanted my day to be special. By the time my bridal shower came around, I was mentally exhausted and ready to marry my man and get the heck out of Los Angeles. Many people had acted a fool during that time, and I was very disappointed. I know I can be tough and what bride is not, but I have a big heart. I am a perfectionist, and I do not like mediocrity and neither did Blake. But it was all good, and I was getting tired of Los Angeles and ready to get away from everyone.

The décor and favors for the bridal shower were nice. I arrived looking fabulous as always and sat at the table waiting for the guests to arrive. My bridesmaids seemed as if they were just going through the motions. No one asked me to bring my Tiara, as most brides-to-be wear at their bridal showers. When most guests arrived, we ate, and then I asked Vivian what was next, so she started a game. After a few games, the two bridesmaids left the room to pay the bill and were gone for a moment. I felt so stupid, as everyone was just sitting around. I was the host trying to keep the flow going. I went out the door and asked them, "What's next, ladies? Everyone is sitting around doing nothing." We played another game and opened my gifts, and that was it.

We took pictures, and then some of the ladies and I went across the street to the Glow Lounge within the Marriott in Marina Del Rey, CA. The waitress gave my friends free drinks and after about forty-five minutes the bridesmaids left. I asked Vivian why she was leaving, and she said Layla was dropping her off at her car. I thought,

No one else could drop her off to her car? I guess my facial expressions said a lot, so one of my other friends said, "Just let her go." My wedding day could not come fast enough for Blake and I to start our new life together.

My friends and I continued to have fun dancing and talking about girlee stuff. The next day, I mailed out my 'thank you' cards to everyone thanking each woman for coming, and I sent a special one to my mom and bridesmaids.

> *"Put no trust in a neighbor; have no confidence in a friend; guard the doors of your mouth from her who lies in your arms."*
>
> -Micah 7:5 ESV

Two Weeks before the Wedding

Our big day was getting close, and we both were getting excited about becoming one and releasing a lot of built up frustration. Then just when I thought nothing else could go wrong, Blake called me yelling at the top of his lungs, which I never thought he would approach me in that manner. Apparently, he had lost sight of our communication class techniques. He said, "Why did you give London a message to give her mom when you two were at the nail shop about her hair without me knowing about it?" In a calm voice, I asked, "What are you talking about? I never gave London a message to give to her mom. Is that what Sarah told you?" He said, "Oh no, Sarah isn't upset, but it's disrespectful for you to do that." I was perplexed, because there was not anything for her to be upset about, and I really did not care if she was, but certainly I did not appreciate her lying on me. I said, "Blake, you never even asked how the conversation went. You're assuming and taking their word for face value, and I'm the one you're marrying. Is this how you treat your once in a lifetime?"

I started to cry, because I was so tired, feeling overwhelmed and stressed from everyone acting out against me, and I had enough. Then I said, "Babe, don't you remember I mentioned to you the conversation London and I had about her hair, and I asked you if we could get it styled in Los Angeles then pay for her to put the braids back in her hair before she went back to school? You then told me you would talk to Sarah and for me not to worry. You would make it happen." I had been relieved when he had said that, because how would London look with braids going back on her head with everyone else's hair, including her little cousin's hair, nicely styled. I would not want to make her feel embarrassed or out of place that day.

I also shared with Blake, I did not appreciate him yelling and accusing me of something I did not do. Blake told me I was sensitive, and he did not mean to yell. He seemed unusually upset about the matter, so I asked him was there anything else going on, because he was really upset. He said he was dealing with a few clients who were getting on his nerves. I believe something else happened that caused him to be very upset. While driving home, I prayed and said, "Lord, some people are so vindictive." The good thing is God knows all of our hearts and sees everything. God will certainly deal with the deceit that is going on. I also prayed to the Lord that I was not going to pay for Blake feeling guilty about the choices he made pertaining to his previous marriage and was not going to feel like I am the help and not the wife in our marriage.

Later in the evening, Blake called me to apologize immensely about him accusing me and not asking me what conversation we had at the nail shop. Although I was hurt how he handled the matter, my love for Blake was truly unconditional, and we know what God says about this type of love, so I accepted his apology.

We moved on, and Blake continued to express his love for me and how he could not live without me. Up until the week of the wedding, the text messages were flowing from both of us in excitement of our big day. We could not wait to consummate our marriage and be one.

Vivian went to pick up the bridesmaid dresses, and the style was not what we talked about. The dresses were too short and not cute at all. I was told the seamstress messed up the design, so I was furious. I phoned the seamstress Cathy and asked her what happened with the dresses. My wedding was in two weeks, so I wanted to know if it would be possible for them to get their money back, because I had another seamstress who I knew would make the dress like I wanted. Cathy said, "Monica, I don't think your bridesmaids are being honest with you. The first time we all met, you showed me the style and length you wanted. When they came for the fitting without you, they didn't like the length and said to make it shorter. I told them if we made the dress shorter it would mess up the pattern, so it's not my fault it's theirs." I could not understand why they thought it was permissible to change the style for my wedding theme. I was so close to saying, "Do not worry about being in the wedding. Just London and I will stand at the altar," because it was becoming too much of a distraction for my big day.

I told Vivian what Cathy had told me, and she responded, "Layla told Cathy to make it shorter not me." Then, I asked, "Vivian, why didn't you tell me the style of the dresses had changed?" She said, "Mo, I did not want to bother you." I had so much on my plate I did not have time to deal with it, and I am certain Vivian sensed my frustration. She began searching for other dresses, which I appreciated.

Thursday before the Wedding

A few days before Blake came to Los Angeles, he booked our honeymoon to Costa Rica, and I could not wait to get there to start planning our future and relax. Two days before the wedding, my dad Michael and I picked up Blake and London from the airport. Blake seemed jittery and gave me a quick hug. His entire mood had changed from the night before when he had said he was so excited to become my husband. London gave me some candy apples, as she knew I love candy apples. I gave her a big hug and said, "Thank you, darling." That was Blake's first time meeting my dad, so they were talking with one another. We went to another terminal to pick up my aunt Lynn. She came early to take some pressure off me, so I could focus on my big day. When she got in the car, she started to talk with London. Lynn is a principal of a high school and is really great with children, but she is a disciplinarian.

When we arrived to the house, Lynn asked me what I needed her to help with first. I said, "Please help London try her dress and shoes on to ensure they fit." Lynn did that and took care of things while I was gone to get my hair washed. Before I left the house, Lynn asked me what was wrong with Blake. I said, "I don't know." She did not think he had the temperament of a groom who was about to get married. I kissed Blake and left. While I was gone, Blake and my dad went to pick up their tuxedoes, and Lynn and London accompanied them.

Blake sent me texts during the day to say sweet things. He asked me if I needed anything, and I said, "Yes, babe. Can you please get me a few boxes and a steamer for my dress? I have a few things to wrap for the hotel." On my way home, Blake called me again and said he was going to get my dad something to eat and asked me if I wanted anything. I said, "Yes, please babe. I'm tired and need to get home to finish some of our décor for the wedding."

When I arrived home, London helped me with the last few décor items, and we taped the boxes. Blake was not saying too much to me, but I was in lala land. But, Lynn was observing everything. Usually, Blake and I would be talking to one another all day, but he was very quiet. Blake told London to get ready for bed, but she did not want to because she was enjoying Lynn and me.

While I was emailing my wedding coordinator the final list, Blake kissed me on my forehead and said he was tired and going to bed. So, he went upstairs to lie down, and I joined him shortly thereafter.

When I looked into Blake's eyes, he looked worried about something. I was concerned because it was a look I had never seen before. I proceeded to get everything done for our big day, as the train was moving quickly, and I had no idea what was ahead.

> *"A malicious man disguises himself with his lips, but in his heart he harbors deceit."*
>
> -Proverbs 26:24 NIV

Rehearsal Dinner Signs

I asked Blake on Friday morning if all was well, and he said, "Yes, babe just tired." Lynn said London was sitting at the bedroom door waiting for us to come out. Before I knew it, London opened the door, although Lynn had told her not to. I said, "Hey, London. Good morning. How are you?" She said, "Fine. I need some lotion out of your bathroom." I said, "Okay." I gave her the lotion, a big hug and asked her to let Lynn help her get dressed so we could all go to breakfast, while I finished some last minute wedding notes for my coordinator to take to the rehearsal dinner. Blake gave London a kiss then went downstairs.

Shortly thereafter, I went downstairs to the kitchen to rinse my glass out, and as I looked out the window, I saw Blake on the porch on his cell phone. I thought that was odd, but maybe he was planning a surprise or something for me. The clock was ticking, and I went back upstairs to get dressed. A few minutes passed by; then, we all headed out for breakfast at M&M's Soul Food restaurant in

Inglewood. I was feeling really down, and Blake had not hardly shown me any affection or said much too me since he arrived like he would usually do every time we were together during the last ten months of our relationship.

When we sat down to eat, he sat on the other side of London. I was quiet, and my stomach was in knots at breakfast, because my spirit was feeling like he had let someone come in between our relationship. He was acting very distant, which was a contradiction from the texts and conversations we had earlier in the week saying how excited we both were. Also, we were both so excited about how our day was going to be so beautiful. I have seen newlyweds and had been one in the past. Usually, the day before the wedding, the bride and groom cannot keep their hands off one another, especially if you have not consummated your relationship. Blake did not even hold my hand or anything, so I was not feeling loved at all.

As we left M&M's, Blake, with a depressed look in his eyes, kissed my cheek. Lynn and I were headed to my fabulous friend Damone Robert's salon in Beverly Hills to get our eyebrows beautifully shaped. Damone is the best in the business, and my eyebrows never looked the same after his glamorous touch.

I called Blake in the car with my sweet voice and said, "I'm not feeling the love from you, and it would have been so nice if you had sat in the middle of your two princesses at breakfast." Why did I say that? Blake became irate and said, "You don't like my daughter?" I said, "What? This has nothing to do with London and has to do with you and me. I'm just sharing with you, since you have not said much to me. And, you could have sat in the middle of us and whispered some sweet nothings in my ear or something. Tomorrow is our big day, and I don't feel the love you were so excited to give me as you talked about earlier in the week before you came to Los Angeles. Blake don't make something out of nothing." He said, "We will talk about this later." As I stated, I was not feeling any affection from him, and I was not rude. My comment was very sincere and spoken with concern.

In hindsight was my comment immature about him sitting in between us? Yes. But, there was not just cause for him to get so upset, seeing how he had said there was not anything we could not ever work out. He had said things to me I did not appreciate. I was already feeling like I had to walk on egg shells with him and no woman should feel this way. Had I huffed and puffed with anger at any time during our relationship, he would have been done with me a long time ago. He could have said, "Oh, my baby doll. Don't worry. On the night of our wedding, you're going to get all the love I have been waiting to give you." That would have been priceless and made all the difference in the world and would have given me some notion the love was still there. A God-fearing man who loves his fiancée unconditionally and like Christ loves the church would not have become so upset, but he would have tried to meet my need of "affection" that was not being met, as we learned in the communication class he signed us up for.

Blake called me back an hour later, because we were to meet at the bridal shop for me to pick up my dad, because he had family to pick up from the airport. When Blake got out the car to let London in the front seat, he was huffing and puffing as though he was furious. I asked, "Babe, you're not going to give me a kiss?" He kissed my lips and said he had to pick up his sister and take her to get a rental car. Blake was not acting like the man who had told me all those nice things throughout the entire year and how I had his support. Lynn and I felt he was just looking for a reason to act that way, but I never imagined he would do what would become my worst nightmare.

Blake arrived back to the house before Lynn and I did and called to ask what else I needed to take to the hotel, and I said, "The boxes on the living room floor." He consented and said he would see me at the hotel. Lynn and I arrived home, and I needed to tape a few more boxes. I noticed the boxes Blake did not take would not fit in my car, along with my dress and other items. I phoned Blake and said we needed the jeep to transport some other items. He said he had most of the children and could not come back. I called Vivian and asked her if she could stop by my house to pick up the items and take Lynn with her. She was more than happy to help.

I went upstairs to get my things ready, and before I left, I noticed Blake had taken the blue suit I bought him but left older clothing items he did not wear. I started to put away laundry I had folded that morning and went to place some socks in the drawer and noticed Blake had taken all the new underwear and tee-shirts I had purchased for him. I thought that was weird, because we were only going to be at the hotel for two nights. My attention was on getting to the hotel for the rehearsal dinner, so I did not have time to ponder on the matter.

We headed to the hotel, and I sent Blake a text to let him know I was on my way. When I pulled up Blake, Jamie and Kyle were waiting in front to help me. Jamie and Kyle were smiling and were so excited about our big day. They started taking things out of my trunk and were asking me if I was ready for my big day the next day. Blake had an attitude and was not smiling and barely gave me a kiss on the cheek. I was not feeling like the happy bride to be, and I was vividly shocked at his coldness towards me.

Harriett, the director of events from the Ritz Carlton, greeted me in the hallway and was looking forward to our big day. I introduced her to Jamie and Kyle. I told her Jamie was my son, and I had him last year. We all laughed, except Blake, who was pouting and acting childish, very immature, and extremely cold hearted. I had never seen any man have such a hard heart and be so cold towards the love of his life. You would have thought I told him I was pregnant with another's man's baby. I wondered if every time I did not do or say something he liked if he would always shut down and not talk to me.

At that moment, God reminded me earlier in the year when Blake told me in the past when his ex-girlfriends would make him mad, he would not talk to them for a while, and they would always call him begging to be back with him. But, he had said he would never treat me that way.

> *"Judge not, and you will not be judged; condemn not, and you will not be condemned; forgive, and you will be forgiven."*
>
> -Luke 6:37 ESV

While we walked over to the rehearsal, I whispered to Blake and asked him if we could talk very quickly, because I felt tension, and I wanted our rehearsal to be harmonious with our family and friends. Blake responded in an aggressive manner, "NO!" My stomach dropped to the floor, and I proceeded to pray in tongues as we continued to walk to the rehearsal.

People were eating hors d'oeuvres. Then, my wedding coordinator rounded everyone up, and I expected Blake to introduce everyone, because my family had not met his family. However, he did not. We went through rehearsal, and it was awkward. My dad and Chris were to walk me down the aisle, and when we arrived to Blake, he was to take my hand after they kissed my cheeks. He took my hand, and we stood there in silence. I tried talking to him, but he looked at me as though I was his enemy. He talked to everyone else, but not to me. I asked Blake if my dad could go on the party bus with the guys that evening, and he said, "No." He was not sure where they were going or what time they would return to the hotel. My dad may have a disability, but he has a lot of sense, and he was the sharpest man at the rehearsal that day. I felt so sad for my dad, because we had already told him he could go. I had to be the bearer of bad news to Lynn. Lynn was irate and was about to let Blake have it, but she said it was not the time or place. She assured me she would tell my dad and not to worry about it.

After rehearsal, everyone went his/her separate way, and in a few hours, all the men were going on the party bus for Blake's bachelor party. Blake and I headed up to his room, and he sat in the chair, and I sat on the bed. He looked at me with hatred and said, "What the hell is your problem?" I said, "I don't have a problem. Since you have arrived in Los Angeles you have been distant towards me and frowning up all the time with an attitude." Blake stood up and screamed so loud at me the security came to tell him to lower his voice.

He said, "TELL ME RIGHT NOW IF YOU DON'T LIKE MY KIDS!" I said, "What are you talking about? I don't have anything against Jamie or London, and I'm appalled and hurt you would even think that of someone you claim to be so in love with. Jamie loves me, and we have a great relationship, because we see each other more often than London and I do. London and I are still getting to know one another, but when we are together, we have fun. London always asks about me and loves to be around me." He said, "You didn't want London to sit by you at breakfast today." I said, "Blake, are you for real? My statement, 'I would have loved for you to sit in the middle of us,' translated to you, I didn't want London to sit by me? My need at the moment was 'affection' from you had nothing to do with me disliking London. I know what this is about. You are cheating on me, caught up in lust, and you're trying to make me the villain. You being the person that does not bite your tongue and has all your friends in check, while we were dating if you thought for one second I didn't like your kids, you would have addressed this with me. We would have talked about this in our pre-marital eleven-week counseling sessions. But, you never mentioned it. This topic never came up. As a matter of fact, all this year, you have told all your friends how great I am with your kids, especially London." Blake just looked at me with a blank stare and did not have a response. He only proceeded to text on his phone.

Kyle came into the room and said, "California Love, what are you doing in here? You know you can't come with the guys tonight." I said, "I'm good. I need to get my beauty rest." Kyle said, "You better get more than beauty rest," as he laughed so hard. Blake acted as though all was well. Kyle said, "Get ready, Blake. We're leaving in a few minutes." My phone was acting up, so I began fiddling with it. Kyle took notice and asked me what was wrong with my phone. By that time, I could not dial out on my phone, because I had dropped it. Blake acted as though everything was copacetic and said, "Yeah, man. I don't know what's wrong with my babe's phone." Blake asked for my phone and tried to fix it in front of Kyle.

I wanted to burst into tears, because Blake had just finished screaming at me, but he suddenly converted back to Mr. Nice Guy when Kyle came into the room. It was like watching Dr. Jackal and Mr. Hyde in action. Kyle walked out, and then I said, "I can't believe you are making this whole thing to be about your kids that we both know is not true. I didn't have to accept your hand in marriage if I didn't want to accept your kids. You assured me I had your support and said all those wonderful things to me that made me feel secure enough to take this journey with you, and now you are treating me like dirt, and I'm way better than this. Something else is going on, and your anger and whatever you are up to has nothing to do with me."

At that time, I wanted to react like the old Monica from my early thirties and say, "You know what? I'm out of here." But, my heart would not allow me to. Then, he said, "I gotta go. The bus is downstairs. I will come by your suite when I get back to talk." We both walked out the room. He got in the elevator, and he mumbled, "I love you so much" with a very sad face. I asked him if he was sure he knew what God meant by loving me unconditionally. Then, the elevator door closed.

I walked up to my room in tears, and I felt I had no one to lean on. Occasionally, when you think people are your support system, they are secretly hoping things do not work out for you. So, I was left to do what I knew to do. I prayed all night asking the Lord for His guidance. The Holy Spirit was extremely lucid. He said, "Be still."

> *"Rest in the LORD and wait patiently for Him; Do not fret because of him who prospers in his way, Because of the man who carries out wicked schemes."*
>
> -Psalm 37:7 NIV

Wedding Day Heartbreak

"Rejection is God's Protection."
-Dr. Kenneth C. Ulmer (Bishop)

The next morning, I woke up looking forward to becoming one with the love of my life and to what was going to be the most beautiful and glamorous wedding one has ever seen. Our wedding was going to be similar to those shown on T.V. that looked like a million dollars. God truly blessed me with the creative gift to bring the bling to life. Blake never came by my suite like he said he would, but I did not think anything of it. I figured he had cooled off and had a great bachelor party.

I meditated on the Word and then called Blake around nine a.m. from the room phone, because I could not dial out on my cell phone. Blake did not answer, so I left him a voicemail. I saw a text on my phone around ten a.m. from Mrs. Becky's hairstylist I connected her with stating she cancelled her hair appointment for that day, because something happened. I could not respond, but I knew then my world was about to be shattered.

Blake returned my call from his car about eleven a.m., and I said, "Hey, what's up?" He said, "I'm not moving forward with today," in a rude voice. My heart dropped out of my chest, and then I said, "Why are you doing this? I know you planned this. That's why you took all the nice things I bought you from my house, because you knew you were not coming back." He said, "You do not like my kids, but right now, I need to see my parents and my friend who is a pastor. I will call you back." Then, he rushed me off the phone.

I knew he had already spoken to his parents, because his mom cancelled her hair appointment. Blake never called me back nor did he come to see me. Blake's call to me was like the one Richie from the movie "Harlem Nights" made to his wife and said he was never coming home, because of Sunshine.

I called Lynn crying to give her the bad news, and she was infuriated. Lynn called my mom and said, "Please, go get your child." My mom, in turn, called Vivian. I started to pray as tears ran down my face like a stream of water, and I asked the Lord again, "What are you trying to tell me?" Any time the Lord does something drastic in my life, He is trying to tell me something. The only other drastic matter in my life was when I got shot, and the Lord definitely was trying to get me to the next level in Christ.

The Holy Spirit was so clear in His answer, the Lord revealed to me, "No man can love you, Monica, as Christ loves the church when he has bitterness toward his own mother and a hard heart. Until he releases the anger and forgives his parents, he will not have the type of relationship he desires and know how to honor and cherish a woman like God says he should with unconditional love." I thought he loved me with all my perfections and imperfections, as I loved him unconditionally.

"A wise son brings joy to his father, but a foolish man despises his mother."

-Proverbs 15:20 NIV

The Lord said, "I have given you all the strength you need to get through this." Calmness came over me, but I still felt like I lost my best friend and the love of my life. Blake was the only man in my life I have ever trusted with all of me, including my heart, only to find out he would be the one to break my heart. Anyone has the right to cancel a wedding, but it is how it is done. Blake did not even have the courage to come look me in my face, because he knew he was lying as to why he cancelled the wedding. He left me to do all the dirty work and tell everyone the wedding was cancelled. The way he handled it was senseless and so very hurtful to me and my family.

We were the poster couple in our eleven-week pre-marital sessions, and I could not do any wrong in Blake's eyes, except for the card incident. That was nothing compared to other couples who had been cheated on and still were moving forward with their wedding. Blake even told one of the pastors in our counseling session we would be unstoppable as a couple, and the pastor agreed. The pastor also told Blake he must treat me like a "diamond" and cherish me. He asked

Blake if he could do that, and Blake said, "Yes," with much confidence.

Vivian, my mom and Bela came to my room. They asked me what happened, and I told them. My mom started crying, and she called Blake and Mrs. Becky and left voicemails. I was sitting on the couch, and my mom said, "You sure are calm, Monica." I said, "I'm hurt, in shock, have cried all that I can, and I'm just continuing to hear from the Lord, who has already revealed some things to me. What else am I supposed to do? If anyone would have asked me to bet everything I owned if I thought Blake would ever do me that way, I would be homeless. Not in a million years would I have imagined Blake leaving me basically at the altar. He knew he was not moving forward, Mom, when he took all the things I bought him from my house yesterday." Vivian hugged me and said she was so sorry. I was numb and really did not want to be bothered.

Bela said, "Let's give it some time to see if he comes around." In the meantime, she would have the hotel take my phone to the Apple store to have it repaired. Colette kept texting me trying to find out my room number and to confirm the time she would be coming to style my hair that day. Vivian called her and told her what happened, and she was utterly shocked. She told the other girls and called back to the room and said they wanted to come be there for me. I was not myself and said okay.

Blake finally called my mom back and sounded like he was crying and angry. My mom said, "Blake, what's going on? How could you do this to my daughter?" He began to tell her I did not like London and he cannot marry someone who does not like his daughter. She said, "That's not true. Why are you yelling? This is not a reason to cancel the wedding." He then told her, "Monica and I need to get more counseling." But, he knew that was not his intent. She said, "Many couples need counseling for several reasons, but this is not the reason you are cancelling the wedding. You have told me and Chris how much you love my daughter and now you treat her this way." Blake yelled, "I DO LOVE MONICA!"

Then, when the London reason was not making sense or being accepted by anyone, he started to say he does not feel like the man in the relationship. My mom again said, "Blake, it seems like now you are just pulling stuff out of the bag. I know for sure that's not true, because when I ask Monica about any plans with you and her, she always tells me it's Blake's decision. And, you told her that's what you like most about her is that she allows you to be the man. I know

Monica can be bossy at times, but what woman isn't? And, you certainly do not mistreat the woman you proclaim to be in love with. You didn't even have the decency to come and meet with her face-to-face." My mom asked Blake where was he, and he said, "About forty-five minutes away from the hotel, but I really don't know where I am."

Blake also talked to Vivian and told her the same lies. Then, he talked to Bela's husband Michael and told him the same thing. In addition, he told Michael, "If it came down to London or Monica having to starve, Monica would starve, and I would feed my daughter." Blake did not even say he would give me a little bit of food and London some food, but he would basically let me starve to death. That said a lot about his love for me. Of course, no man wants his child to starve, but not giving your wife a piece of bread was shocking to me. That was the same man who told me he would lay his life down for me. My mom then asked Blake to come back to talk with her, and he said he would, but he never showed up.

> *"Confidence in an unfaithful man in time of trouble is like a broken tooth, and a foot out of joint."*
>
> -Proverbs 25:19 KJV

It is one thing if he did not want to get married, but the lie he was telling was I did not like his daughter. He was assassinating my character. I never spoke badly about Blake. Not even to this day will I speak badly about him, because he is the love of my life. One thing I despise is when before couples breakup, they both cannot do any wrong, but soon as the breakup happens, one or both of them begins speaking badly about the other person. That is not love. It is not as though he did not have any imperfections, because he did, but I am not the type to tear down my man if I am proclaiming to love him so much. I would only lift up Blake and make him feel like the man at all times.

Vivian went downstairs to get a drink and bumped into Kyle. Vivian ran up to Kyle and asked, "Where's Blake?" He said, "I don't know. We have been trying to call him." Vivian said, "That's messed up what he did to my friend." Kyle began to go on about how I got mad because Blake sat next to his daughter at breakfast. Vivian said, "You know that's not true, and you should have more sense to know if he felt that way he would have shared that with Monica a long time ago. Just like he has all of his friends in check, including you, Kyle." Kyle found her statement to be amusing.

Vivian said, "You're the best man and his best friend. You could not talk with him?" Kyle said, "When he called me and told me why he was cancelling the wedding, I said, 'Man, you two can't work it out after the wedding?' and he said no. Then, I called Blake back at two p.m., since the wedding did not start until six p.m., and he would not change his mind. Blake is stubborn, and once he has made up his mind, it's hard to change it."

Vivian then ran into Jamie and asked him where Blake was. Jamie looked puzzled and said, "We have been trying to find him. When I woke up early this morning, my dad was gone. He called and told me the wedding was off." Jamie was shocked, and he said Blake did not give him a reason, so Vivian said, "Well, he lied and said the reason was because Monica didn't like his daughter." Vivian asked Jamie how he felt about me, and Jamie said, "I love Ms. Monica, and she never treated me bad, so I don't know what this is about."

Tammy was very upset and hurting for me. She stayed at home that day to give me some air and would reach out to me later that week. Colette, Rochelle and tall Tanya came to the room, and Gena went to get my cake. Hansen's Cakes tried to deliver it earlier, but was told our wedding was cancelled. She retrieved our cake and took it to my house. Bishop Ulmer arrived to the hotel the same time Rochelle did, and she told him the news in the lobby. Apparently, Bela had not called him about the wedding being cancelled. Rochelle brought Bishop Ulmer to the suite, and he felt so badly and was shocked. He told me, "God knows best, and He is going to see you through." I started crying and placed my head in my lap as my mom told Bishop Ulmer what happened. He looked in amazement, and he said, "Daughter, this is not about you. There's something else going on, but best believe rejection is God's protection, and even during this dark time, God is with you."

"Be strong and courageous. Do not fear or be in dread of them, for it is the Lord your God who goes with you. He will not leave you or forsake you."

-Deuteronomy 31:6 NIV

Bishop stayed for a few more minutes and said he would follow up with me during the next week and to call him and First Lady at any time. My friends were in the bedroom suite while Bishop Ulmer was speaking to my mom. I could not stop crying and had pain in my eyes. Harriet came to see me and said someone would come give me a massage and to let her know in one hour if the wedding was indeed cancelled. She asked us if we wanted to allow the guests to come in and have a party because everything was already paid for.

No one was in the mood, so we said no. When we spoke to my grandmother Jean, she said we were lucky she was not there, because she would have stood in front of the hotel and informed all the guests to come in, and although the wedding was cancelled, we were going to enjoy the food and have a party. We laughed, because she was not lying. We knew she would have done exactly that.

One hour passed by, and my mom told Harriett to let people know the wedding was cancelled. My wedding coordinator sent texts to the guests to let them know about the cancellation. At that very moment, I did not have anything to give. I only existed and felt like a huge rock was on my shoulders. My mom was disappointed Mrs. Becky did not return her call. I did not want to stay at the hotel, so we packed up everything and left after a few hours.

We went to my house and talked for a while. Colette, Vivian, tall Tanya, Rochelle and Gena were still shocked and never wanted me to feel that type of pain. I had so many sweets, so friends took some home, and we cut the cake. After they left, I sat on the couch, and my dad said, "Monica, are you okay? Don't cry." I know my dad was upset, but he really did not know what to say.

Lynn said, "I'm so sorry, Monica. I knew that coward was up to something and had no intentions on moving forward with the wedding. His attitude was not of a man about to get married. The way you talked about him so much was not the person I met on Thursday, so even I was confused." Lynn further stated, "I observed his mood, and I guess he was mad when I kept telling London not to give adults one-word responses. Blake would squirm any time I said anything to his daughter, but truth be told she got closer to me, because she wants the discipline and she couldn't wait for you Monica to get home. All she talked about was Ms. Monica. So for Blake to accuse you of not liking his daughter is a lie. You know that, right?" I said, "Yes, I do." Lynn said, "At the rehearsal, he came up to me and thanked me for being nice to London. I wanted to say, 'What the hell are you talking about? No one was being mean to her.' Why did he think it was okay for him to treat my niece this way? Monica you just need to thank God for His hands on your life."

She asked me how I felt. I told her, "I never saw this coming. Even with his attitude the last few days, I would never think he would practically leave me at the altar and be so cruel towards me. It is all so clear. He had no intent to get more counseling, as he shared with my mom. This is not the man I fell in love with. He disappeared all day and did not even care how I would feel." She said, "I know, but you need to get some rest. So, how about you take a hot bath, and we will talk tomorrow, okay?" I said, "Okay." I walked upstairs with the little strength I had and ran my bath water.

As I sat in the bathtub, I cried and cried for about two hours. Every tear I had not released earlier came out, and I felt so empty inside and could not believe Blake would no longer be in my life. We were inseparable, and I asked the Lord, "Where do I go from here?"

"Thy shoes shall be iron and brass; and as thy days, so shall thy strength be."

-Deuteronomy 33:25 KJV

Forgiveness in the Midst of the Valley

The next day, I meditated on the Word, and the Lord said to forgive Blake. I immediately forgave him and asked the Lord for strength. One person I do not play with is God, because although people may leave me, I knew God would never leave me. Our wedding was supposed to be a new beginning in my daily journal. But, the ending did not turn out like I thought it would. However, I must remember my life is not my own. It is God's, and He put the unity on hold. I prayed for Blake with whatever he was going through, and I asked God to release the anger he has in his hard heart.

I must say, God has brought me a mighty long way. I appreciate everything Blake did for me, and I wish he had been more mature about the matter and truly not just spoke about God, but had God in his heart. Also, I wished he knew what it truly meant to love a woman unconditionally. Unfortunately, our culture is always looking for the next best thing. Trust me; there will always be someone more beautiful, more handsome, wealthier and more physically fit. That is why it is so important to marry someone who does not talk

Christianity but has a lifestyle of it. No one is perfect, but at least the conscience and conviction will be there with how you treat one another.

> *"My son, give me your heart, and let your eyes observe my ways."*
>
> -Proverbs 23:26 ESV

Even in that situation, as bad as it seems, God has matured me spiritually, emotionally and personally. One thing that comes to mind is I have learned at times you do not have to speak on everything with your mate. That is all a part of growing in a relationship. Also, I have grown to not allow others' attitudes affect me personally and to not wear my emotions on my sleeves, because these issues can affect my life. It takes a strong God-fearing man and woman to endure the trials in a relationship. God has made me realize it is understandable everybody is not always going to like me, be happy for me and cheer for the great things God is doing in my life.

Some great advice Colette gave me is you must place people in categories, and that way you will know how to deal with them. It also removes any high expectations of certain people. As I put this into action, it has truly helped me accept people for who they are and where they are. I have truly learned to look up to God for everything I need.

My rewards come from the Lord Jesus Christ and Him alone. I thank God for what He has done in my life, and I trust Him in every area of my life. I am so excited about where God is taking me in my life and what He has in store for me, because my life is just beginning. I told the Lord at the beginning of 2013, I was on top of the mountain with a new executive job and the engagement to the love of my life.

Now, I am walking in the valley all by myself. I said, "Lord, why is my life always on display for everyone to see. This is not fair. I'm hurt; I lost the love of my life; I have been humiliated; haters are praising the devil; and I feel so discouraged." I wanted to stay in bed all day, but I knew that was not going to happen.

My door was closed, and I heard Lynn knocking the first time, but I ignored her. Lynn came in the second time, and it was about twelve noon. My phone had been ringing off the hook, and I had more than fifty text messages. Lynn said, "Okay, I'm not going to let you lie around all day. You have to get up and eat. This will pass, but you have to take care of you." I started to cry and said, "I can't believe he has not called me. It's like he just skipped town and said forget me. This is so hurtful, Lynn, and I feel like my whole world has been taken from me."

Lynn could not hold her tears back from seeing the hurt in my face and said, "Baby, you are not the first and will not be the last, but you are smart and beautiful. You have a lot to offer any man, and God will bless you with a man who will truly love you like God says he should. Besides, the man God has for you would not want to see you like this. You need a mature man who is not with any games. What I saw of Blake these past few days did not reflect an image of God or all the nice things you told me about him. He seems very shallow, cold hearted and living a double life." I said, "Lynn, I never lied about how he treated me. I'm telling you this is not the Blake I know either. Besides the past few months of his behavior being weird, Blake has always been so lovable towards me, and if this were a movie, everyone would be in shock. You are just as confused as I am."

My mom stopped by to take my dad to the airport with Lynn. I hugged my dad, and he told me everything was going to be fine and he hates to see me cry. I cried even more when my dad left, because he does not say much, but when he said those words, they really touched my heart. I could see the hurt in my dad's face, because I was hurting. I wondered what was going through his mind. They left, and I took a hot bath and meditated further on the Word.

> *"Yea, though I walk through the valley of the shadow of death, I will fear no evil: for thou art with me; thy rod and thy staff they comfort me."*
>
> -Psalm 23:4 KJV

On Sunday morning, when I awakened, I felt like the wind had been kicked out of me. I never miss church unless I am traveling, but I did not have the strength to get dressed. My brother and his girlfriend came by to check on me, which was nice of them. Lynn and I just relaxed all day and talked, which was very therapeutic.

That Monday, Lynn and I went to the movies, and she left the next day Tuesday. I generally workout with my trainer Reggie "The

Machine" during the week, but he said I could rest the week after my wedding issue, but I would need to come back the next Monday.

The day after Lynn left, my friend Peaches called me and said, "Sis, I do not have any money, but I want to make sure you eat, so tell me what you want when I come over, and I will get you some food." I thought, *Wow that is so wonderful*. So many people were reaching out to ensure I was doing well, because they knew Lynn was scheduled to leave on Tuesday.

Peaches came by, but I did not give her all the details of what happened, nor did she ask me. I just told her the wedding was cancelled. The only ones who knew the details of what happened were my four friends who came to my hotel suite and to my home the day of my wedding chaos. Peaches said, "Girl, I don't even care to know what happened. My main concern was to ensure you are okay." After Peaches left, Layla called me on the phone and said, "You know it's not about you right, Monica?" I said, "I sure do." She said, "There's something weird about Blake, but I didn't want to say anything at the time."

Delania, who has always been straight forward, called me and said, "Girl, I'm not going to sympathize with you. Get out the bed, and call me if you need me. You have a lot of life to live. You know how I do it when a man trips on me: Keep it pushing." Delania means no harm, and her friendship has always been genuine and caring. She actually made me laugh.

During that week Colette, tall Tanya and little Tanya, Rochelle and Gena sent me text messages to see how I was doing, which was great. Tall Tanya called me day and night for months and text me words of encouragement to ensure I was okay. She was so transparent with me and shared some of her deepest secrets of the hurts she had gone through. She knew if God did it for her, He would get me through. That was such a blessing, and it helped to energize me. Tanya has been a great big sister to me, and I cannot thank her enough for uplifting my spirits and continuously speaking the Word into my life.

As women, it is important for us to lift one another up and be able to share your inner most secrets with one another. This is something that is lacking in our culture, but I want to change that and help my sisters and brothers in Christ push through their pain. I meditated in the Word, day and night as I have always done. During that valley experience, God gave me visions of so many things, and the visions comforted me at night and carried me through the day.

My mom came by, and we went to lunch that Wednesday. As we ate, she suddenly said in a rage, "I'm going to call the *Steve Harvey Morning Show*, because he would know why a man would do something like this." I said, "Mom, please do not call Steve Harvey, because then everyone will know what happened." She said, "Monica you can't worry about who knows what. So what it happened, and you have to brush yourself off and move on. I still can't believe Blake did this to you, and he still has not called you. What about the counseling he told me you two needed?" I said, "Mom, he just told you that to appease you. It's obvious he never planned to be with me after his one-minute call to me the day of our wedding. Nope, he has not called me, and I have not called him. God told me to be still, so that's what I'm doing. God is the only person I fear, and one should never interfere with what God has planned."

Tammy was my lifesaver, and I was so glad she had moved back to Los Angeles from New York City. Ten years prior, she had relocated to New York City. She came to pick me up to have dinner at Boa Steakhouse in West Hollywood, CA that Thursday. She said, "You look great to have just gone through such a hurtful situation, so keep your head up and a smile on your face."

That night, we had a great time eating and laughing. Tammy is a mature pure-hearted friend, very astute business woman and successful entrepreneur. I am so proud of what she has been able to accomplish in her life. Tammy told me to call her any time, and she would be on her way or if I just needed someone to talk to. When you go through a situation like this, you do not even have the energy to call anyone. So, I was appreciative Tammy always reached out to me and others would too, because I would have remained in the bed all day. I still had two weeks off work, so that gave me some time to get myself together. Tammy and I would go bike riding. She always made sure I was busy, which got my mind off the entire matter. I cannot thank her enough for the time and effort she spent getting me back on track and keeping my spirits high, despite her very hectic schedule.

> *"One who has unreliable friends soon comes to ruin, but there is a friend who sticks closer than a brother."*
>
> -Proverbs 18:24 NIV

One week passed, and it was time for me to go back to church. I told the Lord I needed to hear from Him that day in the service, because I was feeling lost and was unsure what to do next. I felt hopeless, and I knew those feelings were the devil, but it still affected me. Bishop Ulmer's sermon my first day back at church was "I Am with You." Other sermons each week included "The Blessing is in Your Breaking," "Your Latter House will be Greater than your Former and in this Place I Will Give You Peace," "Book of Ruth: Boaz is Coming," "God uses Your Life to get Glory and Draw People Closer to Him," and so many more sermons that answered my prayers from the Lord each week for months. It was like God was not giving me anytime to have a pity party, and God knew where I would be in my life, and I cannot tell you enough how the Word and ministry at FCBC has been a blessing to me. Every week, I knew God was talking directly to me.

The Lord was so clear in His message for me to keep my head up and never let anyone see me sweat. I still had a job to do, and it was nothing but the Lord who brought me through. I may have been smiling, but some days driving to work or at home, I would just burst into tears.

During that time, God expurgated people from my life who did not have my best interest and delivered those friends and mentors unto me who would encourage and support me. The gospel group Mary Mary's song "God in Me" was my song every day. People saw me and thought I had it made, but they had no idea the pain I was feeling. I could not even explain this type of hurt and often wondered how God was going to get me through this dark valley. I know God never gives us more than we can handle, but the excruciating pain was unbearable.

When I returned home each day, my face was on the floor praising God with tears running down my face asking God for more strength to get me through another day. Then, I was watching T.D. Jakes ministry one Sunday after church as I do most Sundays, and he shared his secret verse, as he called it, that gives him strength when he is going through tough times and does not want to get out of bed.

"As thy days are, so shall they strength be."

-Deuteronomy 33:25 NIV

The next week, I was back working out with my trainer Reggie "The Machine." I was trying to keep it together. Then, while I was doing some push-ups, I fell flat on my face and cried my eyes out, due to the hurt and anger inside of me. Reggie said, "Monica, what's wrong?" I said in a rage, "Reggie, I can't do this, and I'm so hurt Blake did this to me, and I miss him so much." He said, "Monica, get up. You're a child of God, and you're going to be just fine. There had to be a reason why God allowed this to happen, so you have to put all your trust in God. I'm not going to let you wallow in this mess. You're not going to miss a day. If you try to, I'm going to come pick you up from your house."

From that day forward, besides God's ultimate strength He instilled in me, Reggie really helped me get my physical and mental strength back, and I contribute my results to his awesome skills as a fitness trainer and big heart as a friend. Soon enough, I was motivated to do my workout routine, and I was on fire. I was starting to look and feel better than I had ever felt in my life.

Reggie, who never gives compliments unless you have earned them, told me one day, "You look great, Monica." I almost fainted, and I knew for certain I was on the right track. Reggie has been telling me for years I need to eat healthier to see better results, and it was not until during that time I finally listened. I cannot thank Reggie enough for caring for me as a little sister and sewing seeds of words of encouragement to me each day during our workout.

My cousin Donna would also call and text me periodically to see how I was doing. She has always been there for me, no matter the situation. That really meant a lot to me. God is so good, because every corner I turned, He placed a person there to keep me uplifted and never allowing me to fall.

Puzzled

Kyle's wife Crystal called me often to check on me. During one of our conversations, she told me people were saying Blake tripped out, and they cannot believe he had not called me. I asked Crystal, "What is Blake telling people?" She said, "That you and he could not see eye-to-eye, which is puzzling, because he would always tell everyone you were so great. Kyle is the only one he told you didn't like London, which even Kyle said, 'Man, you could work this out after the wedding.' He didn't think it was a reason to cancel." I said,

"You know that's not true, Crystal." She said, "Yes, I know, Monica. People who flew to Los Angeles on Saturday wish they had known he was not going to move forward. They could have saved on the flight and hotel." Crystal told me things would get better, and she would keep me in her prayers.

I talked to Jamie, and he told me he was sorry about everything, but his dad has a really hard heart. I said, "I didn't know then, but I know that to be true now. All of this is a real shocker to me, and I would never think he would walk away this easy." He said, "Ms. Monica, my dad didn't talk to me for two years, and we live in the same city. And, he hasn't talked to my mom in twenty-two years, so just hang in there, Ms. Monica and hopefully, he will come around one day." I said, "Thank you so much, Jamie. I appreciate your kind words, and I know you are going to be successful. I wish you all the best." My heart hurt so badly knowing I would not be in Jamie's life to encourage and love him, because I know he really needs that nurturing.

I decided to call Mrs. Becky, because she had not returned my mom's call or mine and besides she was to be my mother-in-law. Mrs. Becky would tell me from time to time she loved me, so I thought we were headed toward a great relationship. When I called Mrs. Becky, I said, "Hello, how are you?" She responded, "Doing great." I told her I was reaching out because I was unsure if she was upset with me, based on what Blake told her why he cancelled the wedding. Mrs. Becky said, "Blake didn't say anything negative about you, Monica. I want the best for both of you." I said to myself, *Blake told all my people I did not like London and that was the reason he cancelled the wedding and assassinated my character, but it did not sound like that is what he was telling his family and friends, besides Kyle.*

I shared with Mrs. Becky I thought she would have called to check on me. She said, "Well, I really do not know you very well and didn't see a need to call." Whoa, that hit me hard. I said, "Okay, well thanks for everything, and I wish you all the best." She said, "You know when one door closes another one opens." I said, "Yep." That was the last conversation we had. I thought about how her lack of familiarity with me never prevented her from stating how much she loved me. I thought as a pastor and a woman there would have been some kind of compassion for how I would be feeling. I would not expect her to go against her son, but how about praying with me and having a genuine concern? I had been looking forward to building a relationship with Mrs. Becky, but it did not turn out that way.

I started to feel so betrayed and hurt even more that no one even cared about my well-being on his side, except Crystal and Kyle. I made a call to Blake's pastor friend's wife Mia. We had hung out once with the guys, and we were building a relationship. I did not have her number, because we did not exchange numbers the last time we had dinner together. I knew she worked at a large bank, so I asked one of the executives I knew in Los Angeles to give me her work number. I phoned Mia, and she called me back later that day. Because she is a first lady of a church, I was hoping just to talk to her woman to woman. Mia said, "Hi, Monica. How are you? I was wondering how you got my work number." So, I told her how.

I told her, "I was simply calling to see what Blake had told you two about why our wedding was cancelled." She said, "All I know is the wedding was cancelled." Again, I thought, *This is weird*. Then I shared with her, "Well, Blake accused me of not liking London, and on the day of our wedding, he phoned me and told me he was not moving forward." Mia said, "Oh, I hadn't heard anything like that." I told her, "I'm certain Blake was cheating on me, and this had nothing to do with London." I asked Mia not to share our conversation with her husband, because I was not trying to start any mess. I was only desirous of learning what Blake was telling others, because I could not understand why he would bash me to my family, but with his family and friends it was as simple as we could not agree, which was a lie. Sure enough, Mia went home and told her husband. Looking back, I am not sure why I even cared what he told people, but I was hurting. He had torn me down to pieces and humiliated me.

The next thing I knew, a friend of mine at the time told me Blake told Josh I was losing it, because I had called Blake's pastor's wife. That made me sick to my stomach, because people have no compassion for how a woman or man may feel who is in that situation, and I could not even fathom how anyone could be so deceitful, cold and callus. Josh had the story all wrong, because Mia's husband is not Blake's pastor. He is his long-time friend. After that foolishness, I sat still as God had told me to do before and did not worry about who knew what. I knew the truth, so what did it matter what he told other people?

> *"Truthful lips endure forever, but a lying tongue is but for a moment."*
>
> -Proverbs 12:19 ESV

Four Weeks Later – The Call

My mom asked me every week if I had heard from Blake, and I would say no. She was just as surprised as I was, because in the past, Blake would call me every morning before I went to work.

Chris was so upset because Blake had not called me, and something did not seem right, nor was the matter sitting right with Chris. After four weeks, Chris decided to call Blake, because he did not appreciate how he handled the situation or the pain I had endured. He left him a message, calling him a coward. Chris knew if he left that voicemail, Blake would definitely call him right back. Blake called right back and said, "Who are you calling a coward?" Chris said, "You know man, how is it that you think it is okay not to give Monica any closure?" Blake started yelling and was very angry. He told Chris he gave me closure the day he called me and said the wedding was cancelled. Chris said, "Man, that's not closure."

Then, Blake lied and told Chris, "Monica told me the day before our wedding she didn't do kids." Chris said, "Blake stop lying. She would not say anything like that." When Chris told me Blake said that, I was shocked.

Chris told Blake he owes me closure and the way he handled things was cowardly and an immature move. Chris also stated he knew some-thing else was going on with Blake, which was the true reason he cancelled the wedding, which had nothing to do with London or me. Chris said, "You also just wasted money not only for yourself but for others." Blake said in an arrogant way, "My friends gave me back the money I lost."

Chris said, "Man, you could have cancelled the wedding weeks prior if you felt Monica didn't like your daughter. That was terrible how you did Monica. No one deserves to be treated that way. Seeing this side of you, if you thought she didn't like your daughter, you would have talked about this in marriage counseling and said something to Monica early on. This is not how a man of God treats a woman you love. In relationships, you talk things out, man. You had no intention on calling Monica to even check on her. Man, you are cold blooded." Blake started to yell again, and shortly thereafter, they hung up the phone from one another.

A few days later, Blake called me and left me a voicemail. I called him back the next day, as I needed to pray for God to humble me, because as you can imagine, my emotions were tumultuous: I experienced belligerence and borderline depression. Blake answered, and his tone was still one of anger, but I was unsure of the reason, because I was the one who should have been angry. He said to me, "Chris said I didn't give you closure, so that's why I am calling you. I thought I had given you closure." I said, "You call a one-minute phone call the day of our wedding closure?" He said, "My reason for cancelling the wedding is that you didn't like London. That's the only issue I have with you." I said, "Well, that is not all you told Chris, and you know that is not true. What gave you the impression I do not like London?" Blake retorted, "You didn't help her get dressed the day before our wedding." I asked, "Are you for real? That's why Lynn was there to help out with London, and it was the day before our wedding. The bride needed help. Besides, do I help her get dressed in Houston, which you never had an issue with? London is nine years old, and the times I had helped her get dressed was by ironing her clothes. You always thanked me for doing that. London would always ask me after she got dressed, 'How does this look, Ms. Monica?' That would be our girl time. Blake, you know you have been cheating on me for the last two months, and that's why you cancelled the wedding."

Blake dropped a bomb and proclaimed with an attitude, "I'm not obligated to you!" My heart dropped to the floor in dismay, and I told him, "I thought when you asked for my hand in marriage, we were committed to one another." He then said in a very cold tone, "I do not want to be your friend, so there is no need for us to talk to one another. Do not call me, as we do not have any business dealings with one another. But, I am going to remain celibate."

I just said, "Blake, I don't know who you think you are kidding, but that would be between you and God." I did not know what to say to the cold-hearted person on the other end of the phone. Then, he said, "Oh yeah, your friends called me this week and ripped you apart." I said, "No one has anything negative to say about me to you, and if they called and ripped me apart with lies, they are not my friends. Furthermore, did you believe what they said about me and who was it that called you?" He said, "No, I do not believe what they said, and I'm not going to tell you who it was." Blake then said, "You called Mia to tell her what happened, but my friends are okay with me not getting married." I said, "Yeah, based on the lies you told them, because no one in their right mind would agree with how you cancelled the wedding."

Blake said, "The wedding was still on Friday night, but you had no meekness." I said, "That's not true, and you know it. You were the one yelling at me and acting like I was your enemy. I think I have been very meek over the past few months, considering your behavior towards me. Blake you planned this, and that's why you took all the good clothes from the house, because you knew you were not coming back." He said, "Whatever." Afterward, he did not have anything else to say, except he had to go and hung up the phone. That would be my last time ever hearing from Blake.

> *"He healeth the broken in heart, and bindeth up their wounds."*
>
> -Psalm 147:3 NIV

I was sitting in my office thinking, *What just happened?* Tears ran down my face. I told myself right then I would never give anyone my heart again, but God would soon heal my heart.

God said, "You will love again with the one I have prepared for you who will love you unconditionally." I had to get it together, because I had a meeting with the president of the network at my job. I prayed for God to give me strength and brushed myself off. I walked over to meet with her, and she asked me how I was doing. I said, "Okay," but my eyes were red. She could tell I had been crying, so she said, "Come on. Let's go on my patio." When we got there, she instantly said, "You are not okay. I can tell, but you will be okay and get through this." We talked, and she gave me some great advice and told me to just say, "Thank you, Jesus!" She reminded me I am a God-fearing woman, smart, beautiful person, and I deserve someone way better than a man who would do me that way. I shared with her a little bit about our conversation before meeting with her, and she added from what I shared with her, "Only a five year old tells someone he doesn't want to be her friend."

After I thought about the comment, it actually made me laugh and she continued to encourage me. Of course, my day would not be the same, and it was nothing but God who gave me the strength to push through.

I felt badly, because I did not tell everyone the truth about my big day, because I was hurt, humiliated and embarrassed. My boss, the president, human resources and my clients were so supportive at work, and I could not have asked for a better network family. Of course, there were women who were jealous about my relationship, but as I have learned, you cannot escape haters. As long as they are around, you know you are making the devil mad. My life was getting on track, and then the unthinkable happened.

The Unthinkable

Moving forward, I wanted to ensure I did not have any unforgiveness in my heart towards Blake, because having unforgiveness blocks your blessings, and if you do not forgive others, God will not forgive you. So, I wrote him an email letter and told him I forgave him. I asked for forgiveness of anything he felt I did wrong towards him. I shared with him how much he really hurt me and his recent actions did not add up to his words during our relationship. I also told him I wished him and whoever he was with all the best. I know the previous statement may sound sarcastic, but when you are in love with someone, you ultimately want the best for him/her and, if I am not the best for him, I want him to be happy. That is unconditional love. I would not want to go through life being with someone who does not want to be with me. Life is precious and whomever God has for me, I would like it to be for a lifetime, not for spare time.

Blake never responded to my letter, which is what I expected, but it felt great to fully forgive him and move on. That helped me to release every emotion I was feeling. I had even told myself I would never give my heart to anyone ever going forward, but it was evident God was slowly healing my heart and making me whole again. I decided going forward I will love like never before, because it is such a spectacular feeling to be in love and to be loved. After writing the letter, I was finally feeling really good and excited about my life and what God had in store for me.

Just when things were moving along, and I was getting back on track, I was sitting in church one Sunday in October, when Bishop Ulmer mentioned in his sermon, "What someone doesn't want to happen is going to happen, and God is not going to stop it, because He wants to get glory through your life. Through you, God is going to draw people closer to Him, and you will be matured to the next level with your walk with God. What's about to happen is not going to feel good, and it's going to seem bad, but if you would just trust God and praise Him through your adversity, He is going to take you to places your eyes have never seen and your ears have not heard."

> *"But as it is written, your eye hath not seen, nor ear heard, neither have entered into the heart of man, the things which God hath prepared for them that love him."*
>
> -1 Corinthians 2:9 KJV

I knew God was speaking to me, because at work our parent company was going through a divestiture with their networks, and we had just laid off 180 people at a huge studio, but when I asked one of my human resource leaders during that time if our department was going to be affected, I was told we would not be impacted. A few months after I joined the company, I figured something was going on when the parent company inquired more often about our processes.

Sure enough, a few days after that church service, I was told my role was being eliminated and several employees would be laid off in other states. I was the only one in Los Angeles, and the parent company would be assuming my role. There was nowhere else for me to go, unless I wanted to relocate to New York City, and that was not an option for me at that time. The network recruited me in April, and my boss felt really bad and said he would not have hired me if he knew the parent company was going to realign their businesses. I had two months to find another place of employment.

On my way home, I listened to the Mary Mary's song "God in Me," and said, "Lord, I don't know what you are doing, but I trust you." God had given me unbelievable strength at that point, because I could not have handled all of what I was going through two years before that time. I kept a positive attitude and shut down from everyone to hear from God. People all around me would say, "You are so positive and look so great, and if I went through the things you are going through, I would just die." I would always tell people, "God is so good and always look up to Him, not man." My smile never left my face, even though I was hurting inside.

Three weeks before my job was to cease, my boss called me and said, "I am going to leave you on the payroll for three more months, because we really want you to find a job." He apologized again about recruiting me from the full-time job I already had. I told him, "No worries." It was not his fault, and I thanked him for his extension, which would give me more time to find another job. When I hung up the phone, I started to praise God in my office and thank Him for His grace and mercy on my life. I had realized through my heartache and my job going away, God had truly matured me to the next level in the Word and truly humbled me in every area in my life.

> *"Do not be afraid or discouraged, for the Lord will personally go ahead of you. He will be with you; he will neither fail you nor abandon you."*

-Deuteronomy 31:8 NLT

The holiday season was a time for healing, and God exposed so many people and things to me of which I needed to dispose. I continued to shut down to hear from God and focus on what my purpose in life really was. I knew God had to remove me from that job in order to get me to where He wanted me to be. I would soon find out what He wanted me to complete and my purpose in life.

10-1 Man

Around the holidays, Tammy and I went out to eat, and I met a retired successful professional baseball player. Tony was chocolate, six feet four, fifty years old and could not resist showing us his six pack. He was coming on strong and offered me the sky, moon and stars. We exchanged numbers, but I was not planning on dating anyone, but I said, "Let me get out the house and enjoy myself."

We met for dinner one evening, and he started to talk about sex. I told him I was celibate to cut the conversation short. He said to me, "Oh, my love. You better start giving it up to someone, because there are ten of you to one of me, and no women I know are celibate. You are a rare breed, and why would a man accept your celibacy, when he can get laid any time?"

I smiled and said, "I love your thought process." He thought for sure he was onto something. I continued, "However, you and I live in two different worlds. You say it's 10-1?" He said, "Yes, darling." I said, "Well, I don't care if it was 20-1 or how about 50-1, or even 100-1. All I need is 'one,' and my God has already prepared that 'one' for me. Unfortunately, it appears you are not the 'one' for me, so I will just sit back and look fabulous and wait for my Boaz."

He said, "Who is Boaz?" I shook my head and said, "I will introduce you to him when he finds me. Besides like Jay-Z said in his song back in the day, but I'm going to change it a little: I got ninety-nine problems, but getting laid is not one of them." We both started laughing. After that, Tony would continue to call me every day until he gave up. I did not want to be bothered, and by then, he knew having sex with him was not my focus.

Tony was just another distraction and attempted discouragement from the devil, and no longer would I fall into the devil's traps for my feet. God's word will never return void, and I know the future He has for me is grand. God truly kept my eyes stayed on Him during this season.

> *"So is my word that goes out from my mouth. It will not return to me void, but will accomplish what I desire and achieve the purpose for which I sent it."*
>
> -Isaiah 55:11 NIV

Tips from Lessons Learned

1. Always look to God and let Him direct your paths.
2. Put all your trust in God's every word, not man's.
3. People tell you who they are and if they can be trusted by how they handle situations.
4. Always surround yourself around people who genuinely care about you and only want to see you happy, never wanting to see you hurting.
5. If a man does not honor his mother, he will not honor you.
6. Women do not have to speak on everything. Just allow God to reveal the truth.
7. Men and women, we must think before we speak, to alleviate any unnecessary healthy debates.
8. Do not be discouraged if things do not turn out as planned. Remember, God's ways are not our ways, and His thoughts are not our thoughts. He has the script to our lives.
9. Your fiancé/fiancée should love you as God says with 'unconditional' love, not 'conditional' – never keeping track of your wrong doings, but being patient with one another's imperfections.
10. It is tough to have a real relationship with someone who has a hard heart. Only God can soften it.
11. Your fiancé/fiancée's friends tell you a lot about him/her, so be observant of the company he/she keeps.
12. Test the strength of a relationship by the adversity you come through together – not just when things are going well.
13. Praise God in the midst of your trials and tribulations. Do not wait until He brings you through. God will see you through much faster.
14. Everyone cannot handle your happiness. Be selective with whom you share your happy moments.
15. Do not allow a relationship disappointment to close your heart. Love like you have never loved before. Life is short and you want to enjoy every bit of it.
16. Strive to be loved for a lifetime, not in his/her spare time.
17. Do not allow family or friends to stress you out and upset your happiness. Realize you cannot control others' behaviors and cannot make everyone happy. It is fine if people do not like you for who you are. Remember, God loves you and will never leave you.

18. You do not always have to cut off those who disappoint you, just thank God for the reveal, put them in a category, and deal with them accordingly.
19. You cannot have high expectations of everyone. Identify the capabilities of people and accept them for who they are.
20. Providence is the seen and unseen activity of God, and if you trust Him with your life, you will never question the decisions He makes for your life.
21. Marriage is sacred and honorable to God. Be mindful of who you ask to share your special wedding day with you.
22. A man or woman of God will never want to see you hurt under any circumstances.
23. God cannot take you to the mountain top, without taking you through the valley.
24. Do not resist the move of God when He is trying to take you to your next season. This is when you become closer to His purpose for your life.
25. What God has for you no man can destroy, but what is not for you, God will overturn.
26. Stay firm with your walk with God, no matter how great your relationship is going and the promises your mate has made to you.
27. It is okay to admit you are hurting and need encouragement. Every man and woman does at some point in his/her life.
28. Learn to forgive and pray for those who hurt you. Doing this will help you heal much faster and be promoted to the next level in Christ.
29. When you pass God's test, He will bring you out looking and feeling better than you ever have before.
30. Blended families can work, if the man, being the head of the household, knows how to manage it.
31. Never have regrets, only lessons learned.

Monica R. Carter

Chapter Eleven
Answer the Call

> *"Because I have called and you refused, I have stretched out my hand and no one regarded, Because you disdained all my counsel, And would have none of my rebuke.... Then they will call on me, but I will not answer; They will seek me diligently, but they will not find me."*
>
> -Proverbs 1:24-25, 28 NIV

I do not know about you, but when God calls, I answer. God is the only person I would never want to have turn His back on me. I knew when I heard Him calling, I needed to answer. It was the New Year of 2014. I was making connections and networking, looking for my next human resources executive role and doing my real estate. The executive level role is a more strategic role; therefore, the interview process is more extensive with meeting several senior executives within any organization.

Over the holiday, I did not get a clear word from God as to what exactly He wanted me to do, but I continuously felt in my spirit God was saying to start 'the project.' I thought the project was getting my Broker's Real Estate license, because I am a real estate professional and should have completed this milestone three years prior and opened my own real estate office. Every time I went to schedule the real estate crash course, the class would be cancelled. This occurred twice. So, I continued with my informational interviews, meeting heads of human resources executives and had planned to attend the crash course in February.

In mid-January, I was cleaning an area in my room where I house an abundance of books. After the disappointment of my relationship with Blake, I stopped journaling. I had been journaling for years, and my wedding was to be the happy beginning of a new chapter in my life. God had been speaking to me about starting 'the project,' but after I was notified about my job, I shut down. Occasionally though, it would enter my spirit again. When I saw my journal, I picked it up, tears ran down my face, and the Holy Spirit was so clear. I then knew 'the project' was God wanting me to still move forward with writing my novel. My novel was always going to be an autobiography about living a celibate lifestyle. During the same week, one of my mentors told me they could envision me speaking to the world about God. I had not revealed to her anything about the book. My goal was to always be a motivational speaker, and she had listened to me speak on several occasions. In the spirit, she saw me involved in more meaningful activities than human resources.

I told the Lord, "I know I am supposed to begin transitioning my novel into manuscript form, but I have already been humiliated more than one could ever endure. Now you want me to share this with the world? I need to find a new job." I was complaining and making excuses, all at the same time.

It was clear God had given me the extra time at my current job to be able to complete my novel. It was ironic that everywhere I went, I met someone who either mentioned people to me who wrote, published books or was an author him/herself. I said, "Okay, Lord. I got it." I reached out to a publisher my friend hired to publish her book and interviewed a second publisher. Ultimately, I hired the one my friend referred me to.

One Saturday evening in February, I began placing my journal into manuscript format. I had four weeks to complete it, before releasing it to my publisher. The devil tried to discourage me by saying, "You are not a pastor or author, and you have never even written a novel." I continued to pray about it with the little strength I had left, and I really felt like giving up.

The next day, Bishop Ulmer was away traveling, so he was not in attendance at church. Pastor K.W., a pastor on our church roster, preached that day in his stead. She said, "My message for today is titled 'Answer the Call.'" I felt myself growing increasingly nervous as I listened to her begin her message. She continued, "It is funny how our cell phones will ring, and we will not answer the call, because we may not feel like talking. God is telling someone today to 'Answer the Call.' The call is not working a job, singing in the choir, ushering, or simply your talent. It's the eternal purpose God has for your life. God may be telling you to write that book, but you are letting the devil put things in your mind, such as I have never written a book before. I am not a pastor or an author. God may be telling you get into ministry, but you have been ignoring the call."

I was shocked and amazed at the words she spoke over the pulpit directly to me, but not surprised, because God has always answered my concerns and given me a word when I needed it. For sure, this time God was pushing me to limits I could not imagine.

When your life is lined up with the Lord and you make your body a living sacrifice, you can hear clearly, and God gives you revelation in every area of your life.

God's purpose for my life is to ensure all women and men know being celibate does not mean you are weak. It does not mean something is wrong with you. It does not mean you will not be popular. Nor does it mean, you will be an outcast. Ladies, you can be celibate and fabulous, and men can be celibate, fearless, and manly. Women, God says to the Proverbs 31 woman, "Your merchandise is good." It hurts my heart when women devalue their worth by being a slave to sex, sleeping with a married man or always being a man's second base, rather than being his one and only. Let us stop falling into the devil's den with this 10-to-1 notion, which somehow encourages women to make desperate decisions. Men will respect you, but you have to give him something to respect and if he does not, why would you want to allow him in your presence?

Men can also be used as sex slaves or toys. There are many women who use men for sex, with no intention to commit to the man. These women are the ones making the late night calls. When men and women engage themselves into these types of situations, they become broken, bitter, abused, miserable, angry, confused, and running from one relationship to the next. Instead of looking up to God, they look to people who give them false hope, a few minutes of pleasure and who do not have their best interest.

This is why it is so important for men and women to heal your mind, body and soul in order to hear from God and be able to answer the call. Often times, 'Answering the Call' is uncomfortable and scary, but if God has put on your heart to answer His call, do not hesitate. This is God's way of getting you to His ultimate plan for your life and promoting you to your next season.

Monica R. Carter

Chapter Twelve
Ten Reasons to Avoid Pre-Marital Sex

Premarital or extra-marital sex is always a losing proposition! God is clear that His wonderful gift of physical intimacy is to be reserved for the boundaries of marriage. Inside of those boundaries, the sexual relationship is a gift that blesses a couple and a family abundantly, and God blesses the oneness that is created. Outside of that biblical commitment, God's word for this is **"fornication."** Here are ten reasons of many to abstain from fornication:

1. It *breaks God's laws and dishonors Him*- search a concordance for the word "fornication." We could stop here- it is all we really need to know.

2. It presents *huge physical risks*- diseases and illnesses are rampant among those who engage in this lifestyle.

3. It presents *huge emotional risks*- a physical and emotional bond without a spiritual commitment is never a winning experience.

4. It presents *huge spiritual risks*- grieving the Holy Spirit and offending a holy God means we forfeit God's best. We never will be fulfilled by dishonoring God.

5. It is *awkward, guilt ridden, unfulfilling, and not representative of God's original intent*- hence, a culture that continually seeks fulfillment with new partners and relationships.

6. It is *disappointing at the physical, emotional, and spiritual levels*- the only physical intimacy that exceeds expectations is that founded on long-term commitment and marital growth.

7. It *creates a spiritual/emotional bond without commitment*- this only breeds resentment, bitterness, and the feeling of being used. It says something like this, "I don't love you enough to commit to you, but I love me enough to use you." These bonds are known as unholy soul ties, which can be very unhealthy and dangerous in fornication and adultery.

8. *It destroys trust*- the best way to have trust in a marriage is to abstain from sex before you get married. Learning to be committed to Christ (in purity) is the best way to learn to be committed to a spouse.

9. It ***creates resentment and frustration***. Sexual intercourse was designed to happen within a committed marriage of selfless love. Outside of that, fornication just breaks the heart and wounds the soul.

10. ***It leaves you empty and searching for real love-*** physical intimacy does not create a loving, committed relationship. It is the fruit of one.

BONUS – You can hear God clearly in regards to every matter of your life, and it is well worth the wait! (Adapted from a statement made by Cary Schmidt.)

Chapter Thirteen
My Life on Display

> *"To them God has chosen to make known among the Gentiles the glorious riches of this mystery, which is Christ in you, the hope of glory."*
>
> -Colossians 1:27 ESV

During my entire existence on this earth, my life has been on display for all to see, whether the occurrences were good or bad. I often wondered why God saw fit for it to be this way. Most people I know would go through their struggles with bad relationships, marital problems or financial issues, but their personal business would never be on display for all to see. When it comes to some of my family members, it is not permissible to share their business and they were not sharing it with the general public either, but rest assured if they became privy to your business, they immediately became *'CNN Breaking News'* and would share with everyone and did not see anything wrong with doing so.

In my life, as you have read, there have been ups and downs since I was born. If God would had given me the script to my life prior to my birth, I would have said, "Put me back in my mother's womb and choose another egg." However, my perspective has since been changed. As I reflected on my life while writing this novel, I am now honored God chose me to display my life for all to see. He knew despite me not wanting to withstand the pressures of my life, I would eventually take His hand and allow Him to lead me. I once was hard headed, and God knew He had to show me He is real or else I would not take the Bible for face value. Remember, I was born in the 'Show Me State' of St. Louis, MO.

I realize everything does happen for a reason. We may not like, understand or agree with it, but when we put our trust in God, we should never fear what He has bestowed upon us. Many times, He is trying to mature us spiritually and personally when we go through trials and tribulations. Although this season has been challenging, it all started to make perfect sense through Bishop Ulmer's sermon.

Dr. Kenneth C. Ulmer's (Bishop) Sermon

"God has put those who bear his message life on display for all to see" (short translation).

-1 Corinthians 4:9 NIV

It was not until February 2014, when God answered my question to Him, as to why my life is on display for all to see. I fully received this message and knew God had me at FCBC for such a time as this. Dr. K.C. Ulmer (Bishop) preached on a sermon called 'Mystery Theatre.' The message was as follows: God puts those who bear His message on 'stage' when no one wants to purchase a ticket. God places those on center stage where half of the audience is rooting for you and the other half is not. In essence, we live our lives in a 'mystery.' The world is the instrument that will record the history of our lives, and the stage we stand on is the stage before the world. We are the actors, and our lives are being betrayed. God is the Producer and Script Writer, and the Holy Spirit is the Director.

The plot revolves around the 'mystery' of God, and the world looks at us and does not understand the storyline of our lives. Yet, God puts us on display (center stage). He positions us center stage so He may tell a story through us. Paul says in Ephesians 3:1-11 NIV, this is a 'mystery.' Keep in mind a 'mystery' is not something that cannot be known, but it can only be known by revelation. It speaks of secrets that you only know if you are in the inside. In other words, God must reveal it to you; we cannot figure it out by ourselves. When we try to discern it in our mind, it makes no sense. When people look at our lives, it makes no sense. Trusting God during adversity and in a bad economy makes no sense.

People looking at the stage are saying, "This is a 'mystery." For example, a fraternity or sorority has certain codes, and these groups do not know each other's codes. One must be initiated in order to be privy these codes. The outsider cannot comprehend it. Even we do not know because we are living our lives as a 'mystery.' It is only when God takes you into the intimacy and secrecy of His own love and reveals it to us that it begins to make sense.

We are living our lives as a 'mystery' and the 'mystery' is God's eternal purpose. God has a purpose for your life and that purpose is part of God's eternal purpose. That means you are not an afterthought. God has a plan and purpose for your life and that purpose came forth in eternity, so that whatever you think is your purpose (talents, gifts, etc.) is only your true purpose if it is connected with eternity. That means, your 'eternal purpose' is what God designed for you even before you were born. Knowing this will help you keep in mind that no matter what God throws at you, you have God's full support.

One of the worst things you can do in a 'mystery' movie is to fall asleep or leave before you know the plot. If you tune out too quickly, you miss the message. Often times when watching a 'mystery' movie, we think we have the answer. Then, we realize when the story lines unfold, it is not what we imagined. But, the script writer knew the opening plot and the end. God has already written out the script of your life, and in the end, it is going to be a wonderful time of celebration and rejoicing. God said, "In the end, I will get the glory, according to my eternal purpose."

God's Purpose for Your Life

God's eternal purpose is a secret word called, 'dwelling place.' He wants to dwell in you in every area of your life. The word 'purpose' means to position or place before. God's purpose is to place your life on display and to lift up your life as His dwelling place, for His desire is to have a place to dwell. God then puts your life on display on stage before a divided audience, before principles and principalities in the heavily realm. This audience also includes holy and demonic angels, which means your life is put on display to an audience that is divided. Half of the audience is pulling and cheering for you, wanting you to win and give you a standing ovation. The other half are demonic beings that are booing every step, phrase and line you cast. They are there to ensure God's plan and purpose does not manifest. God's plan is that He will get glory, because Christ is in you.

Right now, you may be in an uncomfortable or disturbing scene that seems hopeless and seems to have nothing good taking place. Yet, you have in your mind that Christ is in you, and somewhere down the line you will get glory. You must remember your lines, but you must also remember the story line, while remembering the story is bigger than you. You only have a role to play, but you get into character when you remember there is also a supporting cast that builds up the story, you are simply playing a role in.

God wants you to know He has already declared the end from the beginning, and not only will you come out in victory, you will get a standing ovation at the end of the play. The demons in hell will have to declare that you made it beyond every trick and trap that Satan placed for you. God will then dispatch angels that will say:

"I TOLD YOU":
- **Isaiah 54: 17** ESV - *no weapon that is formed against thee shall prosper and every tongue that shall rise against thee in judgment thou shall condemn. This is the heritage of the servants of the Lord, and their righteousness is of me, saith the Lord.*
- **Psalms 30:5** ESV - *For his anger is but for a moment, and his favor is for a lifetime.* **Weeping may tarry for the night, but joy comes with the morning.**
- **Isaiah 40:31** ESV - *But* **they who wait for the Lord shall renew their strength;** *they shall* **mount up with wings like eagles;** *they* **shall run** *and* **not be weary;** *they shall walk and not faint.*
- **Revelation 3:8** ESV - *I know your works. Behold,* **I have set before you an open door, which no one is able to shut.** *I know that you have but little power, and yet you have kept my word and have not denied my name.*
- **Deuteronomy 28:13** ESV - *And the Lord will make you* **the head and not the tail,** *and you* **shall only go up** *and* **not down,** *if you obey the commandments of the Lord your God, which I command you today, being careful to do them.*
- **Philippians 4:19** ESV - *And my* **God will supply every need of yours according to his riches in glory in Christ Jesus.**

The 'mystery' is the audience will not know how God did it, but by the time the credits roll at the end of the movie, God will get the glory. People do not understand how the script will end. Some have written you off already, but tell them just keep watching the movie. It is not over yet, because God has created the script of your life, and He is in full control. Be faithful and make your body a living sacrifice, so God can dwell in you. Let those who come up against you laugh and talk, but I guarantee you God will have the last laugh.

Do not permit the devil to cause you to throw in the towel. He is the defeated foe, not you! Because you already know how the story will end, start praising Him and do not give up.

Put your faith to work, and let God get the glory through your life! The trick of the enemy is for you to walk off stage. The devil will say, "If I hit him/her hard enough, he/she will walk off the stage."

God is saying to His sons and daughters from **1 Corinthians 2:9-** *"But, as it is written, 'What no eye has seen, nor ear heard, nor the heart of man imagined, what God has prepared for those who love him.'"* Everyone is not going to be able to handle God's glory in his/her life. Where God is about to take you, everyone cannot go. If God dwells in you, you must make a conscious effort to empty yourself and allow God to overtake your life and set up residence in you.

Get ready! Get ready! You are about to receive an Academy Award!

-Dr. Kenneth C. Ulmer (known as "Bishop")
Sermon – "Mystery Theatre" (Feb. 9, 2014)
Faithful Central Bible Church
331 W. Florence Avenue
Inglewood, CA 90301
www.faithfulcentral.com

Conclusion

> *"I beseech you therefore, brethren, by the mercies of God, that ye **present your bodies a living sacrifice**, holy, acceptable unto God, **which is your reasonable service.**"*
>
> -Romans 12:1 ESV

In the scripture above, our Lord Jesus Christ is simply saying fleeing from fornication and not committing adultery, which both creates unholy soul ties, is your *reasonable service*. As mentioned, most men and women I have talked to expressed living a celibate lifestyle is a challenge, which is definitely true. However, it is only *one* challenge in a long list of many other challenges we all face in our lives on a daily basis. If we examine the life of Jesus, we will soon learn He had many challenges. Yet, He still sacrificed His life for us. Knowing this is reason enough to *surrender* your life to the Lord Jesus Christ and adhere to the word of God.

My last life event truly made me realize in order to receive all God has for me, it is imperative for me not only to continue to live a celibate lifestyle, but 'surrender' my *life* plans to God. No matter what one, three or five-year plan I have on paper, it may not be God's plans for my life. So, I have surrendered all of me to God, because He has the master script to my life, and He is not going to revise it.

As you have read, throughout my life, I have walked through some valleys and reached some mountains, but through every life experience, I have developed into a better person, become much more astute in the Word, gained a meeker spirit, and have lived a happier life. I now know the ultimate goal is for God to get the glory through every obstacle in my life. I fully understand God knew it was coming. In preparation, He has already given me the strength to handle it. Through my life, I have solace knowing, people will be saved and He is taking me to the next level in Christ and into a new season. No longer will I hesitate moving to the next seasons in my life. When God calls, I will follow.

I have also learned in life *change* is inevitable, whether it is in your personal life or career. Furthermore, it is not the change you should focus on. Rather, it is how are you going to prepare yourself for what is next in your future. Do you walk around feeling sad about what is not in your control to change, or do you focus on what you can change? What you can change is your attitude about the situation and position yourself so Jesus can take you to the next level in your life. Always remain optimistic and know that with change comes opportunities, fresh starts and new ventures in your life!

I pray my goal was accomplished in writing this novel, which is to encourage and enlighten my brothers and sisters to know you can be *'Celibate Fabulous and Fearless.'* Despite what the world says about premarital sex, be a challenge, unique, know your self-worth, step out on faith, and surrender your life plans and bodies to the Lord Jesus Christ. Watch God take you places you could never imagine.

I guess in the end, I thought a *prince* was good enough for me, but now I know God will bless me with a *King*!

God bless you all, and thank you so very much for supporting me. I pray sharing my life story has healed many hearts, saved souls, enlightened you on the dangers of pre-marital sex and adultery, and has encouraged many people to live a righteous lifestyle that is pleasing to God!

> *"I have said these things to you, that in me you may have peace. In the world you will have tribulation. But take heart; I have overcome the world."*
>
> -John 16:33 NIV

About the Author

"Faith makes a Christian, Life proves a Christian, Trial confirms a Christian, Death crowns a Christian."

-Unknown Source

First and foremost, Ms. Monica R. Carter is a beautiful, spirited Woman of God, consummate business woman, entrepreneur, author, motivational speaker, licensed realtor, and extravagant event planner.

In addition to juggling many professions, she is a human resources executive and has worked at several fortune 500 companies. Predominately and most importantly, she is well grounded.

Monica is a woman who believes there are no limits to what she can accomplish. Some may wonder how she is able to juggle all that she does. It's because her foundation starts with her faith. Her motto is…. "I can do all things through Christ, who strengthens me." Everything she does may look glamorous and easy, but many aspects of her life have not been without challenges or obstacles. There have been many sleepless nights with working often times until the wee hours of the morning, but throughout life's challenges, there was only one person who lifted her up: the Lord Jesus Christ.

Monica was born in the 'Show Me State,' St Louis, MO. However, she has been in Southern California since she was four years old. She received her M.B.A. degree in 2001 from University of Phoenix by attending evening classes, while working over sixty hours a week.

Monica has been a licensed realtor for over ten years and extravagant event planning has always been in her DNA.

She definitely puts the wow factor on any event! As an author, Monica has always wanted to complete and publish her first novel: *Celibate Fabulous & Fearless.*

This novel serves as her autobiography and includes experiences of tragedy, deceit, love, pain, grace and mercy. She also covers the importance of living a celibate lifestyle as a single Christian woman and man, dangers of pre-marital sex and the benefits of living for God.

No! It is not something you will find at any corner bookstore or just church gatherings; it is the essence of her personality, which includes humor, emotions, faith and perseverance.

Monica is excited to be releasing her debut novel, which she hopes will motivate people all around the world and inspire them to come hear her speak.

In doing so, they can see for themselves when she enters a room, she definitely lights it up with her witty, charismatic charm, and she is a very inspirational speaker. Not to mention, she is on fire for God!

www.ingramcontent.com/pod-product-compliance
Lightning Source LLC
Chambersburg PA
CBHW070643160426
43194CB00009B/1564